Procurement and Public Management

Procurement and Public Management

The Fear of Discretion and the Quality of Government Performance

Steven Kelman

THE AEI PRESS

Publisher for the American Enterprise Institute

Washington, D.C.

For Shelley, Jody, and Rory

Distributed by arrangement with

University Press of America
4720 Boston Way   3 Henrietta Street
Lanham, Md. 20706   London WC2E 8LU England

Library of Congress Cataloging-in-Publication Data

Kelman, Steven.
  Procurement and public management : the fear of discretion and the
quality of government performance / Steven Kelman.
    p.   cm.
  ISBN 0-8447-3712-7
  1. Government purchasing—United States.   2. Computers—United
States—Purchasing.   I. Title.
JK1677.C65K45   1990
353.0071′2—dc20   89-48765
                                                           CIP

AEI Studies 502

The AEI Press
Publisher for the American Enterprise Institute
1150 17th Street, N.W., Washington, D.C. 20036

Printed in the United States of America

Contents

Acknowledgments

This work could not have been possible without the kind and generous cooperation of a large number of government officials involved in computer acquisition management in the federal government. They include those who agreed to be interviewed for the Government Computer Managers Survey and especially those at various agencies who gave extremely generously of their time and of their patience in allowing me to do the case studies discussed in this book. I owe these men and women unending thanks. I hope that this work will contribute at least something toward improving their ability to do their jobs effectively and, hence, to our ability as citizens to get good performance from government. In addition, a number of managers at private firms who agreed to cooperate with this research were also very helpful, especially Guy Battista, at Shawmut Bank; Sy Gilman, at Ford Motor; John McCullogh, at United Technologies; and Chuck Blasewich, at Motorola. Paul Pittman and Mike Wall were cheerful and helpful as research assistants; Paul also assisted in some of the interviewing of government computer managers.

A number of institutions provided generous financial support to make this research possible. These include the Pew Charitable Trusts (through a grant to the Kennedy School of Government at Harvard), the Center for Business and Government at the Kennedy School, and the American Enterprise Institute for Public Policy Research. Chris DeMuth, of AEI, provided continual encouragement.

My colleagues at the Kennedy School have been a constant support of intellectual stimulation; I am constantly grateful to them. Mark Moore's ideas on public management are, I know, a source of insight to all his colleagues. In addition, helpful comments on a draft of this manuscript were generously provided by Eugene Bardach, at Berkeley; Michael Barzelay, at the Kennedy School, Michael Burack, at Wilmer, Cutler & Pickering; Karl Davidson, at the Department of Commerce; John DiIluo, at Princeton; Jack Donahue, at the Kennedy School; Frank McDonough, at the General Services Administration; Jerry Mechling, at the Kennedy School; Senator Howard Metzenbaum; Robert Reich, at the Kennedy School; John Springett, at the

Department of Defense and the Kennedy School; James Q. Wilson, at UCLA; and my wife, Shelley. Their comments widened my perspective and corrected errors of fact and judgment. Those that remain are my responsibility.

1
Introduction

The procurement system in the federal government is in trouble. The management of the public sector in general is also in trouble. Neither of these is a controversial statement. The only question is: What is the source of the trouble?

For procurement particularly, the conventional answer, enshrined in media accounts and congressional hearings, is that the source of the trouble is a lack of competition in awarding contracts. The lack of competition, the story goes, is in turn engendered by cozy relationships between government officials and contractors (itself the product of revolving doors or even payoffs) and by the indifference that sometimes afflicts people not responsible for watching the bottom line. As a result of the lack of competition, according to conventional wisdom, the government pays contractors too much and gives "wired" awards to contractors who do not deserve them. The conventional solution to these problems is more competition.

I, too, believe that the government often fails to get the most it can from its vendors. In contrast to the conventional view, however, I believe that the system of competition as it is typically envisioned and the controls against favoritism and corruption as they typically occur are more often the source of the problem than the solution to it. The problem with the current system is that public officials cannot use common sense and good judgment in ways that would promote better vendor performance. I believe that the system should be significantly deregulated to allow public officials greater discretion. I believe that the ability to exercise discretion would allow government to gain greater value from procurement.

This is a study of how the federal government buys computer technology—computers, computer networks, computer applications, and computer support services.[1] It is undertaken partly in the belief that computers have come to play an increasingly important role in the ability of government to do its job well. Spending by the federal government for computer hardware, software, and services has increased dramatically during the 1980s, from $9.1 billion in fiscal year 1982 to $17.4 billion in FY 1988, even at a time of shrinking federal

1

programs. (Computer spending rose as fast in civilian as in military agencies, so the increase cannot be attributed to increases in defense outlays.)[2] Perhaps even more important, the uses for computers have been changing. Traditionally, computers (in industry as well as government) were introduced mainly into routine back-office functions, such as payroll or accounts payable processing, far removed from the organization's mission. More recently, computer applications have moved from the back office to the front office, from mission-support to mission-critical functions. Computers are now used to track down money that drug dealers have laundered, to locate stolen cars, to help make decisions about farmers' loan requests, to determine priorities for toxic dump cleanups, to answer inquiries from citizens, and (in the case of organizations such as the Federal Aviation Administration) as the heartbeat of the organization's operation. How well computer systems work and how creatively they are used have become important in how well government works.

The interest in computer procurement in government, however, goes beyond this. Lessons derived from problems with computer procurement can be applied, to a greater or lesser extent, to the functioning of the government procurement system in general.[3] Procurement of goods and services by the federal government from the private sector currently amounts to $200 billion a year—almost 20 percent of the federal budget. Put another way, procurement at *all* levels of government averages approximately $450 billion a year— almost 10 percent of the GNP.[4] And there has been increased interest, particularly during the last several years, in contracting out government activities, that is, procuring them from the outside rather than producing them inside. With numbers of this magnitude, even small percentage improvements in the social value generated by government procurement management are significant.

Beyond the announced policy of not competing unnecessarily with the private sector, the government frequently has good reasons to buy the goods and services it needs from outside rather than producing them itself. By buying outside, an organization can focus on its own areas of real expertise, while allowing the selling organizations to use their expertise and to take advantage of economies of scale in research or in production. Moreover, when something is no longer needed, an organization can more easily stop buying than it can shut down part of its own organization and stop making it. These arguments for buying rather than making, apply not just to government purchases from the private sector, but to the private sector's purchases as well. General Motors does not make the steel for its cars, it buys it. Few companies produce telephone services for themselves, write their own advertising, or perform all their legal services in-house. But if the procurement system does not work well, the government will lose potential benefits from buying rather than making.

Finally, a study of government computer procurement sheds light on our philosophy of management of the public sector. The procurement system is highly regulated. Government agencies may not simply purchase what they want from whomever they wish. Voluminous rules govern both contract award and contract administration. The rules are embodied in statutes, in the 744-page *Federal Acquisition Regulations (FAR)*, and in the thousands of pages of supplementary rules for specific agencies (of which the Defense supplement is most important) and for specific kinds of acquisitions (of which the *Federal Information Resources Management Regulation*, governing computer-related procurements, is the most important).[5] The rules cover how to determine and specify needs, how to select vendors for award, and how to administer a contract once signed. The extensiveness of the government's regulation of itself are familiar to observers of civil service rules, administrative procedures for government rule making, and the myriad internal procedures within agencies. In general, such regulation reflects a fear of granting discretion to public officials. An answer to why the procurement system is in trouble may also tell why management of the public sector is in trouble.

The data regarding computer procurement that form the empirical base for this book were gathered from several sources. The first is a series of case studies of all nine contracts awarded in fiscal year 1985 on the civilian side of the federal government for computer hardware, software, or services, with an expected value of $25 million or more. That year was chosen as the most recent that would allow conclusions to be drawn about contractor performance under the contract. The agencies covered in the nine case studies are the Department of Agriculture, the Customs Service (two cases), the Immigration and Naturalization Service, the Veterans Administration, the Internal Revenue Service (two cases), the Federal Aviation Administration, and the Environmental Protection Agency. The case studies are presented in Appendix B, and findings from them are interspersed throughout the text.[6] One cannot necessarily generalize from these cases to the thousands of computer procurements made each year in the government, most for considerably smaller dollar amounts. But these cases do provide a good source of data for experience with procurements that have a major impact on how government agencies perform.

Other sources for this book are surveys I conducted of senior civilian federal government computer managers (Government Computer Managers Survey) and of senior computer managers in the largest 350 corporations listed annually in *Business Week* magazine (Private-Sector Computer Managers Survey). Since the activities of the government and private-sector computer organizations are similar, differences in the procurement process and in how vendors performed appeared to be of interest. In addition I spoke with computer and purchasing department managers at four companies about their philosophy of computer purchasing. I also interviewed senior marketing managers for government sales at five major computer vendors on their perceptions of differences between marketing to the federal government and to large commercial customers.[7] For a further discussion of how the cases were selected and written, and of the various surveys, see Appendix A: "Research Methodology."

The findings from the case studies and the various surveys provide considerable insight into the performance of the vendors who sell computer systems to the government and to large private firms.

In only three of the nine cases were government officials largely satisfied with the performance of the contractors. In four cases, they were dissatisfied, and in two cases their judgments were mixed. Furthermore, two of the three vendors that received high marks had reason to believe that computer buyers outside the government might be watching the vendor's performance on the government contract in making their purchasing decisions.

Some examples of problems were:

• In the procurement of a system to automate local offices at two agencies within the Department of Agriculture, no vendor informed the government in their bids that meeting the government's specifications required a complex Rube Goldberg-like system that would be far more expensive than the agency expected. All the vendors bid an expensive solution that met the specifications but made little substantive sense.

• The vendor providing local-office computerization equipment to the Department of Agriculture, as well as the one providing similar equipment to the Customs Service, exaggerated the ease of use of the equipment and the extent to which the software was commercially proven. The Customs Service system initially worked so badly that one local manager threatened to throw it into the Pacific Ocean.

• When the IRS contracted for the replacement of the mainframe computers at its service centers, the winning vendor bid computing power not capable of meeting the agency's requirement. It passed a benchmark test of the capabilities of its computers by shady (or even improper) measures. Then the vendor failed to advise the agency about problems with how the IRS was proceeding on its software

4

conversion, although that might have helped to avert the disaster that overtook the new system when it was introduced during the 1985 tax filing season.

- To operate and maintain databases and other systems at the Environmental Protection Agency, the vendor provided managers and technical personnel who were inexperienced and then transferred them as they became experienced. Complaints of this nature were heard in other case studies as well.

- At the Immigration and Naturalization Service, the vendor provided (and billed for) management personnel called for in the contract but who were shown by experience to be unnecessary.

- The vendor providing a packet-switching data-communications network to the Customs Service used increases in the actual system demand over the levels to increase the equipment it sold the government and to increase the cost far beyond what the vendor had bid.

- Vendors repeatedly interpreted contract language in ways favorable to them and harmful to the customer. In the IRS mainframe replacement contract, after abandoning the computer language it had bid on the contract, the vendor disputed the meaning of the "support" it was committed to give for that software. The Customs Service thought that the word "site" referred to a local Customs Service office; after the contract was signed, the vendor, said the word referred to subunits within each office. The vendor had signed a contract to provide site preparation costs at a fixed price, but then billed the government for a larger than anticipated number of sites. Similar differences arose over the "local area network" the vendor had bid a fixed price to provide.

- A vendor initially provided the Veterans Administration with office automation equipment at the very low prices it bid on a multi-year contract. But the prices of equipment bought later under a provision allowing technological upgrades were far less favorable.

In one of the nine cases, the internal operation of the procurement system itself was directly responsible for difficulties. The Immigration and Naturalization Service procurement of local-office computerization equipment became mired in a bid protest by a losing vendor who said the contract was wired. An expensive compromise solution led to a General Accounting Office report and finally to the cancellation of the original procurement by Congress. In the IRS mainframe replacement, the procurement system forced IRS technical officials to award the contract to a vendor they did not believe should have won.

The case study material also provides a chilling example of good vendor performance going unrewarded. In only one of all the nine case studies—the purchase by IRS of computer support services—was the customer wildly enthusiastic about the vendor's performance. (This was also the only one of the three cases of customer satisfaction where the vendor did not have reason to believe that nongovernment customers would be looking at how the vendor performed on the government contract.) The contract had to be recompeted early because IRS customers were so pleased with the vendor's work that budget authority under the contract was used up far more quickly than originally anticipated. After this research was completed, and just as this book was going to press, it became known that this vendor *lost* the recompetition of the contract. (In fact, the vendor's proposal was not even admitted into what is called the "competitive range," that is, those proposals that form the basis for further negotiations between the government and finalist vendors.)

These woes should be kept in perspective. The record generally tends toward the mediocre and undistinguished rather than the catastrophic. It reveals an attitude by vendors of trying to squeeze the last drop out of the customer rather than to engender customer good will. Of all the case studies, only the officials of the Internal Revenue Service in the support services acquisition case said that the contractor went out of his way to accommodate the customer.

Results of the Government Computer Managers Survey and the Private-Sector Computer Managers Survey tell a similar story. Each group was asked what percentage of time they were dissatisfied with the performance of their vendors. Among the government respondents, the average dissatisfaction level was 24.5 percent; among private-sector respondents it was 16.3 percent.[8] Although those accustomed to the heady brew of Grace Commission–style horror stories about government performance might find these differences flat and fizzless, they do show that government managers are 50 percent more likely to be dissatisfied with the performance of their computer vendors than are their private-sector counterparts. Put a different way, government officials are dissatisfied with vendor performance on almost one additional contract in ten. These numbers paint a picture of contractor performance on government work that is not a screaming scandal but is hardly a record of distinction.

These judgments of vendor performance were confirmed in a second survey question regarding the degree of satisfaction on the organization's most recent major contract.[9] On a scale of one to ten, government respondents gave vendors an average rating on their most recent contract of 6.9; for the private-sector managers, the average rating was 7.8.[10] Only 48 percent of government managers rated vendor performance at eight or above, compared with 74 percent of private-sector managers. On specific elements of vendor perform-ance, the differences between the government and the private sector were close to those on general satisfaction. On two questions, the differences were greater—on "keeping promises" (7.0 government mean vs. 8.0 private-sector mean) and on "sticking to the contracted delivery schedule" (6.2 government vs. 8.4 private sector).

Finally, both surveys included a question designed to measure the extent to which they believed vendors overpromised about their products and services. At opposite ends of a seven-point scale were two statements: "In my experience, vendors frequently overpromise in a major way about what their products can deliver, how fast they will be ready, and so forth"; and "Vendor overpromising is only a small problem." Table 1–1 shows the distribution of responses: public sector managers are considerably more likely to perceive vendor overpromising in advance of contract award than are private-sector ones.

The difference between these results in the private and public sectors is not, as the conventional view would have it, caused by less competition in government contracting, at least as competition is understood in most debates on procurement. Indeed, something closer to the opposite appears to be true.

The conventional view is that government procurement consists of cozy deals and lazy trods down paths of least resistance. Yet, 78

TABLE 1–1

PERCEPTION OF GOVERNMENT AND PRIVATE-SECTOR COMPUTER
MANAGERS OF OVERPROMISING BY VENDORS
(percentage of responses on a seven-point scale)

		Government	Private Sector
"Frequently overpromise"	1	11	1
	2	11	8
	3	30	22
	4	11	16
	5	7	27
"Overpromising	6	26	23
a small problem"	7	4	4

NOTE: Percentages add up to more than 100 because of rounding. For exact question wording, see text. The number of managers in the government sample was 27 and in the private sector 153.
SOURCE: Government Computer Managers Survey and Private-Sector Computer Managers Survey.

7

percent of the most recent major computer contracts in the Private-Sector Computer Managers Survey were signed with firms the company had previously used, compared with 58 percent in the Government Computer Managers Survey.[11] Furthermore, 28 percent of the most recent major contracts in the Private-Sector Computer Managers Survey were awarded without soliciting more than one bid, on a sole-source basis.[12] Such sole-source procurements were concentrated in purchases of mainframe computers, where private firms were inclined simply to purchase a new generation of machine from their existing vendor. Even for major purchases other than mainframes, 18 percent of purchases were sole-source contracts. By contrast, none of the most recent major procurements discussed in the Government Computer Managers Survey was a sole-source contract.

Nor is this view about excessive coziness in government supported by data on the comparative market share of the major computer vendors in the public and private sectors. If the picture of uncompetitive government procurement were correct, one would expect it to be reflected in the market share of IBM, the vendor with most to gain from all the alleged features of the government system. As the largest computer vendor in the world, it has the most lucrative post-government jobs to offer government officials. Its size also makes it the safe path-of-least-resistance where the riskiness of the technology creates possibilities for scapegoating when things do not work out. ("Nobody ever got fired for buying IBM," is a saying in the commercial world.) Indeed, the worry that lack of competition favored IBM motivated the decades-long drive of Congressman Jack Brooks for more competition in computer procurement.

Yet IBM's market share in the federal government is considerably lower than its share in *Fortune* 1000 companies—34 percent in government versus 76 percent in *Fortune* 1000 companies.[13] By contrast, some smaller vendors (most dramatically Unisys, with an 11 percent government share versus a 3 percent *Fortune* 1000 share and the IBM-compatible mainframe vendor Amdahl, with a 13 percent federal market share compared with 5 percent in the *Fortune* 1000 world) are overrepresented in government. Whatever the incidence of "sweetheart deals" and "lazy" decisions in the federal government (if indeed that is a correct description of such arrangements), it appears to be less than in the private sector.

During the summer of 1988, the U.S. Postal Service got into trouble with Congress, the General Accounting Office, and the General Services Administration Board of Contract Appeals by awarding a sole-source contract to generate suggestions for cost savings in the Postal Service to a new company that H. Ross Perot had established. The award clearly contravened federal procurement regulations, but the Postal Service said it was not subject to those regulations. Probably because of Perot's name recognition, the *New York Times* and the *Washington Post* reported the events. In the midst of the controversy, a small article about it appeared in *Purchasing,* the trade journal for private-sector purchasing managers. The article noted:

> The Postal Service's top procurement officer, recruited from the private sector to bring reforms to post office buying practices, is learning the hard way that the government is, indeed, different. John J. Davin, a former GTE vice president widely respected among industrial purchasing pros, has revamped postal procurement practices since he came aboard in 1986 following a scandal that saw one member of the postal board of governors admit to fraud. . . . Now he is seeing the Postal Service come under Congressional scrutiny again—this time for something that is common in industry: a sole-source contract award.[14]

When the Post Office canceled the contract, the postmaster general, whose experience was in the private sector, told a Senate committee that the kind of contract that had been signed was "perhaps more typical of the private sector than the government."[15]

The Government Computer Managers Survey asked respondents to place themselves on a seven-point scale, with this statement at the number one: "The way we organize procurement in the federal government is a good way to procure appropriate (computer) technology at good prices"; this statement at number four: "The way we organize procurement neither helps nor hurts our efforts to do our job right"; and this statement at number seven: "The way we organize procurement is a serious obstacle to accomplishing our mission." Government computer managers expressed a considerable degree of unhappiness with the current system. The mean response was 5.5; only 14 percent of respondents placed themselves on the favorable side of the scale.[16] Earlier in the survey when the same managers were asked whether changes in the system in their view would have "a major positive impact on your ability as a computer manager to do your job," their criticisms were rather conventional, centering on the delays the system imposed and the layers of review and oversight to which they were subject (see table 1–2).

Although the delays and the second-guessing are problems, the argument of this book is that the problem with the current system goes deeper. It is that the fear of allowing public officials to use good sense and good judgment in procurement works against both the selection of the best contractor and the quality of performance of those that are selected.

TABLE 1–2

CRITICISMS BY GOVERNMENT COMPUTER MANAGERS OF THE CURRENT
PROCUREMENT SYSTEM
(percent)

Process takes too long	29
Too much oversight/too many layers of review/easy for vendors to protest	15
Give managers more responsibility/don't assume we're crooks	15
Competitive procedures allow unqualified vendors to bid/win	11
Miscellaneous other criticisms (not mentioned more than once)	18
System basically all right as is	21

NOTE: Responses were coded into categories from open-ended answers. Percentages add up to more than 100 because of multiple answers. The number of managers responding was 36.
SOURCE: Government Computer Managers Survey.

The fear of discretion makes it more difficult to select the right vendor because public officials cannot use important information that could help predict vendor performance if that use requires judgment that the system forbids officials to exercise. The most dramatic example of the information that may not be used is information regarding the past performance of vendors on earlier contracts with the organization. Such information is at the heart of countless decisions in everyday life about the future performance of others. Yet it is ruled out because biased or corrupt decision makers might pick and choose from a vendor's past actions as an excuse for an unfair contract award. Moreover, unwillingness to allow officials the discretion to depart from "free and open competition" can prevent the government from obtaining more value from vendors. Officials cannot offer as an incentive for good performance a promise to award future contracts. For the same reason, vendors are less likely to invest in developing creative ideas that the customer had never conceived, as opposed to ideas for effecting what the customer has already developed. Indeed, the greatest costs of the current system may well be those least recognized by participants—the creative ideas and suggestions that are never made, that suggest that participants may not know what they have missed.

This volume suggests, then, that the fundamental problem with the procurement system is that it undermines the government's ability to get the most for its money and reduces the quality of government performance. In my view this is a problem that extends more broadly into public-sector management as well.

2
Procurement Regulation and Official Discretion

The procurement regulatory system has three goals:

- *equity*—to provide fair access to bidders in competing for government business
- *integrity*—to reduce the chances for corruption in the procurement process
- *economy and efficiency*—to procure at the lowest possible price for goods or services of the quality desired

Taken together, the goals of equity, integrity, and economy embody a vision of the goals we should seek from government organizations with deep roots in our tradition of thinking about public administration.[1] One might note, however, that nowhere included among these goals—or emphasized in the tradition of thinking about public administration out of which they grow—is the goal of excellence in the performance of the organization's substantive tasks. Perhaps the reason was that most tasks government organizations performed when the traditional doctrine was developed were rudimentary and straightforward. If they were performed equitably, honestly, and economically, the rest followed more or less automatically. When the nineteenth-century federal government distributed land to homesteaders or pensions to war veterans, the tasks required little more than equity, honesty, and economy in their performance. The same was true when the government procured pencils and paper to write with or coal to heat the offices.

Although the goals of equity, integrity, and economy appear repeatedly across the entire domain of traditional American public administration doctrine, perhaps only in the area of procurement has an institutional arrangement been developed that is seen as simultaneously promoting all three goals. This, of course, is the arrangement of awarding contracts through what the procurement statutes and regulations call "full and open competition." Competition lowers prices; hence, it promotes economy. Competition equitably extends access to the system to everyone. If procurement decisions are made based upon who wins a full and open competition, officials involved in procurement are more difficult to bribe, because a corrupt decision in favor of a bidder who would have lost the competition is easy to detect.

Conversely, the evils arising from a lack of full and open competition are seen as occurring simultaneously in all three areas. Corruption denies citizens equitable access to the procurement process and raises the prices government pays. Chairman Jack Brooks of the House Committee on Government Operations referred to the alleged $435 paid for a hammer by the Department of Defense as an example of "the sweetheart deals that occur daily . . . throughout the Federal Government"—thus linking high prices to favoritism.[2] Congressman Brooks has stated that lack of competition for contracts was wasting the government billions of dollars a year.[3] Only "full and open competition," he believes, can prevent giant companies such as IBM from dominating the government computer market and charging monopoly prices to the agencies that are "in bed" with them.

The economy and especially the equity and integrity goals of the procurement system in the federal government reflect the demand for a high standard of probity in public officials.[4] Our democracy has been, and continues to be, a source of pride for Americans. Since the founding of the Republic, this pridefulness has been nourished by the vision of America as a democratic experiment in a world just emerging from absolute rule. In the late 1950s, Gabriel Almond and Sidney Verba asked Americans, together with citizens in four other countries, which things about their country they were most proud of.

> Eighty-five percent of the American respondents cited some feature of the American government or political tradition— the Constitution, political freedom, democracy, and the like—as compared with 46 percent for the British, 7 percent for the Germans, 3 percent for the Italians, and 30 percent for the Mexicans.[5]

The authors found that features of our political system were far more frequently cited as a source of pride than any other aspect of American society, such as our economic system, religious values, or position in world affairs. These views persist. In a 1976 survey, Americans were asked whether they agreed more with the statement, "I am proud of many things about our form of government" or the one, "I can't find much in our form of government to be proud of." Seventy-six percent of respondents said they were proud of our government.[6]

The prideful view of government holds it to a specially high standard of probity because of the visibility of the example it provides.

As early as 1792, Congress passed laws prohibiting officials from gaining personal profit from office and enjoining conflicts of interest. This legislation was far more advanced than British legislation at the time. Employees of the U.S. Mint, for example, were subject to the death penalty for counterfeiting.[7] In the prideful view, people should also have equal rights in their dealings with government organizations, whether as job applicants or as suppliers. Such equal treatment makes a statement, consistent with our democratic values, about the dignity of all and the respect owed to all. Government officials should treat similar cases similarly—two people wanting passports should not be treated differently because of bureaucratic whim or political favoritism. Unmotivated exclusion of firms from the right to bid for government business, or favoritism in the selection of contractors, would violate our beliefs. The prideful view is offended by public corruption; it demands economy and honesty in handling public money. Newspapers usually cover procurement issues because of scandal. Kickbacks or bribes to government officials in connection with procurement are news. Favoritism toward a vendor—particularly a big one—is news.

A cynical view of government also has deep roots in our history. America was born in an armed struggle against government tyranny. Many of our people came here to escape government power. In the late 1800s, Mark Twain quipped about politicians being America's only native criminal class. During the Depression of the 1930s, people working too slowly were compared to employees of public work programs. The statutes, regulations, and cultural norms that govern the procurement system reflect the view that, left to their own devices, government officials will not live up to the ideals we hold. We fear that their contract awards will be tainted by personal cronyism, partisan backscratching, or outright bribery. In the hearings on major revisions in 1949 of the federal procurement statutes, a lead witness noted:

> A lot of people think that every person who is employed by the Federal Government has his hand in the Federal Treasury, and that if he is not carefully guarded by two or three armed men he will get away with the Treasury of the United States. . . . Practically every law governing the procurement and disposal of property is based on the assumption that the Government employees are crooks.[8]

In addition, government officials are suspected of being slothful and heedless. They fail to get good products at good prices because they are not spending their own money and there is no bottom line to worry about in government. Finally, agencies are suspected of being pressured to award contracts to politicians' constituents or contributors.[9]

If we are suspicious that politicians will abuse and oppress us, that nervousness turns into dread with regard to bureaucrats, who lack the legitimacy of popular election enjoyed by congressmen, senators, and presidents.[10] Hence the important strand in our thinking about the proper role of nonelected government administrators. Woodrow Wilson argued that nonelected government officials should be kept from any discretion at all but should simply execute decisions made by others. The enormous corpus of American administrative law is about limiting the ability of appointed officials to make decisions they wish, rather than decisions guided by their agency's statute or by the views of citizens.

In a world where we trusted government officials more, we might establish the goals of integrity, equity, and economy for government organizations without establishing elaborate rules to regulate official behavior. We might simply inform public officials of the goals, direct them to act accordingly, and hold them accountable for the results of their actions, rather than looking over their shoulders each time they act. Instead, we fear discretion because we do not trust officials to live up to high standards of probity unless we keep a close eye on them. We establish therefore a system of public management based on rules. The prideful side of our view of government is reflected in our selection of goals for the behavior of government officials, emphasizing honesty and fairness. The cynical side is reflected in our selection of means to achieve those goals. That mixture is reflected in the notion of a government of laws, not men. Laws are rules, and men are individuals exercising judgment in particular cases. When we seek a government of laws rather than men, we express both an ideal of fair and impartial treatment, and a fear that such treatment will not be forthcoming if we leave it to the judgment of the individuals who actually make up the government.

Equity, integrity, and economy are goals that, more than many, are amenable to transformation into rules. The goals themselves have the character of relatively clear injunctions about expected behavior—"don't take bribes," "get the lowest price for what you want to buy," and "treat everyone the same way." These commands can be translated into specific rules—"award the contract to the lowest bidder," "evaluate bidders on criteria established before you knew who the bidders would be," and so forth. (Compare this with the difficulty of making a clear behavioral injunction of, say, getting vendors to make creative suggestions to the government.) Whenever a procurement scandal occurs the reflexive reaction is to tighten the regulations.

The problem in government is not lack of accountability, as is sometimes suggested, but the nature of the accountability. Government people do not lead sheltered lives: they are indeed held accountable, often publicly and painfully so, if they violate rules, even if the standards of probity themselves were not violated. We see this, for example, in the tradition of strict accountability for how government funds are spent. The attention government organizations get when they do something scandalous reflects both our high expectations and our great worries about their achievement. What is missing is demand for accountability for the quality of the government's performance.

The Development of the Procurement Regulatory System

Traditionally in America, the institutional expression of the goals of equity, integrity, and economy—and the clearest declaration of the animus toward managerial discretion in procurement—was the system of advertising procurements to all comers and awarding contracts by a process of sealed bids.[11] The contract award went to the lowest bidder who met the specifications the government had presented.[12] Making an award based on low price alone was a brilliant solution to the problems perceived by the system's framers. It promised taxpayers the lowest possible prices for what government was purchasing, it gave everyone an equal chance to compete for the government's business, and it reduced drastically the opportunity for corrupting public officials because it took the decision about contract award out of their hands. A classic statement of this view appears in a Supreme Court decision from 1940.

> The purpose of statutes requiring the award of contracts to the lowest responsible bidder, after advertising, is to give all persons equal right to compete for Government contracts, to prevent unjust favoritism, collusion or fraud in awarding Government contracts, and to secure for the Government the benefits which flow from free and unrestricted competition.[13]

In response to efforts by congressmen to obtain contracts for friends in the first part of the nineteenth century, sealed bidding was introduced. The first of a series of laws requiring sealed bidding was passed in 1809. A statute enacted in 1861 made sealed bidding the rule for letting government contracts and remained, with a number of legislated amendments and exemptions, the basic procurement law of the United States for almost one hundred years.[14]

Much of the history of American procurement regulation reflects the tension between the ideal of sealed bidding and the grudging realization that it was hopelessly inappropriate for a good deal of government procurement. Specifications were too complicated or imprecise to allow a simple declaration by bidders that they could meet them. The government also wanted to buy products, mainly weapons, that had never been produced, so a fixed price could not be quoted at the time of contract award. Trade-offs between quality and price made more sense than specifying a single level of quality and having vendors bid their lowest price to attain it. Requirements for procurement by sealed bid were suspended for the military services during World War I and World War II.

During much of the twentieth century, in the recognized alternative to sealed bids, a contractor has been selected after bidders present the government with proposals explaining how they plan to perform and for what price. These alternative methods caused anxiety, however, "over the degree to which public managers should be allowed to exercise judgment regarding the expenditure of public funds."[15] As Ralph Nash and John Cibinic write in their casebook on procurement law, "It is precisely because of the greater flexibility and discretion afforded (by competitive proposals) that Congress has maintained a preference for formal advertising in the procurement statutes."[16]

In 1947 Congress acknowledged the contradiction between the statutory support for sealed bidding and military procurement reality in the Armed Services Procurement Act. That law continued the traditional policy of favoring sealed bids, while providing a list of exceptions allowing other methods. This regime was extended to civilian procurement by the Federal Property and Administrative Services Act two years later.[17] Many of the statutory exemptions were simply modifications of exemptions that had already been made by earlier amendments to the original 1861 legislation. In addition to allowing nonsealed bid procurements in a national emergency, the statutes allowed them for professional services, for developmental and research work, for drugs and medical supplies, and for situations in which a significant investment is required to produce an item. In any departure from formal advertising, however, a statement of "determination and findings" had to be signed by the contracting officer and often by one or more of his superiors.

The 1947 and 1949 statutes created a procurement regime with a statutory preference for sealed bids but with a list of exceptions allowing other procurement methods. In dollar value, the exceptions became more common than the rule. The *Report of the Commission on Government Procurement* in 1972 noted that although the greatest number of federal procurements were awarded using sealed bids, only 10 to 15 percent of contract award dollars were awarded that way.[18]

The first, somewhat tentative, suggestion that sealed bidding be removed from its preferred status came in the 1972 congressionally mandated *Report of the Commission on Government Procurement*. In language that appears to have been carefully selected to recognize the strong tradition of support for sealed bidding in government procurement, the *Report* recommended

> that formal advertising, the competitive procurement method exhibiting the greatest safeguards against favoritism, be preferred whenever market conditions are appropriate for its use. Competitive negotiation should be recognized in law for what it is; namely, a normal, sound buying method which the Government should prefer where market conditions are not appropriate for the use of formal advertising.[19]

More than ten years later, with the outcry over perceived abuses in defense procurement in the early 1980s, Congress finally passed a new procurement statute. The Competition in Contracting Act of 1984 attempted to discourage sole-source procurement partly by raising the status of procurement by competitive proposals in the way the Commission on Government Procurement had suggested. In this statute, the preference for sealed bidding disappeared. Both sealed bidding and competitive negotiations were defined as methods for "full and open competition"; the statute merely offers guidance about when one is more appropriate than the other. A strong distinction is drawn, however, between sealed bidding and competitive proposals on the one hand, and sole-source procurement on the other.

To soften this fairly major change from a long preference for sealed bidding, the legislative history of the Competition in Contracting Act tried to justify it as a way to remove the barrier to competition arising from the lack of distinction between competitive and sole-source negotiations.

> Due to the lack of direct restrictions on non-competitive contracting, the exceptions to formal advertising are often applied inappropriately to justify the use of sole-source procurement. Revisions are needed in the present statutory framework which would shift the focus from having to justify the use of negotiation to having to justify the use of non-competitive negotiations.[20]

The statutory and regulatory environment is thus designed to reduce to a minimum sole-source procurement—that is to say, procurement where only one source is solicited or where negotiations are conducted with only one source.[21] Sole-source procurements are believed the least likely to meet the procurement system's goals of equity, integrity, and economy.

Disputes erupted after the sole-source procurement provisions of the Competition in Contracting Act were translated into regulatory language in the *Federal Acquisition Regulations*. Initially, the regulatory language stated that an agency could procure sole-source when "the required supplies or services are available from only one source." As a commentator on the Competition in Contracting Act noted, this provision appeared "to be less restrictive than the statutory exception, which requires as a further condition that no other type of property or services will satisfy the agency's needs."[22] Similarly, the original *Federal Acquisition Regulations* language regarding sole-source follow-on procurements was not as restrictive as the statutory language.[23] In both cases, the language was changed following congressional objections.

When sole-source procurements are undertaken, written justifications are required that vary in their onerousness and in the number of concurrences with the size of the proposed sole-source procurement. Justifications must include information about efforts the government had undertaken to locate possible alternative suppliers and an explanation of the reason that specifications suitable for full and open competition could not be developed.[24] For proposed sole-source contracts with a value between $100,000 and $1 million, the justification must be signed by an official specifically designated within the organization as a "competition advocate," who is expected to be unsympathetic to any sole-source requests. For sole-source procurements valued at more than $10 million, the justification must be approved personally by the agency's senior procurement official.[25] If a sole-source procurement is to be justified based on the most nebulous of the exemptions established in the Competition in Contracting Act—that "it is necessary in the public interest" to use some procedure other than full and open competition—that justification must be signed by the head of the agency and the justification submitted to Congress within thirty days. (There has not been a single instance since passage of the Competition in Contracting Act in 1984 of an agency's using the "public interest" exemption.)[26] All justifications for sole-source procurements are accessible to people outside the government under the Freedom of Information Act.[27]

Procedures for Acquiring Computers

The major computer systems that this book examines are not acquired through sealed bids, but through competitive proposals. Procurement by competitive proposals involves publication of a request for proposals (RFP) that tells vendors what the government wants. Bidders respond to the RFP with a written proposal and, often in computer procurements, with a live test demonstration during which the bidder's equipment is made to perform preestablished tasks. The government then selects the vendor whose proposal is best according to the criteria in the RFP.

This alternative to sealed bidding is intended to allow greater exercise of judgment where sealed bidding would threaten an anomalous or disastrous outcome. Theoretically, procuring by competitive proposals creates a great deal of discretion. The government has considerable freedom in deciding how to evaluate proposals and it need not make an award to the low-priced bidder. In practice, however, prodigious efforts have been made to control unbridled discretion and direct it into preestablished paths.

The three major limitations on discretion in procurement by competitive proposals are the rules and practices for establishing the government's requirements, the criteria by which proposals from vendors are evaluated, and the information that may be used in evaluating proposals against those criteria. The hope is to discipline discretion by making the contract award process as much as possible a structured reaction by government officials to the initiatives of others. The requirements for what is procured are seen as being ultimately set by Congress when it establishes the responsibilities and mission of the organization. The evaluation of vendor responses is based on proposals developed by the vendors themselves. Public officials become somewhat passive receptacles toting up scores in a game others play.

The first way that the system domesticates what might otherwise be unbridled discretion is by procedures for the establishment of the government's requirements for what it is purchasing. "Requirements" express in the form of specifications what the government wishes to purchase—how much computing capacity, what sorts of applications, what servicing or training capabilities, and so forth. Discretion is limited because the government in its specifications can ask for no more than what it requires to meet its "minimum needs" (in the language of the *Federal Acquisition Regulations*).[28] The theory is that those needs are exogenously expressed by the program missions ultimately based in statute. Those involved in the procurement process in theory therefore merely flush out preexisting needs and craft them into the language of specifications. The idea is that this process, if correctly carried out, involves little discretion because the officials are not determining needs but translating already existing needs established by Congress into purchase specifications. The regulatory guidance is clear that specifications in an RFP must be tied to agency requirements, which in turn reflect the agency's mission. In pursuit of these goals, agencies do expensive and time-consuming planning exercises and requirements analysis efforts in the early stages of the procurement process. A requirements analysis is undertaken early in the process to prevent government officials from wastefully seeking the unnecessary or from favoring certain vendors by tailoring specifications to that vendor's capabilities rather than to agency needs.

It must of course frankly be confessed that the theory of "discretionless" requirements emerging from an exogenously established agency mission is in significant measure mythical. At any interesting level, the nature of the government's computer "needs" is a matter of judgment. For instance, do lawyers "need" a computerized system for locating cases for legal research? If so, what features does such a system "need"? Government officials have significant discretion in determining such specifications despite all the language about needs.

Discretion is also limited by the demand that specifications not be so unduly restrictive that they inhibit competition. Any specification, however, is to some extent exclusionary. If a specification says that automobiles must run, those who cannot make them run would be excluded, but no one would object to such a specification. At the other extreme, a specification might require paper tablets of a shade of yellow, as measured by a spectrographic test, that only one vendor produces. Such "wired specs" favor one vendor and eliminate competition on a contract. According to the *Federal Acquisition Regulations* "agencies shall specify needs in a manner designed to promote full and open competition."[29] Specifications may "include restrictive provisions or conditions only to the extent necessary to satisfy the minimum needs of the agency."[30]

In developing criteria for evaluating vendor proposals, agencies are permitted considerable discretion. The regulations insist that "price or cost to the Government shall be included as an evaluation factor in every source selection," but the award need not necessarily be made to the lowest-price bidder.[31] In purchasing large-scale computer systems agencies also consider technical excellence and managerial capabilities. Factors that might be included under those broad rubrics are ease of use, upgradability and expandability, reliability, and the quality of the implementation plan for system installation.

Many RFPs include both mandatory and desirable features (the latter now often referred to as "evaluated options"). Desirable features are those that, if included, gain additional points for the vendor.[32] In a procurement for word processors, desirable features might include a capability to justify the right column or to vary the typeface. Vendors include them in their proposals only if the additional cost is justified by the additional benefit to the vendor in the technical evaluation.

Although the system allows considerable discretion in determining evaluation criteria, such discretion is far from unlimited. Just as specifications must be related to the agency's requirements, so too must evaluation criteria. Evaluation factors such as management capability, ease of use, or upgradability "should be justified on legitimate agency requirements, like any mandatory requirement. [They] need not and should not be included unless clearly relevant to the agency's mission."[33] This rule tends to exclude benefits to an agency that are hard to quantify. Most users of complex computer software, for example, would regard it as a positive that there exists a user group of customers who compare notes, meet with company representatives about ways to apply the product, and offer suggestions for product improvement. The government may not use presence of a user software group as an evaluation factor, however, unless "there is a clear showing that the direct, identifiable, and quantifiable benefits of membership in such an organization outweigh the attendant costs."[34]

The system also domesticates discretion by requiring all evaluation criteria to be stated in the RFP. "An agency," the *Federal Acquisition Regulations* state, "shall evaluate competitive proposals solely on the factors specified in the solicitation."[35] Officials cannot decide what criteria to use or how to weigh them after they have seen the proposals, because they could say that a favored vendor's proposal was strong in the areas the agency had suddenly come to regard as crucial. By demanding that the RFP include all criteria, the system seeks to guarantee that vendors know how they will be judged and can compete fairly.

The system seeks to tame discretion through the rule that vendors may be judged only on their written proposals and in accompanying live test demonstrations. This feature, like other central features of the evaluation process, results from the culture of procurement and not the regulations, although it may be seen as an application of the general doctrine that administrative decisions must be based solely on material appearing on the written record.[36]

This doctrine means that government officials may not evaluate vendors on other information they have sought out strictly on their own initiative or on information and impressions they have accumulated simply as living, breathing human beings. Officials may not base a contract award decision on a phone call to a friend who has had experience with a vendor or on an article in a magazine about the vendor. Otherwise, officials might arbitrarily select just the facts that would justify a biased or corrupt decision. If, by contrast, evaluation is based on information that vendors themselves provide, then the officials cannot make a biased selection of facts. The problem is that the possibility of a biased selection of facts by the vendors is heightened.

Since the vendor's written proposal is the centerpiece of its efforts to get a contract, it is normally a complex and lengthy document that can cost the vendor more than a million dollars to produce. Proposals are typically divided into technical, management, and cost sections. In the technical part vendors explain how they plan to meet requirements described in the specifications, such as which combinations of computer equipment they propose for processing specified volumes of data, how the technology will be upgraded, and how service will be provided at all the government's locations.

Proposals are evaluated by one or more panels, consisting of agency technical experts and users, that consider vendor technical and management proposals and by contracting personnel who evaluate cost proposals. Independent of the rest of the agency, technical evaluation panels work closely together with each other, often full time for a period of weeks and even months. The panels must document their reasons for the scoring given each proposal on each evaluation factor, and they may not see the cost proposals, because they are supposed to make judgments only about technical merits.

Final source selection is made by a source selection officer, typically the contracting officer in charge of the procurement. Often, the contracting officer will simply add up cost and technical scores, awarding the contract to the bidder with the highest score. The regulations, however, do not require this. If the technical scores are close, contracting officers usually award the contract to the low bidder.[37]

The system seeks to ensure realization of the equity, integrity, and economy goals by establishing extensive mechanisms for protesting procurement decisions to outside bodies. These include opportunities to protest both before an award is made (over the nature of specifications or evaluation criteria, for example) and after the award has been announced. A principle of American administrative law is that administrative decisions may always be appealed to an outside review body. About one-third of the most recently awarded major contracts that respondents discussed in the Government Computer Managers Survey were protested.

The bid protest system is intended to help keep the agencies from violating procurement regulations, because vendors have an incentive to act as private attorneys general in bringing violations to the attention of the legal system. Case law on the application of the procurement regulations to specific situations provides guidance on such otherwise nebulous concepts as unduly restrictive specifications or the government's minimum needs. Many concepts and provisions embodied in regulatory and statutory language first appeared in legal decisions on bid protests.[38]

Until 1970 there was only one accepted forum for bid protests, the General Accounting Office. Subsequently forums for litigation have increased. The federal courts, for example, now hear bid protest cases. And the Competition in Contracting Act established a new bid protest forum, for computer-related procurements initially on a trial basis only, in the General Services Administration Board of Contract Appeals.[39]

Traditionally, the General Accounting Office used informal procedures. Protesters sent in a written protest document, and the procuring agency responded with a written reply. The hearing official could call the parties together, but the conference was not an adversary proceeding; there was no written record, testimony, or cross-examination.[40] GAO rules did not allow discovery (that is, legal requirements on the agency to produce internal documents for the protester to examine). By contrast, the federal courts, which now also hear protest decisions, follow the adversary procedures used in other court trials, including discovery, witnesses, and cross-examination. When the General Services Administration Board of Contract Appeals was established in the Competition in Contracting Act as a bid protest forum for computer-related procurements, Congress made its procedures far more judicial than those traditionally used at the General Accounting Office.

The General Accounting Office has traditionally been a protest forum that was cheap but unfriendly. It was cheap because of its lack of formal procedures; a protester could lodge a protest by filing a simple written document explaining his objection to an agency decision. It was unfriendly because it deprived protesters of protections they might have in a trial (such as access to internal agency documents). In addition, the body tended to put a heavy burden of proof on the protester. Congressional debates over the 1984 Competition in Contracting Act included a good deal of criticism of the bias against protesters.[41] The GAO has now adopted rules that make its procedures more trial-like.[42]

The courts and the General Accounting Office have traditionally applied a burden of proof that made it difficult for the protester to win, demanding that agency actions have been "arbitrary and capricious" or something similar. By contrast, the GSA Board of Contract Appeals has adopted a more lenient "preponderance of the evidence" test for its bid protest decisions; it could decide against the agency if a mere weight of the evidence supported the protester.[43] The difference in burden of proof is reflected in the outcomes of decisions. At the General Accounting Office, about 10 percent of bid protests have traditionally been decided in favor of the protester; at the Board of Contract Appeals, the figure is typically more than half.[44] Because of high protest success rates for computer-related procurements, government officials must regard a protest from a losing vendor as a distinct possibility. The high cost of preparing proposals encourages losers to protest to justify to their own management that the contract loss was due to favoritism—or simply in the hope of recovering proposal costs as part of a settlement.

Given the complex procedures and the possibility of protest, the procurement process for major computer systems generally takes at least two years. The biggest blocks of time go to requirements analysis, specification drafting, and proposal drafting by bidders. Proposal evaluation also demands considerable time and energy. The system builds upon itself: complex evaluation processes require expensive proposals that in turn increase the propensity to protest. The risk of protest in turn encourages agencies to make the evaluation process even more complex.

The Role of the Contracts Function in the Procurement Process

The main participants in the procurement process for computer technology are the technical computer people (and, to some extent, the program officials who are the end users) on the one hand and the contracting people on the other. The technical people are responsible for the organization's substantive computer work. They are the primary ones whose exercise of judgment the system seeks to constrain.

The contracting officer, by contrast, has a different agenda. Contracting officers run the process itself and are charged by the regulations with the responsibility to "encourage that contractors receive impartial, fair, and equitable treatment from the government."[45] Their expertise comes from their knowledge of procurement regulations. By law, they sign the contract itself, as well as various procurement-related documents, including determinations that various regulatory requirements have been met. (As contracting officers point out, with a flair for drama and perhaps hyperbole, it is they who "will go to jail" if the rules have been violated.) The contracting officer's role tends to set him in institutional conflict with the program and technical people, who have less concern for the regulations, particularly the various competition requirements.

The contracting people are the agencies' own in-house leash holders. While there are some exceptions, in general contracting officers often try to reduce the exercise of discretion by the technical or program people, partly through their role as guardians of the regulatory process. As the ones who almost always know the regulations better than the technical or program people, they advise these others about how to proceed. (Few of the computer managers in the case studies had ever run a major procurement before.) They insist on reviewing and signing documents—although their ability to spot, for example, restrictive specifications is limited by the deficiencies in their knowledge of computers.

The contracts people generally serve as a lobby for allowing less discretion than the regulations do. The *Federal Acquisition Regulations* do not mandate that price be the most important criterion, and the technical and program people, with their concern for performance and technical excellence, tend to wish to give it a low evaluation weight. Contracting officers, however, favor a higher weight to price and lower weight to less intangible evaluation criteria, such as management capability. Making a judgment about the possibility of upgrading a computer system, they believe, is a straightforward process, without much risk of unwarranted discretion, but judging bidders' management capabilities is far more nebulous. Moreover, contracting officers tend to favor leaving out requirements, especially when they restrict the number of vendors who could bid. One frequently hears from contracting officers the phrase, "the government is in the market for Chevrolets, not Cadillacs," reflecting the minimum needs philosophy of the regulations. Program and technical people, by contrast, are inclined to ask for as much as possible, even at the cost of excluding vendors. Some contracting people argue that agencies should steer clear of "desirables" in their specifications, listing instead only the mandatory requirements that all bidders must meet to be eligible for contract award. Generally contracting people support the use of fixed evaluation weights, with award going to the bidder with the highest number of points. (In some agencies, contracting officers prefer to retain the freedom to award the contract to the low-price bidder regardless of how the scores come out.) Indeed, I was repeatedly surprised how many common procurement practices are not mandated by the procurement regulations, but come from a procurement culture that has developed in contracting offices.[46]

The institutional role that contracting people play resembles that

25

of purchasing managers in the private sector. In the conventional view, purchasing managers tend to be more sensitive to price and to soliciting competition than the engineers and other users are. The stereotype of the purchasing agent has been "the kind of man John Ruskin described when he said, 'There is hardly anything in this world that some man cannot make a little worse and sell a little cheaper, and the people who consider price only are this man's lawful prey.' "[47] One text on purchasing management states that "the ability to get a 'good price' is sometimes held to be the prime test of a good buyer," although texts on purchasing management make clear that this is an incomplete view.[48]

In the private sector, this purchasing culture originated because cost savings are a ready measure of the performance of purchasing people. In government, the source of the unique knowledge and expertise of contracting officers is the regulations. They are evaluated by how few regulatory violations they allow or how few "waves" the procurement causes. Because exercise of discretion generates the congressional investigations and media stories, contracting officers tend to be safe rather than sorry. Given their lack of program responsibility for what is procured, they have little to compensate them for taking risks.

Public Management

The ability to define, direct, and coordinate the behavior of large numbers of people through rules is one of the great achievements of the human experience. Rules make it possible for ordinary people to accomplish extraordinary tasks by summarizing an organization's past learning and experience into forms that can in turn be taught to new employees. They allow a complex task to be divided more easily into parts that are within the reach of mere mortals and then coordinated because each person knows that the others will follow the rules. Because they give employees direction about how to behave, rules are a good tool of control by management. Max Weber, the first great modern organizational theorist and the coiner of the word "bureaucracy," stood in awe of what a system of rules allowed an organization to accomplish. He wrote that

> the decisive reason for the advance of bureaucratic organization has always been its purely technical superiority over any other form of organization. Precision, speed, unambiguity, knowledge of the files, continuity, discretion, unity, strict subordination, reduction of friction and of material and per-

sonal costs—these are raised to the optimum point in the strictly bureaucratic organization administration.[49]

Despite Weber's awe, however, the problem with rules has also preoccupied organizational theory. The problem is that general rules may be inappropriate to particular situations and that existing rules may become generally inappropriate if the environment has changed. In such cases, individuals should be given greater discretion in making decisions. Otherwise the organization will pay the price of encouraging inappropriate behavior. More seriously, a mediocre level of organizational performance results when people mechanically apply rules to situations that call for more than mechanical behavior and when rule-boundedness stifles creativity and the striving for excellence.[50]

The proper combination of rules and discretion varies among organizations because their environments are more or less routine and more or less changeable. Various organizations are also more or less able to recruit people capable of exercising discretion, and they are more or less able to control employees using means other than rules.

An additional factor in balancing rules and discretion in government organizations comes from the mixture of high standards and fear we have regarding government, which usually favors the use of rules. This consideration is orthogonal to the considerations of task variability, speed of environmental change, and skills of employees that are standard in the thinking about the proper combination of rules and flexibility in the literature on organizational design. That literature, however, takes the quality of the organization's substantive performance as the guiding goal. Determinations about the mix of rules and discretion in the domain of public-sector management have proceeded on a separate track, largely heedless of the impact of such determinations on the quality of government's substantive performance. The orthogonal agenda in public management arises from our prideful and cynical views of government. But it can easily create a situation where government organizations become rule-based, not because such rule-boundedness is the best way to produce effective performance given the particular conditions in which a given government organization works, but because such rule-boundedness is seen as required to avoid the scandal that would arise if our standards of probity were violated. To design an organization to minimize scandal, rules are developed that tell people what they should and should not do. Clearance points are multiplied as further checks. The hope is that all this will stop malfeasance.

A bias against discretion can be seen in American political science literature on government organizations. Often, the surprising—and mildly shocking—research finding is that bureaucrats, particularly lower level bureaucrats, do, indeed, enjoy some discretion. Such "irreducible discretion" is frequently regarded as if it were the name of some sort of disease. Even as sensitive an observer as James Q. Wilson refers to "controlling discretion" as "*the* problem of administration."[51] Writers about business organizations, by contrast, stress the need for an environment where initiative and achievement are encouraged.

The apprehension about discretion that lies at the heart of the procurement system is, as mentioned in the introduction, hardly unique to procurement management. Many specific features of the procurement system, ranging from the demand that decisions be based on information supplied by the bidders to the provisions for protest, apply to the procurement process general doctrines of American administrative law.

As a strategy of organizational design, rules have a cautious character. When we design organizations based on rules, we guard against disaster, but at the cost of stifling excellence. Excellence requires the ability to demonstrate distinctiveness, but rules imply uniformity. Government officials deprived of discretion that could produce misbehavior are at the same time deprived of discretion that could call forth outstanding achievement. If an organization's tasks are standard and its environment slow to change, this won't create any particular problems, since creativity or innovativeness are unnecessary. When that's not the case, rule-bound organizations are accidents waiting to happen. In subsequent chapters we shall see how these general principles apply to the specific case of government procurement.

3
The Tyranny of the Proposal

In selecting a contractor, government organizations hazard a guess and place a bet. They must decide which of the vendors seeking the work will provide the best mixture of good performance and good price. For major high-technology systems, the bet is risky because new, large installations, especially those at the cutting edge of technology, may not work as hoped. The decision is a guess because a prediction must be ventured about the behavior of contractors in the future. The process of vendor evaluation should be seen as an effort to gather information that will improve predictions.

When making a tough, risky decision, one should use all important information and take advantage of all available learning. The theme of this chapter is that public officials are less likely to make the best decision about which vendor to select because the procurement system denies them important information that would shed light on future vendor behavior. The system domesticates the information government officials may use in making contract award decisions to the written proposals vendors submit. This denies the officials other information that might guide such decisions. The system also prevents some of the information that can be used from being given the significance it deserves, and stops government officials too early in the process from learning more about what they want and how much they want it.

What Is Hard to Figure Out before Contract Award?

Some features of contractor performance are easily established prior to contract award, and others become clear only afterward. The more difficult it is to determine aspects of contractor performance prior to contract award, the more important will the role of judgment be in making appropriate decisions about vendor selection.

Government computer contracts are mainly fixed price contracts; contractors bid a firm price to undertake the work presented in the RFP. It therefore might appear that the prices a contractor will charge the government are an example of something that can readily be determined before contract award. This, however, is not always true, for several reasons. Large multiyear contracts now typically contain what are called technology refreshment clauses that allow a vendor during the life of the contract to offer new generations of hardware or software that meet or exceed the performance of the equipment in the contractor's proposal, provided the price is the same or lower. Given the rapid replacement of computer equipment with new boxes showing constantly improving price-performance characteristics, the equipment (and the prices) that vendors bid in response to the original RFP quickly become largely irrelevant.[1] Whether the price the government gets on subsequent generations of equipment under a contract is a good one or not does not depend on the prices bid at the time of the original contract. Merely to get prices slightly under the prices for the older generation of equipment when new equipment is developed may not be much of an achievement if market prices for the equipment are plunging rapidly. Good prices at the time of the contract award therefore do not necessarily predict good prices in the future.

There is a second reason that even fixed-price bids at the time of contract award do not necessarily predict prices in the future. The government may not be sure at the time of the RFP exactly what the volume of its requirements will be. For example, in the case of the data communications network acquired by the Customs Service, in one of the case studies, the agency was not sure how much traffic would have to go over the lines. Or the agency may not know precisely what configurations of equipment, such as microcomputers, printers, and minicomputers in a local office, it will require. This was true in the case study of the procurement of the Immigration and Naturalization Service for computerization of local offices. In such situations, the government asks vendors to propose prices under a set of stylized usage assumptions or equipment configurations. For example, if the stylized assumptions involved delivering 500 configurations of a stand-alone microcomputer with dot-matrix printer and 50 configurations of a similar microcomputer but with a laser printer, the evaluated bid will be calculated by taking the unit prices of the computers, dot-matrix printers, and laser printers and multiplying them by the number of different configurations set forth in the RFP. If, however, the agency's usage assumptions were too low, a contractor may state after contract award that the quantities of equipment the government will need to purchase are considerably, and perhaps disproportionately, larger than the amount of equipment originally bid, or else the system will not function under the new usage figures. Similarly, if the relative quantities of different kinds of equipment that the government buys differ from the relative quantities in the RFP, the government may end up with worse prices than expected. To return to the example above, a vendor might have bid a very low price on dot-matrix printers and a relatively high one for laser printers. The low price on the dot-matrix printers gives the vendor a good total price, since the assumption in the RFP was that ten times as many dot-matrix as laser printers would be purchased. But if instead the government ultimately buys few dot-matrix printers and many laser printers, the price the government pays will be less favorable. In both examples, the price bid at the time of the proposal will not have predicted the future well.

A similar example occurred in the recompetition of the Environmental Protection Agency operations and maintenance computer services contract in the case studies. The winning vendor, who was the incumbent, lowered hourly wages from the existing contract on a number of labor categories, a change that was crucial in the reaward. Shortly after the contract was signed, however, the contractor sought to recategorize existing personnel already at agency sites to higher labor categories that were as expensive as before.

The difficulty of predicting a system's performance is even more difficult than predicting prices. For specific, well-defined machine tasks, gauging future performance beforehand can be straightforward. One can determine before a contract is awarded whether a microcomputer contains a certain amount of memory or whether an office automation software package can automatically renumber footnotes in a text when a new footnote has been added. Even with stand-alone microcomputers, however, some future performance is more difficult to determine, such as whether the vendor will deliver the computers on time, whether they will frequently break down, whether they will be serviced well if they do break down, how well the software will be updated and debugged, and how many new software applications will be written that are compatible with the computer.

The quality of performance of networks, of on-line access to databases, of real-time processing using those databases, and of other forms of complex computer systems is even far more difficult to predict. Unforeseen difficulties may include architectures that do not work as hoped, performance degradation, or countless other ails to which complex multiuser computer systems are prone. "What you know for sure is that things will go wrong," one of the private-sector computer managers interviewed told me. "What you want to be sure about is that when something does go wrong, the vendor is going to do his best to make it right." It is difficult to know in advance how a vendor will react to the unexpected, because at the time of contract award he naturally proposes the expected.

After the contract has been signed, one form that a poor contractor attitude can take is customer abuse—taking advantage of foreseeable errors, loopholes, and ambiguities, or of foreseeable changes in circumstances, to the customer's detriment. In a government context, such customer abuse is associated with phenomena that go under the names "buy-in" and "get-well." A "buy-in" in contracts for major weapons systems might have a small component for initial development work that is bid competitively, followed by full-scale development and final production negotiated on a sole-source basis. The buy-in involves an unrealistically low bid for the initial portion, with the hope of making up for early losses later. (The high prices for later work constitute the contractor's effort to "get well" from early losses.) Buy-in and get-well can also apply to computer contracts that are bid on a fixed-price basis, using features of long-term computer contracts described earlier, such as the size of discounts on new technology or the additional equipment said to be required to meet increased performance demands.

When the time comes to negotiate prices on new generations of equipment under a contract, the vendor has a strong bargaining position. If negotiations break down, the vendor can continue to sell the government the old equipment at the prices he had bid at the time of the RFP; the new generation would have rendered the old virtually impossible to sell to commercial customers, so the inventory would probably have to be written down anyway. At the time of contract award the customer does not know how strongly the vendor will press that advantage. In the case studies, complaints about these forms of customer abuse were common. The contractor selling the Customs Service its packet-switching network said that it had to dramatically increase the equipment to meet agency traffic demands that were higher than in the RFP. The contractor gave the Veterans Administration far less generous discounts on technology upgrades than the discounts bid on the first generation of equipment under the contract.

Another category of customer abuse can occur when the customers have misunderstood their own needs or failed to understand problems that meeting those needs would create. Such problems are likely to be the rule and not the exception in complex procurements of high technology. "We always make mistakes in our specifications. We're not smart enough to get it right all the time," one private-sector computer manager told me. Performance specifications in the original contract may be impossible to meet or may meet the specification without accomplishing what the government wanted. Different requirements in the contract, such as a design specification and a performance standard may contradict each other. Or achieving certain specifications may be far more expensive than the government anticipated.

Problems with specifications occur so frequently in government that an entire branch of contract administration law, referred to as the law of "constructive change orders," is devoted to them. The basic tenet of this body of law is that when defects in government specifications create performance problems for the contractor, the government should compensate the contractor for measures it must take to make performance acceptable.[2]

This is reasonable enough if indeed the contractor could not reasonably have known of the defects. A potential for customer abuse occurs when a vendor at the time the contract goes out for bid realizes that there are problems with the requirements. The vendor may choose to inform the customer of the problem or to remain silent. The vendor who remains silent may sell the unsuspecting customer unnecessary equipment. If meeting the original specifications creates problems the customer did not anticipate, the vendor may, after contract award, suggest some change that adds to the quantity of equipment sold or to the hours of technical support.

Buck Rodgers, former vice president of Marketing for IBM, states his company's policy in these situations as follows:

> A lot of salespeople make a go of it by taking the path of least resistance. "Give 'em what they want, and let them worry about it if they make a mistake" is a common attitude. . . . I've been in competitive selling situations where the customer wanted a smaller, less expensive installation than I *knew* he needed. I could not sell him what he wanted, without feeling that I wasn't benefiting him. Not if I had done my homework. Not if I had spent days on his shop floor studying his operation, interviewing his foremen, engineers, and production people. It's exactly the same if I concluded that what the customer wanted was more equipment than he needed. When I tried to increase or decrease a client's order, it was because I *knew* I was right. It's a matter of integrity.[3]

A textbook on purchasing management gives the example of a household furnishings contractor who supplied draperies to an apartment building in San Francisco. After the draperies shrank nine inches within a few weeks because of the San Francisco humidity, the owners asked the vendor to replace the draperies with preshrunk fabric. The vendor in turn contacted the mill from which it had bought the material.

> The mill initially refused, explaining that the cloth was not preshrunk because the specifications did not call for pre-shrinking. The contractor admitted the mill was technically right, but . . . contended that the mill, as a capable supplier, should have known that preshrunk cloth is a necessity for foggy areas such as San Francisco, regardless of any omission in the specification. The mill subsequently replaced the drapery material.[4]

Compare this with the approach of a top government marketing manager for one major computer vendor, who stated in an interview with me:

> Our attitude is: "Bid what they ask for, not what they want." We look at a government specification and see it has loopholes and errors. We don't tell the government that the specification won't do the job. You win the contract, and then you go back to them afterwards and say, "By the way, the thing you specified won't work. We need a change order."

The most dramatic example of this problem in the case studies involved the U.S. Department of Agriculture. None of the vendors bidding on the contract informed the agency that its specifications required a very expensive, duplicative computer architecture that would have been unnecessary had the specifications been modified slightly.

Formal disputes over contract administration were uncommon in the case studies and in the Government Computer Managers Survey. Only one of the nine case studies was marred by a significant level of contract disputes, though 33 percent ($N = 30$) of the thirty government computer managers reported "a lot" or "some" contract disputes in their most recent major contract. Nevertheless formal disputes are a bigger problem than they appear to be in the private sector. One study of purchasing agents and sales managers reported that none had ever been involved in a contract dispute that had actually proceeded to trial, and only a minority had been in a dispute where lawyers had been involved.[5]

All these instances of customer abuse tell the same story: it is extremely difficult to know at the time of contract award whether or not a vendor will exploit every loophole.

The opposite of customer abuse is customer coddling—not holding the customer to the letter of his contractual commitments, and going beyond what the contract requires the vendor to do after circumstances have changed. A textbook on purchasing management notes:

> Regardless of the managerial skills of a buyer, he will periodically encounter difficulties from which only a friendly supplier can extricate him. Even the best sales and production forecasts are vulnerable to error. Emergencies of many types continually arise in business. For example, unexpected increases in sales cause material shortages. Unforeseeable declines in sales and plant breakdowns cause material excesses. As a result of unexpected and material shortages and excesses, some orders have to be cancelled, others spread out, and still others increased or accelerated. Purchasing departments must have suppliers motivated by goodwill to cooperate with them in such emergencies.[6]

Another book cites a vendor that did not hold IBM to its contractual commitment to buy at least $1.5 million of furniture in a year when an economic recession reduced IBM's needs. The same vendor, during materials shortages in the wake of the 1973 oil crisis, increased its inventory levels at no additional charge so that IBM's delivery times would not suffer.[7] During the unforeseen supply shortages of the 1970s, some vendors were solicitous of their customers, and others were less so.[8]

One important element of customer coddling is technical assistance, a vendor's suggestions to the customer about ways to reduce costs and improve quality or operations. Part of the reason to buy something outside rather than to make it oneself is to take advantage of the skills that vendors have developed and the broad range of contacts they have with other customers and other situations, from which they get new ideas. For example, in the IRS service center mainframe replacement case, the manager wished the vendor had said in 1983 and 1984 that the agency was overly ambitious in its software conversion plans. Such advice could have helped the agency avoid the 1985 tax-filing season disaster. The vendor, however, failed to provide such technical assistance. Vendors may make such suggestions when competing for contracts, of course, but technical assistance, properly provided, is a process that continues after contract award as well. The quality and quantity of such assistance cannot easily be determined prior to contract award.

When buying complex computer systems, customers are buying people as much as equipment. They want from a vendor a set of capabilities (people who are well-trained and experienced and who work using a good set of company procedures) and a set of attitudes (people who will try hard, who will not take advantage of the customer). William Davidow, former vice president for Sales and Marketing at Intel, the semiconductor company, recounts how his firm won an important contract at Ford Motor Company:

> Ford Motor Company wanted to develop the world's best electronic carburation system for its cars. To accomplish that, Ford needed a very advanced microprocessor. A number of companies competed fiercely for Ford's business. Intel won the contract, not only because its device was superior but because Intel's management got to know every key manager at Ford. By the time Ford made its decision, the automaker not only felt good about the microprocessor, it felt great about Intel. Building confidence was a long and difficult process for Ford, but it had to be done. Wouldn't you be careful if the millions of cars you produced were dependent on a twenty-dollar part?
>
> To Ford, Intel's management commitment was an intangible factor. But it was enough in Ford's mind to be a significant differentiator.[9]

When customers are buying capabilities and attitudes more than hardware, they will have difficulty judging at the time of contract award how good the performance of a vendor will be.

The capabilities and attitudes of the people working on the contracts examined in the case studies varied greatly. A few vendors seemed consistently to go out of their way to please, such as the contractor selling computer support services to the Internal Revenue Service whose people did work over again at no charge even when problems with the work were the customer's fault. In other cases contractor personnel were described as enthusiastic but inexperienced, because vendors used agencies as on-the-job training sites for people and moved their people off the contract as soon as they had learned something. In still other cases, experienced teams fielded for the purposes of obtaining the contract award disappeared almost immediately thereafter. In all these situations, vendor performance after a contract is signed could not easily be ascertained at the time the contract was awarded.

A final category of performance that is hard to predict before it has occurred is how well a vendor will do in the future to stay abreast of technological change in subsequent generations of products. If a company stops keeping up technologically during the life of a contract, the customer may be in trouble.

In summary, myriad considerations involving the performance of a computer vendor cannot easily be determined at the time of contract award. These include the ingenuity and attitude of the contractor's people in overcoming difficulties, servicing equipment that goes down, and being helpful to the customer, as well as the ability of the vendor to keep up with changes in technology. How important should these considerations be in deciding which vendor to select? In purchasing high technology, especially considering the risks inherent in installing major new systems, the general view in the private sector is that these considerations are very important. William Davidow, formerly vice president of Marketing at Intel, writes:

> Customers evaluate suppliers on how well they will perform and on how much they can be trusted. Customers ask of a potential supplier: Will you be ready to fix the software bugs? Will you really be available to service my equipment in two hours? Will you really be in business five years from now? Will you really complete work on the software modifications on time? . . . High-tech is high risk. . . . A high-tech buyer, more than most, will be biased to the supplier he or she believes will assure success.[10]

Buck Rodgers of IBM writes about the importance of customer coddling:

> Most customers are not looking for the cheapest solutions to their problems. The quality of the equipment they invest in is certainly important to them, but even more important is the quality of the people whom they must depend on to service it. *They're buying peace of mind and a good night's sleep.* Customers perceive IBM as a company they can count on in a crisis. There's no doubt in my mind that IBM has earned that perception . . . because it is willing to make an extra effort and an occasional sacrifice to help a customer. . . . After Irv Levey acquired this book for Harper and Row, he noticed that almost every business machine in the publisher's New York headquarters was an IBM. He asked Bill Baker, the company's comptroller, "How come? Are they cheaper? Are they superior? Why IBM?" They're not cheaper, Bill Baker was sure of that. And he couldn't swear that they were absolutely the best machines available. But one thing Baker was sure of: IBM's service organization was the best in the world. They were totally dependable and, at times, did incredible things for their customers. Then he told Irv about a time when the customer's main computer, in Scranton, Pennsylvania, went down because a very inexpensive small part malfunctioned. It was very unusual for this part to cause a problem, and there was no replacement for it

anywhere in the area. However, IBM quickly located one in Colorado, sent a jet to pick it up, and had the computer in full operation within twenty-four hours of the mishap.[11]

In making major computer-purchase decisions in the private sector, one study found, "buyers generally considered the vendor's future capabilities to be key: capabilities to provide continuing streams of useful products."[12] A large-scale survey of purchasers of computer dumb terminals found that respondents ranked "service response time," "service available at point of need," and "overall quality of service," as the top three (of thirty-three) factors in selecting a vendor.[13] In one survey of production and maintenance managers, both groups ranked technical assistance as next to the most important characteristic of a good supplier, just behind reliable delivery (for production people) and after-sales service (for maintenance ones).[14] If salary and other limitations prevent government from retaining the best technical people, then good technical assistance from contractors is even more crucial in the public than in the private sector.

Such considerations are sometimes called intangibles, but this appellation is only partly correct. After contract award, such considerations are extremely, sometimes painfully, tangible—as anyone who has dealt with incompetent repair people or who feels he must check to see if his wallet is still there every time he leaves a meeting with a contractor can testify. These considerations are quite intangible before contract award, however, since they cannot be directly tested the way a specific product feature can.

Search and Experience as Sources of Information

In evaluating vendors, public officials undertake behavior that traditionally in the literature on the economics of information has been referred to as "search." Search, in the economics of information, involves reading printed information about the performance characteristics of alternative products or inspecting products physically, or both. Government search behavior prior to contract award consists of reading proposals that vendors submit in response to an RFP and of any live test demonstration that vendors perform prior to contract award.

The search process that government organizations undertake prior to contract award does, of course, provide much useful information not only about dimensions of contractor performance that are easier to discern in advance, such as the specification for the performance of a machine, but also about those that are more difficult. Through search one can gain at least some idea of the ability of contractors to offer intelligent ideas, by seeing how intelligently they respond to the problem the government hands them in the RFP. A contractor's proposal can show how close the contractor's service centers lie to the customer's installations, the size of their parts inventories, or the education and experience of the technical people who will be working on the contract.

Search-gathered information gives only a dim hint, however, of the quality of post-award vendor performance in terms of technical assistance, service responsiveness, or the quality of vendor management.

There lies the problem for public officials making decisions about vendor selection. As noted in the previous chapter, government contracts are to be awarded to vendors solely on evidence contained within their proposals and accompanying live test demonstrations. Important information about the government's actual costs under a contract and about how well the vendor will perform cannot, however, really be communicated in a proposal. How can the government predict from a written proposal the zeal a vendor will display in solving an unexpected problem? How can the government tell from a written proposal how successfully a vendor weeds out incompetent repair people and motivates the others to fix things efficiently and properly? How can the government determine from a written proposal whether the vendor plans to assign nine lawyers to comb the contract in search of ambiguities to exploit after the contract is signed?

What normal people in their everyday lives do when faced with such a situation is to rely on the other main source of available information besides search—namely, experience.[15] We cease to rely exclusively on what we can learn around the time of decision and extend our information horizons to include information based on how people, organizations, or products we are considering have performed during our previous encounters with them. The use of information about past behavior to derive conclusions about future behavior is so common that people would hardly go about their daily lives without it. Proverbs tell the tale, in this case ones such as "once burnt, twice shy." Without the ability to use past behavior to predict future behavior, entire concepts such as "reputation" and "credibility" would vanish. We would be left to judge a person's likely future honesty without reference to his honesty in the past and his likely future diligence without reference to his past diligence. Social interaction would become far more difficult because we would lack the crucial information that makes it possible. People would try to substitute for the inability to draw inferences from past behavior by complex, but always incomplete and abusable, formal contractual

39

commitments and performance bonds signed at the time they agreed to interact.

The use of one's own past experience as a guide lies at the heart of economic life. Information derived by consumers from experience with one purchase will be crucial in their choices about whether to buy the product again; if I buy a certain candy bar once and do not like it, I am unlikely to buy it again. In deciding whom to promote to a better job, bosses look at how well individuals have done in past assignments. Studies of jobs with above-average injury rates demonstrate that they show higher quit rates than similar jobs with lower injury rates; workers, ignorant of the risks when they start the job, learn through on-the-job experience and adapt their behavior accordingly.[16] Crucial to modern macroeconomic theory is the idea that people adapt their expectations of the future based on their experience in the past; people who experienced high inflation last year are likely to expect a continuation of high inflation this year.[17] Even when selecting a teaching assistant for a course I teach, I base the decision on my knowledge of how candidates did as students in the past.

Faced with the problem of predicting future performance on dimensions not communicable through written proposals, the government procurement system abdicates. Information based on experience, which might be useful—indeed crucial—in making good contractor selection decisions, is generally ruled out by the system. Allowing the use of such information, it is feared, might produce unbridled discretion. Even when using such information is allowed, it is given less weight than it deserves. The government becomes far more dependent than it should be on words and assurances contained in the written proposals made just before contract award. "You're stuck just evaluating them based on the promises thay make," one respondent in the Government Computer Managers Survey said. "We deal with written lies." We need go no further than proverbs such as "actions speak louder than words" and "the proof of the pudding is in the eating" to grasp the limitations of the information on which government officials are required to rely. Consumers normally use information garnered from both search and experience in making decisions about what to buy, but public officials lack the freedom to make use of one entire, enormous, informational domain.

The most important information that is excluded by relying on written vendor proposals is information based on the experience that one's own organization may have had with a contractor. Agencies have frequently had earlier contracts with one or more of the vendors bidding for work on a new contract. (If a previous contract is being recompeted, the prior experience may in fact have been on the kind of work being awarded now.)

Unbelievably—and appallingly—almost all computer systems buyers in government consider themselves forbidden to use information about the past performance of a contractor on earlier contracts within the agency when they make decisions about new contract awards. (The exception is for the barebones determination by a contracting officer that the vendor meets procurement requirements for "responsibility.")[18] *In the Government Computer Managers Survey, 85 percent of the respondents answered "no" when asked, "Are you allowed to factor in your own prior experience with a vendor here in this agency in making award decisions?"* "There is," one respondent to the Government Computer Managers Survey lamented, "no history in government procurement." "Our procurement process is such that taking our past experience with a vendor into account is extremely hard to do," another respondent to the Government Computer Managers Survey stated. "It seems to start from scratch each time around." The case studies also make this point clear. None of those involved in *any* of the cases reported being allowed to use information about the work the vendors had done at the agency in making contract award decisions. In four of the nine cases, the agencies had had prior experience with one or more of the competing vendors, but in no case was that experience part of the evaluation process. In the local office computerization procurement at the Department of Agriculture, the agency had had positive experience with one of the two top bidders, but that experience counted only in making that vendor a "sentimental favorite," not in awarding evaluation points—and that vendor failed to win the contract. In the Veterans Administration office automation procurement, the agency had significant prior experience with all three of the vendors who bid—and awarded the contract to the vendor with whom their prior experience had been the poorest. Officials at the Environmental Protection Agency could not even use information from prior contractor performance in evaluating the vendor for the same contract.[19] In none of the cases did indifferent or disappointing past experience stop the contractor from receiving the contract award, and only in one case—the acquisition of mainframe computers and custom software by the Federal Aviation Administration—was the winning vendor one with whom the agency had dealt and been satisfied. (Even in that case, the vendor might not have been selected had it not bid the low price.)

Officials at the Internal Revenue Service devoted enormous effort to determine how good a job vendors would do in computer services consulting, where it is notoriously difficult to predict performance from a written proposal. The agency demanded that vendors present in their written proposals elaborate plans for how they would staff hypothetical assignments (but did not require that bidders actually *perform* anything). These contortions strike an observer as an almost painful exercise in what conscientious public officials go through when the use of common sense and good judgment are not among the available options. A pathetic comment was made to me by a person of enormous good will and devotion to his job in charge of this procurement at the IRS. He told me proudly that one other person involved in the procurement knew about a bidder with whom the IRS had had terrible experience but "was careful not to tell anyone on the panel, so as not to bias the evaluation process." In the private sector, consulting business is typically awarded in small contracts to a large number of vendors. Future business is then granted or withheld on the basis of performance. In that way, a few consultants come to do a large amount of business with the customer—but the evolution toward the large volume of business is based on information carried from past performance. Such a strategy would be illegal for the government: additional business could not be awarded without "full and open competition," and performance on previous jobs could not count.

The recompetition in 1989 of this same IRS computer support services consulting contract—the results became known after this research was completed and just before this book went to press— provides what can be characterized only as an appalling example of what happens when past performance may not be taken into account. In all nine case studies, the customer was more enthusiastic about Vanguard Technologies, the winning vendor in the original 1985 IRS contract, than any other vendor. Customers told stories of phone calls quickly returned at any hour of the day or night, of reports with which the customer was dissatisfied redone at no extra charge, and of the time IRS misspecified what it wanted in a training program Vanguard was supposed to provide, only to have Vanguard volunteer to redo the training at no charge to IRS despite the agency's acknowledgement that the mistake had been its and not Vanguard's. An internal IRS survey showed seventy-three of seventy-six IRS users satisfied with Vanguard's work for them. Indeed, there was so much customer demand under the contract that it had to be recompeted early because the agency ran out of budget authorization for purchases under it.

In the recompetition of the contract (which occurred after this research was completed and the reactions of IRS people to Vanguard's performance already recorded), however, Vanguard lost to a vendor IRS had not worked with. It lost because its written proposal was adjudged inferior to that of the winning vendor. In particular, the RFP again included a hypothetical situation to which the bidders were to respond, and Vanguard's response to the hypothetical situation was judged poorer than that of the winning vendor. The fact that Vanguard had prodigious experience responding to such situations was not taken into account. Indeed, Vanguard's performance played no role in the evaluation process at all. "Evaluating performance is something that's frowned upon," according to one official involved in the recompetition. "Just because the contractor does work for the government and does a good job, it doesn't mean he can get the business again." This same official went on to say that he took "pride in the fact that we're so objective" that the agency did not let experience with Vanguard affect its evaluation of Vanguard's written proposal.

The procurement system thus removes public officials from what probably is the single most useful bit of information to help predict the performance of contractors in the future. How did General Motors learn about which steel suppliers were likely to treat them well in time of crisis? By looking at how they had performed earlier when a crisis did hit in 1974–1975. How did GM learn about which ones were likely to do a good job keeping up with technology in the future? By seeing which ones reacted quickly with a changed investment program to the increased price of energy in the past.[20] According to one empirical study of industrial purchasing behavior, of all the variables that influenced purchasing decisions, past experience "was found to be the *only* variable that entered *all* of the buying decisions."[21] The authors quote one manager: "My concern is not with what the supplier *promises* to do for me at this time. By the time I find that out, it's too late. What I'm interested in is what he has done in the past, for me and to some extent, for others."[22] When informed of the failure in government procurement to look at past performance, private-sector managers I interviewed generally gave physical displays of incredulity—such as an eyeballs-toward-the-air "there-they-go-again" expression of those who believe that government is habitually daffy. All of those interviewed stated some version of the same words: "How can they say you can't take into account the single most important factor in making these decisions?"

There is no provision in the *Federal Acquisition Regulations* that prohibits using information from the past performance of vendors on contracts in one's own organization. The inability to do so has emerged in the procurement culture from the doctrine that vendors may be evaluated only on their proposals. Judgments about how a contractor performed in past dealings with the organization do not fit into the model of domesticating discretion into a structured reaction to the actions of others. Judgments about the performance of contractors at one's organization are a composite of countless individual incidents and experiences—the time the project manager came (or did not come) after a power outage, the indifference or solicitude shown when unexpected problems arose, the attitude during price negotiations on the latest technology upgrade. Because past performance is such a composite, specific evaluation criteria to measure such performance are difficult to structure in advance, so that any information used would risk being unsystematic. To allow officials to pick and choose among an endless stream of facts and impressions creates the clear potential for whim, arbitrariness, or prejudice. Furthermore, to reduce the likelihood of unfair influence, members of a technical evaluation team are generally not permitted to talk with colleagues at the agency about their experiences with bidders—or even to tell others who the bidders are. In addition, taking account of a vendor's past performance with one's organization would conflict with "free and open competition," since a vendor with no past experience there could not get the credit for good performance given to another.[23]

Formal ratings schemes might be developed within the spirit of the procurement culture for quantifiable aspects of vendor performance, such as the proportion of times a vendor does not come for a repair. Such measures would, however, capture past performance only to an extremely limited extent; futhermore, because of bid protest decisions, to be discussed shortly, such data would have to meet a high standard of representativeness and statistical reliability.

As with many of the limits on using information to be discussed in this chapter, the system doubtlessly works better in practice than in theory. Responding to a follow-up question to the one about whether they were allowed to take past performance at the agency into account, which asked whether "you feel this gets done informally," 71 percent of respondents to the Government Computer Managers Survey responded that they thought it did.[24] Most of them, however, stated that it did so only to a very limited extent, and the tenor of comments suggested that many respondents saw the inclination to take one's past experience with a contractor into account as some sort of irreducible flaw of human nature, like a craving for fattening foods or kinky sex. To quote the comments of several respondents:

> I think we're all influenced, whether we want to believe it or not, by our life experiences. We try not to allow it to influence our evaluation.

> You're always prejudiced. But it shouldn't happen.

Yes, a panel member is biased by prior negative experience, but we try to limit this.

Staging live test demonstrations to observe contractors' solutions in practice might appear to supplement the contents of a written proposal. To some extent, it does. The case studies, however, exhibit many limitations of live test demonstrations. The most dramatic example occurred in the Internal Revenue Service center computer replacement. There, the winning vendor adapted the software on its computers to meet the specific characteristics of the benchmark tapes, and it bid computer capacity that was insufficient to meet real-life requirements similar, but not identical, to those on the tape. In the procurement of computers for local offices of the Customs Service, none of the problems that surfaced at these offices immediately after contract award with the equipment running day-in and day-out showed up in the live test demonstration, which demanded only a one-time demonstration of the computer's ability. A somewhat better method of determining a vendor's likely postaward performance is the design competition used by the Federal Aviation Administration for a new "host" computer for the air-traffic control system. The competition lasted about two years, however, and required the agency to fund two competitors' development efforts. It was a time-consuming and expensive way to deal with a problem that could have been addressed more easily by looking at the past performance of the competitors.

One may attempt to force vendors to include negative information about past performance in their proposals, although that may arouse lawyers and procurement people and prompt bid protests. In connection with the procurement case study on the Enviromental Protection Agency's operations and maintenance, the agency's chief computer manager recounted a recompetition involving a vendor that had performed terribly in another contract but was nonetheless about to be awarded the contract again. Angered and upset, the manager demanded written interrogatories regarding specific elements of the vendor's past performance.

> I said, "This time I'm going to rock the f--king boat." I ranted and raved. Everyone had to put their thinking caps on to come up with a way to deal with this because I was carrying on like a crazy person. It was uphill. The system doesn't make it natural or easy.

One of the few respondents in the Government Computer Managers Survey who said he was allowed to use information about past performance on agency contracts expressed the way he did so: "If you don't trust the firm, you work harder to check for loopholes or things being slipped through in their proposals. Or you can raise a question during your structured interactions with them that comes out of your experience." An innovative approach used by one very small agency whose chief computer manager was interviewed in the Government Computer Managers Survey was to ask vendors for names and telephone numbers of all their customers for the previous three years, including those who had stopped doing business with the vendor. The requirement to list all customers leads to the inclusion of previous contracts at the agency itself. The agency phoned only former customers, in the belief that they were more likely to be honest and frank. Such an approach might not work at a more visible agency: the guardians of procurement purity might ask, for example, why only a subset of the customers that bidders had provided were phoned and not others.

Past performance at one's own organization is not the only important information that public managers are restricted from using in making contract award decisions. Officials may not apply impressions developed in interaction with vendors during the procurement. Government and contractor representatives often meet to discuss questions about the proposal or to negotiate the terms of the vendor's bids. The specific result of these sessions may, of course, become part of proposal evaluation, but not what was revealed at the meetings about how alert, enthusiastic, creative, or smart the vendor's people were. Points cannot be added or subtracted based on how a vendor's people look you in the eye. There is no room for the information about vendor commitment or eagerness that gets communicated in ways other than dry prose. Contrast this with the private-sector computer manager who told me that a vital factor in making an important purchase was that the winning vendor had sent a higher level of management to make its presentation—suggesting that the firm had a higher commitment to the business. Or, even more (melo)dramatically, contrast the attitude in government with an account of how Tom Mitchell, the president of Seagate Technologies, a computer disk drive supplier, seeks customers:

> During a convention in Las Vegas last year, Mitchell spotted Jack Tramiel, head of Atari Computer, at a craps table. Seagate had been trying for years, without success, to sell hard disks to Atari. Mitchell walked over to Tramiel and dropped to his knees. "Please, let us be your disk drive company," he implored. Two months later Seagate drives were on their way to Atari.[25]

During a live test demonstration, government officials can observe the vendor's staff, but usually can use only information on how well the

46

vendor performed in the test. In only one case study did this influence the management quality points that vendors received. Interestingly, in the Department of Agriculture local office computerization case, the contracting officer believed that it was indeed appropriate to use information from the live test demonstration in this way—but the head of the management evaluation team was not even present at the live test and had no idea that he could use such evidence.[26]

Finally, although 91 percent of respondents to the Government Computer Managers Survey felt that judgments about a vendor's future capabilities were important in making contract awards, only 37 percent thought they were given much consideration in the government.[27] The consideration appears too intangible to be tied to any specific requirement of the government and might violate the demand that the discretion of public managers be limited by basing evaluation criteria on demonstrable government requirements.

Alternatives to Past Performance Information

The government evaluation process attempts to handle some of these ex ante intangibles in two ways. Some efforts are made to force some intangibles into the written proposal system. And winning vendors must commit themselves when they sign a contract to language designed to capture some elements of performance that were difficult to evaluate at the time the award was made. Neither technique works particularly well. The information that can be evaluated as part of a written proposal is often not particularly good, and it does not weigh heavily as an evaluation factor anyway. The contractual language does an incomplete job of capturing the relevant dimensions of the performance it is supposed to ensure. Contractual commitments are difficult to enforce in any event.

All the case study procurements included an evaluation criterion called "corporate experience," "management capability," or something similar. RFPs generally required bidders to present information about the company's sales and financial stability. They also required bidders to describe some number of recent projects on which they had worked that had requirements similar in nature and size to those of the contract the agency was planning to award. For these projects, bidders generally had to give the name and telephone number of someone in the customer organization to call for a reference. Vendors were also generally required to provide résumés for the key personnel (that is, the top managers) they planned to assign to the contract if it were awarded to them.

Although agencies are not allowed to consider information about the past performance of vendors on previous contracts at their own

47

TABLE 3–1

Opinions of Information Obtained from Vendor-provided
References
(percent)

References candid/information useful	41
References not candid	10
References not candid/specific mention of fear of lawsuits on the part of references	7
Reference information not useful because vendors provide names of only satisfied customers	14
Information references provide not valuable; respondent digs to get information from other than vendor-provided references	10
Procurement people object to using this information	7
Don't use this information	10

Note: Responses coded into these categories from answers to open-ended question. Percentages add up to less than 100 percent because of rounding. (N = 29)
Source: Government Computer Managers Survey.

agency, most agencies can consider the testimony of vendor-selected references from other sites. (In two of the nine case studies, contracting officers forbade the use of management capabilities as a scored evaluation factor for the program people to examine; only the contracts office could use it, to determine whether the vendor met the minimum requirements for being declared "responsible.") This acceptability of vendor-provided references in a world where one's own experience cannot be used seems peculiar, since vendors will hardly cull references from their least satisfied customers and since people in other organizations know less about the procuring agency's needs than the agency's own people who have dealt with the vendor before. This policy, however, follows a peculiar logic that surely only procurement-system aficionados can fathom: information from one's own agency is subject to bias because the agency controls what to use, but information provided by the vendor is not under agency control and therefore not subject to agency bias.

In the case studies, only one of the four agencies that called references believed they had learned anything significant from those calls. The case study material suggests that references were often called to check only the objective facts such as whether the vendor had completed the work as stated and whether the work was comparable to that in the contract being awarded.[28] Respondents to the Government Computer Managers Survey disagreed about the extent to which vendor-provided references ever provided any useful information—in particular, whether references ever said anything negative (see table 3–1). Approximately 40 percent found information from vendor-provided references useful, while the rest found it lacking for one reason or another. Aside from a rosy bias in the vendor's selection of references, some respondents felt that even dissatisfied references would hesitate to reveal negative information for fear of damaging the relationship with the vendor or risking vendor lawsuits for defamation. Any information from references that influences the evaluation process must be written down and could fall into the contractor's hands if the award is protested. (During a discussion about the usefulness of references, a private-sector computer manager said if he knew that his comments were being written down, he would never say anything negative about a vendor.) Other respondents to the Government Computer Managers Survey felt reference checks did often provide useful information. "We ask them specific questions that ask them to state facts, such as how long it takes to get a hold of the right vice president at the company when you've got a problem," one respondent stated. "We try to get the best information we can by schmoozing with the references," another respondent said. "We take calls to references very seriously, because we can't use the best source of information, which would be our own past experience." Ten percent of the respondents stated that they used information from customers not on the contractor-provided list. One of these respondents stated: "The references the vendor provides never say anything bad. So I ask those references to give me other references, and I call them. Those references will provide good information. This is probably illegal. But I'm responsible for doing this job."

If an agency wishes to develop any measure of customer satisfaction independent of vendor-provided references, it must develop a formal survey. "A statistician can help design a sample and questionnaire to ensure the reliability of findings," according to the regulatory guidance on the issue, which also reminds people that "if there are ten or more nonfederal respondents involved, a survey must be cleared with [the Office of Management and Budget] under the Paperwork Reduction Act.[29] The very use of surveys has been the subject of bid protests. The use of such quantitative data has been ruled permissible, but very high standards have been established for sample sizes and representativeness, so that, for example, reliance on performance data developed by third-party information vendors, such as Reliability Plus in the computer area, has frequently been ruled out, even though these sources are considered good enough for private-sector work.[30] And it would almost certainly be impermissible to use, for example, market-share data of various vendors as a proxy for degree of customer satisfaction, a practice commonly used in the private sector on the commonsense grounds that firms would not remain big or grow fast if they were not doing something right for customers. (In one of the important decisions being made by one of the private-sector computer managers I interviewed, they picked the fastest-growing firm in the market segment they were examining. "They have a tremendous growth rate," the manager told me. "They must be doing something right.") Nor is one permitted to confer informally with friends at other organizations who have experience with the vendor in question—though my interviews suggest that this occasionally occurs anyway. In the private sector networks of colleagues at different firms rely on each other more than on references that the vendor provides. Nor could one use stories one has read or heard through the trade that suggest that a company's products are performing poorly or well. In the private sector, vendors worry a great deal that reports of problems will damage their credibility in the marketplace. All these practices would be condemned on the grounds that government officials might arbitrarily or discriminatorily pick and choose from among a larger universe of possible information. In sum, departing from vendor-supplied references in the government is not easy.

Beyond the limitations of the information the government collects from contractor-provided references is the strikingly small weight the entire factor of corporate experience and management capability is given in the evaluation process. In the nine case studies, this factor counted on average only 8 percent of the total for all evaluation criteria.[31] It counted as low as zero in the Federal Aviation Administration host computer procurement and the Customs Service local office computerization procurement and as high as 30 percent in the U.S. Department of Agriculture local office computerization procurement. Even these terribly low figures included not only actual experience at other sites but also other management subfactors, such as corporate financial stability.

Only 26 percent of respondents to the Government Computer Managers Survey felt the system allowed them to give sufficient weight to the management capabilities of different vendors when making contract awards.[32] Procurement offices and the General Services Administration do not favor efforts to weigh management capability heavily as an evaluation factor, given its intangible nature. As one respondent to the Government Computer Managers Survey stated, "When you allow these subjective criteria to enter into a procurement, you open the door to protest. Procurement officers want to get the procurement through, not meet your needs." The contracting officer on the Customs Service local office computerization procurement stated: "All my technical people want to give lots of points for management. I always say it's not necessary. If you get a negative report, how do you know how reliable it is? Let's get away from subjective things like that." Given the leveling that occurs among major contractors because of identical scores on elements of management capability, such as financial stability, it would be almost impossible for the award decision on a major contract to be determined by contractors' scores on the corporate experience and management capability factor.

Contracts people tend to rely on contractual language to make the intangible concrete—and do not bother to weigh the factor heavily because any vendor who wins the contract will have to sign such language as a condition for contract award. The same contracting officer at the Customs Service who opposed giving any weight to management capability concluded her argument by stating, "Remember, this is a contract. You've got legal coverage for their stuff not performing, or breaking down, or not being right."

The tiny weight given the criterion of management capability would appear to form part of a vicious circle. The procurement system limits the information that agencies may consider about past vendor performance so that the information they *are* permitted to use possesses only limited value. The system furthermore displays a residual skepticism about allowing intangible information potentially tainted by bias and mere personal judgment to be used in making contract award decisions. In a world where the information is unlikely to be terribly helpful and where it fails to make much difference anyway, participants in the system develop contempt for the entire exercise. In only half the case studies did members of the technical evaluation teams even bother to telephone the references that vendors provided, and some of those who did call checked essentially only the honesty of the vendor's claims about the nature of the work, not the quality of performance. In general, variations in final scores on the management capability evaluation factor tended to be insignificant.

Perhaps the saddest thing about this vicious cycle is that it appears to have created an attitude among some in the government, including some program people, of disregard for past performance as an indicator of future vendor performance. Managers working both on the Federal Aviation Administration's host computer acquisition and on the Internal Revenue Service's computer consulting contract—people who gave every indication of caring sincerely, even passionately, about choosing the right vendor and obtaining high-quality

51

work from contractors—stated to me that one did not learn much from a contractor's past performance, since performance varied so much across contracts and over time. In the Federal Aviation Administration's host computer procurement, where the agency actually staged a two-year design competition for the hardest part of the work, the RFP for the full-scale procurement amazingly allowed only modest weight to the bidders' performance during the design competition that had just occurred! This performance was documented by extensive written records, so regulations would not have prevented its use. If the design competition performance had been given significant weight, however, it might have led the less successful vendor to drop out of the final bidding, leaving only one bidder, or to protest the weight given that factor.

Such attitudes are especially unfortunate for two reasons. When we use the term "bureaucrat" as an epithet, we have in mind the psychological disassociation of rules about how to do one's job from the injunctions of everyday common sense. A normal person surely would not purchase a brand of soup again if he had gagged on the last one. When that same person refuses to consider past experience in judging contractors to work in one's organization, something unhealthy is going on. I regret a situation where a conscientious government official proudly recounts that somebody knew about the agency's terrible experience with a vendor and was "objective enough" not to share this information with the technical committee evaluating a new contract. Our system for managing in the public sector may rob the people in it of their faculties to such an extent that, like a person on a mind-numbing drug, they no longer even realize that they are missing anything. The more pervasive and generalized such disassociation becomes, the less public officials are likely to realize how to behave appropriately on the job. These attitudes are unfortunate for a second reason as well. By weakening the realization that the current way of doing things violates common sense, the creation of an attitude that denies the importance of past performance reduces pressures to change the way the procurement system currently works.

A similar pattern—of limiting the information officials may use for evaluation, of assigning the criterion itself inordinately low weight, and of trying to deal with problems through contractual language—applies to the evaluation of the people vendors assign to key management positions. People are crucial, of course, but the evaluation process does not contribute much in evaluating them. The quality of these people is judged on written résumés that bidders are required to submit for key personnel—no room here for Tom Mitchell of Seagate Technologies not being too proud to beg. Even within the confines of a totally résumé-based evaluation, the evaluation process makes it difficult to assess a résumé with any flair or creativity. The limiting of evaluation criteria to those stated in advance in the RFP removes the possibility of reacting to idiosyncratic warning signals in a résumé—Why did this person have ten jobs in ten years? Why did this person take twenty years to advance to a level in the organization that most people attain in five? One contracting officer told me, with regard to a person who had held ten jobs in ten years, that such information could not be held against that person because "under our key personnel clause, after all, we only require a commitment to work for us for 60–90 days"—surely an example of literalism in the requirements process gone wild. Evaluation based only on demonstrable agency requirements discounts achievements such as having graduated summa cum laude in engineering from Cal Tech or having won professional awards, since it would be hard to argue that such accomplishments are a precondition for doing a good job. Neither, of course, may agencies use their own knowledge of individuals whose résumés have been submitted. So résumés tend to be rated on the most mechanical of prestated evaluation factors, such as presence of a certain educational credential and the years of experience the person has had doing tasks related to the procurement, without regard to the quality of performance on those tasks.

A customer must know about more than a few key managers assigned to a project to judge the quality of a contractor's people. One point made by some of the private-sector computer managers was that buying from IBM gave a customer access not just to whomever IBM's local people working on the customer's account happened to be, but also, if problems arose, to the experts in the entire IBM organization. Such people never have their résumés evaluated in the government, because they are not "assigned" to the contract. The dozens or hundreds of people assigned to do the daily contract implementation work never have their résumés evaluated either.

After the contract is awarded, the key people in the vendor's proposal may or may not actually remain on the project. Companies cannot retain employees as if they were chattel, and people do get divorced and leave for the South Seas, get sick, or even die. At the same time, contractors might promise employees with star résumés and then move them away for use in bidding on a different project. Agencies may not use information from past performance, however, that would shed light on how likely the contractor is to engage in this form of customer abuse.

Instead, the government relies on a contractual clause, called the "key personnel clause," which stipulates that the vendor may remove from the contract those managers defined in the RFP as key personnel only with the permission of the procuring agency. Despite this contractual clause, complaints from agency officials about substitutions of key personnel are legion. "They're always proposing people they don't send," one respondent in the Government Computer Managers Survey stated. "There's lots of ruse in the proposal-writing business. You get a great team from the proposal, but it's not who you get." As managers see it, they have little leverage in resisting efforts by a contractor to switch key personnel, since basically the only weapon the government has is the drastic threat to cancel the entire contract. "My boss is not interested in hearing that I'm cancelling a contract and that it will take two years to get another one awarded," said one respondent to the Government Computer Managers Survey. "I have no leverage, and contractors know that and count on that." In addition, there were persistent complaints about very junior people, at the trainee level, being assigned in large numbers to contracts—and then disappearing as soon as they had received their on-the-job training at government expense.

Here, as well, the practice may be better than the theory. A contracting officer at the Environmental Protection Agency referred to "discrepancies" their office saw between the conformance of the formal résumé to the evaluation criteria and the score the evaluators had given the résumé. It turned out that such "discrepancies" often resulted from informal judgments that something was fishy. "They'll tell us, 'We have this funny feeling about this person.' *Or worse, they'll say, 'We know this person from another contract, and she's a deadbeat.'*" The tragedy is that contracting officers regard these judgments as something to hunt down and eradicate rather than something to nurture.

The situation with "key personnel" clauses also creates a vicious cycle. There were two case studies in which one would have thought that the quality of people was especially crucial (the Environmental Protection Agency operations and maintenance recompetition and the Internal Revenue Service computer support services contract) since the agencies were buying not equipment but only people. Yet even in those cases the quality of key personnel was not heavily weighted as an evaluation criterion, and the managers involved did not seem to take the exercise of evaluating key personnel particularly seriously. Since "key personnel" disappear with such regularity anyway, these managers did not devote huge efforts to assessing the résumés in bidders' proposals or fight to get "key personnel" assigned an important evaluation weight.

The same story can be told with regard to service quality, which in government means repair of equipment that is not functioning. The evaluation process assesses formal measures of service capability such as numbers of service technicians available and, particularly, the location of service facilities near the offices where equipment will be placed. Service is given very low weight as an evaluation criterion, and the evaluation criteria that do exist give the government little idea of the quality of the repair people vendors send to service equipment.

The government attempts to ensure good service performance after a contract is awarded through contract clauses. Vendors commit themselves to appearing at the customer's site to repair equipment within, say, four hours and to giving the government certain dollar credits if the equipment is not running a certain percentage of the time in a given month. These commitments, however, fail to capture the differences between good and bad repair performance. Response time is too blunt an instrument. As one respondent to the Government Computer Managers Survey noted: "Service is an attitude. I want them to respond to priorities as they relate to the customer. If there's a critical system in the Administrator's office, I don't want them to wait four hours. If something is down that's not totally critical, I can wait a bit longer." Nor does the language capture the differences in attitude. IBM shipped an unavailable part by air from a remote location to help a private-sector customer, but the contractor in the Department of Agriculture local office computerization case study raised bureaucratic issues about machine identification numbers whenever customers called for repairs.

Monthly downtime credits are intended to reflect the quality of repair work, since presumably bad repairs lead to more downtime credits. One problem is that there is a difference between having a machine down for one eight-hour day, having it down twice for four hours, and having it down four times for two hours each, even though the numbers show them as identical. Beyond that, government people generally consider the credits too small to serve as a deterrent. Moreover, the regulations usually require a prodigious paper trail, and vendors often insist that they should not have to pay because the fault is the government's. According to responses in the Government Computer Managers Survey, downtime credits are seldom invoked. The same goes for the use of liquidated damage clauses (penalties for nontimely delivery) that the government uses to attempt to get good performance in meeting contracted delivery schedules. "If timeliness is important, put a liquidated damages clause in the contract," argues a Customs Service contracting officer, to justify the failure to give points for management capability. Because of hassles and legal problems, however, such clauses are rarely enforced.

Contract Award and the Early Establishment of Award Criteria

Central to the model of domesticating discretion in government contract award is the notion that the government must tell vendors in advance not only all the things it wants but also how much it wants them. What the government wants is set forth in its specifications; how much it wants them are set forth in its evaluation criteria. By requiring that evaluation criteria be set forth in the RFP, discretion is limited because the government is prevented from changing the grounds for contract award after it receives proposals, something that would pave the way for favoritism toward the vendors officials like.

The *Federal Acquisition Regulations* require that the RFP state the relative importance of different criteria, such as "price is the most important evaluation criterion, followed by technical excellence, followed by management capability" or "technical excellence is more important than the other evaluation criteria combined."[33] Exact numerical weights (such as price counts 60 percent, technical 30 percent, and management 10 percent) are not required. Nor need an agency make its award to the vendor whose proposal gets the highest score.[34] The government may therefore award contracts to the low-priced vendor even if another vendor scored higher on points. Thus, discretion is allowed in order to give priority to the evaluation criterion that is least based on discretion—price.

In practice most agencies choose to present exact evaluation weights, often in great detail, in RFPs. Of the nine case studies, for example, exact weights were stated in six of the cases, and in the other three, exact weights were given for every criterion but price. Many agencies feel they are on safer ground if they provide exact weights, since their decisions will then seem less subjective, particularly in cases of bid protests. In all case studies that specified points, the RFP stated that award would go to the proposal with the largest number of points—in some cases, the RFP even noted that point scores would be calculated to two decimal places.

This attempt to domesticate discretion also limits the ability of government officials to make the best selection of a vendor. Specifications and evaluation criteria are frozen before the agency can learn more about what it wants from the vendors.

To be fair, the model that the government uses of establishing criteria in advance and then judging proposals against those criteria does correspond to a common notion of how one ought to make rational decisions. According to this common view, one should first determine one's goals, then evaluate alternatives against those goals, and finally choose the alternative that best meets the goals. An RFP should set out the government's goals, the vendor proposal should outline different alternatives, and the government should then evaluate proposals against the RFP. Such a method appears plausible.

Most organizations acting outside the constraints of the procurement regulatory system, however, do not make decisions this way. In a fascinating study of decision-making processes (during the 1960s) in corporations deciding about their first purchase of a computer, Eberhard Witte concluded that in only four of the 233 situations investigated did the decision-making process correspond to the classical view.[35] The most striking finding was that information-gathering about the problem, of the kind necessary to elucidate goals, was not concentrated toward the beginning of the process. Instead it continued at high levels throughout—reaching its peak around the time of the final decision.[36] Use of fixed evaluation criteria and fixed evaluation weights in making procurement decisions is extremely uncommon in private firms. Indeed, in fully 41 percent of the most recent major computer acquisitions discussed by respondents to the Government Computer Managers Survey, no RFP was developed at all, something that would be unthinkable in government.[37] The decision not even to write an RFP reflects the importance often attributed to keeping the process as flexible and open to learning as possible.

Social psychological literature on the relationship between attitudes and behavior is relevant here. Relationships between initial attitudes and final behavior cannot be taken for granted and in fact are often weak or even nonexistent.[38] For our purposes, initial attitudes may be analogized to the fixed-in-advance sets of requirements and evaluation weights used in the procurement process, while final behavior is analogized to what people eventually do. In ordinary life, without restraints that force behavior into a mold established in advance by attitudes, initial attitudes are an imperfect guide to what people eventually do. The weight and direction of our attitudes change after the initial measurement.

When reality so consistently departs from a theory about how things should be done, it is wise, before concluding with a sigh that people are alas imperfect, to see whether reality reveals something the theory neglected. In selecting and weighting goals and then evaluating alternatives, what is forgotten is the gradual learning about what one really wants and what really is important that occurs slowly in the decision process.[39]

A key insight is expressed by Herbert Kelman:

Action is the ground on which attitudes are formed, tested, modified, and abandoned. . . . Attitudes develop out of the person's interaction with an object in a particular motivational and cognitive context. As he continues to interact with the object (directly or indirectly), the attitudes are tested, exposed to new information, sometimes filled out and shored up, sometimes changed.[40]

People generally make better decisions over time not only because of experience they have had with the products or services they buy, but also because they learn more over time about what they want. The issue is not simply what one learns about the features of different brands of a product—how well, say, various cars handle in different road conditions or how reliable they are. It is often difficult to know what one really values in a car the first time one buys one— how much handling is valued as compared with reliability. Frequently, one does not even know at the beginning how cars might be judged—say, brake-stopping distance, frequency of routine maintenance, or warranty protection. And it is also difficult to know the best ways to gather information about different features. In the buying process, one learns not only about the features of products but also about oneself.

Translated to procurement, cogitating abstractly and noncontextually about questions such as whether a vendor's management should count for 5 percent or 50 percent differs significantly from confronting a real decision with real information about different vendors. If, for example, a vendor is just barely able to provide service, sufficient to be adjudged responsive to the RFP specifications, should the worst that happens be that the vendor gets a low score on something that counts a mere 2 percent toward the contract award? If every reference says that a vendor did a barely acceptable job, should that vendor really be marked down only 3 points out of a maximum 100? Or, if every reference says the vendor has helped the customer in every possible way, should that vendor really receive only 2 more points out of 100? Should the Department of Agriculture in the local office computerization case have modified its requirement in the RFP about "off-the-shelf" software when it saw vendors propose software that had just been announced prior and had no significant customers? Should the IRS in the service center mainframe replacement case have included a prohibition against fine-tuning computers for the benchmark test after one vendor bid equipment that was tuned to pass the benchmark but could not work in the agency's production environment? If the résumé of a key manager in a vendor's proposal looks suspect, but not in a way that fits the preestablished criteria for evaluating résumés, does one really simply wish to hold up one's hands and lump it? Or is the inability to do anything about such situations part of the problem with the procurement system? In the confrontation with reality, one learns new things about what one wants and how much one wants it.

This is particularly true when those making decisions have little previous direct experience on which to base their initial attitudes. Without such prior experience, write the psychologists Russell Fazio and Mark Zanna, "an individual is forced to, in some sense, 'guess' his or her attitude."[41] Fazio and Zanna have built a research program on the premise that the link between attitudes and behavior is vitiated by lack of experience in the area addressed by the attitude. They find, for example, that the relationship between students' attitudes toward participation in psychology experiments and their decisions actually to participate in such experiments were strongly influenced by whether or not they had had direct experience with such experiments.[42] The authors found similar attitudes about a housing crisis among college freshman who had simply read about the crisis and those who had actually lived in temporary quarters. But the correlation between those attitudes and behavior designed to do something about the crisis was far greater for students living in temporary housing.[43] This result is especially relevant to government procurement because few participants have had experience with a major procurement—and more generally since low pay at middle and upper management levels tends to give the government an inexperienced workforce in computers.

Learning in the course of doing occurs with regard not only to the attributes of what one wants but also to the nature of what one wants. Requirements analysis in the government procurement process does involve surveying the experience of users and others with direct experience. But to cut off the needs-identification process with the development of an RFP is to constrain learning artificially. One of the private-sector computer managers I interviewed provided a fascinating example of the problem with this in a discussion of the evaluation process on a major contract. During the course of the evaluation process for the procurement (which involved mainframe computers and some mainframe applications software), one vendor brought some of their people to give presentations designed to demonstrate the quality of the technical support people available at company headquarters to help the customer if need be. These support people demonstrated some software applications that these vendor computer scientists had developed internally for the vendor's own use. But the customer engineers present at the meeting didn't react to the quality of the people as much as they salivated over the software itself, which would be extremely helpful in technical work these engineers were doing. The customer proceeded to inform the vendor that if the vendor would provide the customer with that particular applications software, the customer would award the contract to that vendor, though the vendor's prices were considerably higher than those of the competition. The vendor replied that the software was proprietary and internal, and could not be released to the customer; the customer countered that unless the software was provided, the vendor would lose the contract. The vendor relented, agreed to provide the software, and was awarded the contract. In this case, the customer learned somewhat serendipitously (in connection with information provided by the vendor for a different reason) late in the procurement process about a feature that it had never thought to request but that was actually of decisive importance. Had specifications been frozen earlier, the customer could never have gotten something it wanted. It would have given the contract to a vendor less able to satisfy its needs.

By contrast, a recent case appealed to the General Services Administration Board of Contract Appeals shows the problems the government experiences. Evaluation criteria in the RFP gave only modest weight to the user-friendliness of the word-processing software. One proposal, however, came with word-processing software so difficult that the evaluators—worried about what would happen when the word processor reached the desk of the agency head's secretary—realized they should have given user-friendliness a higher weight than they had originally done. After they did so in the course of the evaluation process, the contract award was thrown out on appeal.[44]

A Note on Price and Contract Award

As was noted in the previous chapter, the classic statement of the fear of discretion in government procurement was the award of contracts to the lowest bidder. Indeed, 65 percent of the most recent major contracts discussed by respondents to the Government Computer Managers Survey were awarded to the low-priced bidder, compared with only 41 percent in the Private-Sector Computer Managers Survey.[45] In every one of the case studies, the lowest priced bidder won. Furthermore, just over half the respondents to the Government Computer Managers Survey stated that if the low-priced bidder was about to be denied award because of technical inferiority, an additional review would be conducted within the organization.

The continuing prominence given low price in government procurement does reduce the discretion of public managers. It has not been treated extensively in this chapter, however, because an analysis of data from the Government Computer Managers Survey found no correlation between price alone as an evaluation criterion and satisfaction with the vendor. An analysis of responses to a question asking whether the winning vendor of the agency's most recent contract was best or not in technical and price evaluations did show, however, a correlation of 0.4 between award to a low-priced, technically inferior vendor and dissatisfaction with vendor performance.[46] This suggests that there is indeed a connection between price and quality and that low-priced solutions cost the government in satisfaction with vendor performance. Problems in performance, then, seem to relate not so much to formal evaluation criteria giving price a high weight as to informal pressures to award contracts to low-price bidders, regardless of other factors.

Conclusion

The procurement system requires officials to buy computers for the government in a different way than they would for themselves. The animus against their using information from past performance is rooted in the fear that, with unbridled discretion, public officials might arbitrarily pick and choose in order to favor one vendor. This is an animus that separates government officials from their normal faculties as thinking human beings. The private-sector comparisons mentioned in this chapter were not made, as is so fashionable, to demonstrate how much smarter people in the private sector are, but how anyone would behave if not shackled by a system that forbids them to use their heads.

4
Getting the Most out of Contractors: Competition and Informal Long-term Relationships

One of the greatest ironies in the way that government organizes procurement is that requirements for "free and open competition" are often seen as an effort to bring government's behavior in line with that of the private sector. And the major criticism one hears of government procurement practice is that it is insufficiently competitive. In fact, if by "competition" one means the principles of "free and open competition" in government procurement, government shows more competition than private-sector purchasing does. In the private sector, companies have learned the advantages of developing informal long-term relationships to get the most value from vendors. Such relationships increase the incentive for vendors to perform well and to provide technical assistance. Free and open competition is likely to diminish the value created by these relationships.

Traditionally sealed bidding has been favored by government as the purest embodiment of the ideal of free and open competition. Putting a set of specifications out to sealed bid and automatically awarding the contract to the lowest bidder may be viewed by some as the perfect way to introduce businesslike practices into government. But it is virtually unknown in the business world itself. According to one text in purchasing management, government use of sealed-bid procurement is "in marked contrast to industrial purchasing practice and sound purchasing theory."[1]

Studies of industrial purchasing show considerable customer loyalty to existing suppliers. One study found that half of the sample of firms had sought no new suppliers of freight transport services during the previous ten years; another study of the purchase of components by an electronics firm found that only 6 percent of all purchase orders went to an "isolated source" (a vendor that had received only one order during the period under investigation).[2] Source loyalty, of course, need not imply sole-source relationships because firms often have more than one established source. Nonetheless, a moderate amount of sole-source behavior occurs as well. A study of companies purchasing machine tools found that 30 percent had solicited only one bid.[3]

Hardly anyone would argue that private firms are less motivated than government agencies to get the most from their vendors or that competition is not a valuable tool for getting it. But private firms have also discovered that limiting free and open competition is also a valuable tool for getting more out of vendors. Because government may not modify competition in the same way, it has a difficult time reaping the benefits of such modifications.

Customer relationships with vendors in industry are often long-term and informal. They are long-term in that customer and vendor work together for a long time. They are informal so that vendors know they can be cut off on short notice. Two main factors work toward creating such standing relationships: the incentive for good performance created by the linkage of past performance with future orders; and the site-specific knowledge that vendors gain from working for a long time at a customer's operation. Each creates value for the customer, and each modifies free and open competition.

Government agencies do have long-term formal contracts with vendors. Large computer contracts, for example, often run for five years or more. Indeed, the length of the procurement cycle, driven in the first place by "full and open competition" requirements, has the perverse effect of locking the government into long contracts simply to avoid reinvesting the time and effort involved in "free and open" competitive procurements.

Two differences exist between these formal long-term contracts and the informal long-term relationships that will be discussed in this chapter. The first is that informal relationships are contingent on continued good performance by the vendor. Normally such relationships, once established, continue for long periods, but the contractor is never guaranteed the business.[4] The second difference is that government contracts are typically limited to some specific and delineated (though often sizable) tasks, rather than encompassing a menu of work throughout the customer's operations, tied together by common patterns of incentives and learning.

Past Performance and Incentives

The previous chapter discussed past performance as a guide to future performance in deciding which vendor to select. This chapter focuses less on information about how well a contractor is likely to perform than on *incentives* to perform well. The most powerful incentive is to tie performance on the current contract to future business.

Although the distinction between the information and the incentive effects of past performance may be artificial, I use it here because of the implications for full and open competition in procurement. As a source of information, a vendor's past performance in one's own organization has privileged status compared with information from other organizations only insofar as it is more reliable. In considering the incentive effects of using past performance to award new contracts, the strength of the tie to past performance in one's own organization becomes much more powerful and the linkage more integral. To generate the incentive for a vendor to do his best in my organization, I must link his opportunity for future work for me with his performance for me. In addition, when informational content of past performance is emphasized, it is useful mainly as a tool in judging who is most likely to perform best. When the incentive effect is emphasized, the quality of performance is seen more dynamically, as something that can be not only predicted better but also influenced.

It is hardly surprising that, just as past performance is important as a source of information both in our everyday lives and in purchasing decisions by businesses, so too is past performance crucial in its incentive function. A simple version of a free-market model assumes consumers can become informed about products by gathering all relevant information during prepurchase search. Such a model achieves maximum welfare for consumers with only one round of purchase decisions. Good producers are rewarded immediately, and bad producers are punished. A more sophisticated model is based on the notion that good producers are rewarded by consumers over time and bad ones are not. Incorporating learning through experience into the model turns repeat purchases into the reward-and-punishment mechanism. Bad producers are not immediately eliminated, but lack of repeat purchases because of consumer disappointment eventually kills them off. (Consumer dissatisfaction tends to be considerably higher in service industries, where quality is less standardized, than in goods industries where the repeat-purchase mechanism functions better.)

As for industrial customers, one textbook on purchasing management makes the point succinctly: "The greatest reward a customer can give is assurance of future business in response to satisfactory performance."[5] One study found that two considerations led firms to look for new suppliers: "dissatisfaction with current supplier" and the "introduction of a new component." Furthermore, in none of the cases did the look at a new component cause the firm to switch suppliers, but all old suppliers that prompted dissatisfaction were dropped.[6] Another study of equipment buyers observed that "missing scheduled delivery dates, delivery of a product that fails to perform satisfactorily, not providing prompt service or repair will quickly remove a bidder from a list" of those eligible to compete for company business.[7] Heinz buys bottles for its ketchup from a number of suppliers and over the years has increased the share of its business to the one most willing to work on improved bottle design. General Motors based the amount of business it gave its different steel suppliers on their delivery performance and technical contributions during the energy shortage of the 1970s. The company also rewarded suppliers that contributed most to parts design.[8]

Obviously, if the government cannot use past performance as a source of information on future performance neither can it use past performance as an incentive. As one of the federal marketing managers for a large computer company said, "Good will doesn't help you win. In the private sector, vendors know that if they perform badly, because of their flexibility the private sector will get rid of them. The government can't do that." The same manager noted that his own marketing people, particularly the new ones coming from the private sector, have a hard time believing this. "My sales reps say: 'The Army hates [Vendor X]. The Army won't give them another award. We're bidding against them, so we'll win.' I have to tell them it isn't that way. The government can't take past performance into account."[9] One wonders what incentive the management of Vanguard Technologies now feels in government contracts in light of the amazing situation where its extraordinary performance for the IRS counted for nothing when the contract was recompeted—and awarded to a different vendor.

The reward of repeat business is a powerful incentive for achieving good vendor performance. Since good vendor performance is of value to customers, customers will be inclined to offer such rewards: if a vendor performs well, the customer will informally commit to continuing to do business with him. But the implication of that commitment is that the customer will not set up a competitive auction where all may bid for the business. To use past performance as an incentive means moving away from "full and open competition" and toward long-term relationships with a few suppliers. This happens through a process of natural selection: poor vendors are eliminated, leaving only the good ones. "If a vendor had successfully performed the service before or was currently performing the service in a satisfactory manner," Johnston and Bonoma report in their study of capital equipment purchasing, "that vendor was often the only one solicited."[10]

A buzzword in purchasing circles these days is "early supplier involvement"—involving a supplier with the company's people in the development of specifications for a product.[11] A survey of purchasing managers and design engineers undertaken in 1988 by *Purchasing* magazine found that 88 percent of purchasing managers and 69 percent of design engineers believed that suppliers played a more important role in the customer's design team today than a decade ago.[12] To work on such design teams, however, the vendor must be selected before specifications have been laid out. "You can't have quotes and bids if you want to involve suppliers in the design stage," one private-sector purchasing manager, deeply committed to early involvement, noted in an article on the subject in *Purchasing*.[13] More generally, firms may leave specifications quite vague when a contract is signed and work out the details later. One study of procurement of nonstandard machine tools noted that "final specifications [were] not made until after the supplier has been selected."[14] This form of technical assistance could never function without both the information that past performance provides as a guide to vendor selection and the practice of rewarding or punishing suppliers based on past performance, so that suppliers who abused the privileged position provided by early involvement could be eliminated next time. These practices add value for the customer in his relationships with vendors, because they increase the amount of technical assistance vendors offer and allow the customer to take advantage of learning in the course of the project.

In government, these practices would be illegal, since vendors cannot be selected before the government has laid out its requirements. Even if they were legal, they would be inadvisable, because they leave the customer vulnerable to exploitation that can be counteracted only by a system of swift retribution against vendors who take advantage of such purposeful vagueness. Not permitting rewards and punishments based on past performance eliminates this source of customer value to the government.

In addition, the inability to reward past performance makes vendors less likely to provide preaward technical assistance. A federal marketing manager for a major computer vendor noted that there was little reason for his company to develop new ideas for the government, because they would then be subject to a competitive process, which would not reward the vendor for his ingenuity.

> It doesn't help to develop applications and then see them compete your ideas to (other vendors). When the procurement system does its best to take away competitive advantage, you have to seriously consider what your options are. We don't employ (our company's normal) value-added mar-

keting techniques, because we have less probability of positively affecting the outcomes.

A federal marketing manager for another vendor stated, "A government agency comes to us and says that they want us to help them with a solution. But we can't help, because they'll just go out with an RFP and compete it." The government experience with regard to vendor attitudes in cases of defective specifications is reflected by a burned government manager in one of the case studies who said, "The problem is that they give you the answer to the question you ask, not to the question you should have asked but didn't know to ask." In the Department of Agriculture local office computerization case, the agency ended up with an expensive, Rube Goldberg solution because none of the vendors informed the agency of the defects in the specifications or that such a solution was the only way to meet them. In the Immigration and Naturalization Service local office computerization procurement, when IBM pointed out that the centralized solution in the RFP was inferior to a decentralized solution, another vendor protested that the government should reopen the contract with new specifications for everyone to bid, rather than reward IBM for its efforts.

Vendors are unlikely to improve as long as the government is in no position to reward the ones that point out problems instead of merely changing the specification to allow everyone to bid. "Why bother to be altruistic?" a federal marketing manager for a large computer company asked me rhetorically. "You just go back to a level playing field."

The dilemma is that rewarding vendors for pointing out defects in the specifications requires granting managers freedom to use their good judgment. When agencies do allow them to comment on draft specifications, vendors do raise questions about the government's specifications. Usually, however, such questions are raised only if specifications create a competitive disadvantage for the vendor. What is needed is the ability for the government to reward vendors for pointing out defects in the specifications even when defects do not competitively disadvantage them. (All vendors were happy to bid on the Department of Agriculture's specifications that would allow any of them to sell the government unnecessarily expensive equipment.) Creating that ability requires letting government officials use their judgment to decide which issues are raised simply to remedy a competitive disadvantage and which are genuinely intended to help the government.

The ability to reward or punish past performance also affects the propensity of vendors to coddle (or abuse) customers. The musical chairs games with key management personnel and the overuse of inexperienced trainees are problems constantly complained about in government but never in my conversations with private-sector computer managers. In an example in the last chapter, a drapery company that had not specified preshrunk fabric for material for use in San Francisco nonetheless insisted that the supplier should have known that preshrunk fabric was needed in that climate and therefore should replace it. The textbook from which this example was drawn notes that

> in industry, suppliers have a strong incentive to interpret specifications in a way that is fully satisfactory to the buyers. If a supplier's product turns out to be unsuitable for the purpose intended, the supplier knows the buyer is free to take his future business elsewhere.[15]

The authors then contrast this situation with that in government procurement.

> The government, on the other hand, is normally not free to take its business elsewhere as a result of such experience. . . . In the absence of being able to prove clearly that the contractor has not met the specifications, the government must accept delivery of the product, and keep the supplier on the bidders' list as a qualified vendor in good standing.

A fascinating study by Stewart Macauley of "non-contractual relations in business" discovered that more than 60 percent of the orders a large manufacturer of packaging materials received from customers were placed without any agreement on terms and conditions or without any legally binding contract at all.[16] That business can proceed this way creates value in flexibility and forgone negotiation costs. Although one would hardly purchase a major computer system in the private sector without a contract, many contractual provisions about service levels, liquidated damages, or commitments to keep key personnel on the job that are common in government computer contracts are unusual in the private sector, because the incentive for obtaining repeat business serves as a substitute.

One acceptable, though roundabout, way to reward a contractor for good past performance in government is to assign greater weight to criteria that give an incumbent vendor a higher score, such as "knowledge of agency requirements" or "quality of key personnel." The criteria themselves do not reflect good performance directly. Any vendor who has had the contract has an advantage over competitors in knowing the agency and its requirements, and any incumbent has key personnel with significant experience doing the work of the agency. These advantages occur whether or not the vendor has performed the job well. Nonetheless, an agency that has been happy with a vendor's performance can, within limits, favor that vendor by raising the weight given such criteria. (Competitors can also compete by submitting résumés of people with excellent experience, even if not at the agency.)[17]

There are, of course, limits to favoring well-performing incumbent vendors this way. The approach is most applicable in people-intensive (rather than equipment-intensive) contracts, such as those for consulting services or facilities management, which have a tradition of assigning significant weight to the qualifications of key personnel. Excessive deviations from the normal weights given these criteria are, however, likely to evoke protest. Moreover, this technique applies to recompetitions of the same contract more than to competitions for new contracts where some vendors have experience with other areas of the agency's operations.

Site-specific Knowledge

The other value of long-term relationships that tends to limit full and open competition comes from investments made in that relationship by both parties. The notion of "transaction-specific" or "idiosyncratic" investments tied to dealings between specific customers and specific buyers (or to specific workers within a firm and that firm) has been central to the pathbreaking work of the economist Oliver Williamson. Similar ideas are also key to the notion of an "invisible handshake" and the distinction between "auction" markets and "customer" markets in the last work of the economist Arthur Okun, *Prices and Quantities*. Barbara Bund Jackson has developed a similar distinction in the industrial marketing literature between "always-a-share" markets, where the cost of switching among suppliers is low, and "lost-for-good" markets, where switching costs are so high that once a vendor loses a customer, he is unlikely ever to get the customer back.[18]

The work of Williamson and Okun may be seen as a reaction to the auction notion of competition in traditional neoclassical microeconomic theory, which assumed that a passel of anonymous sellers and buyers competed in a spot market with short-term contracts for standardized products. Okun and Williamson, who develop the argument in much greater detail, point out that a significant part of the value of many products and services comes from investments made by both customers and suppliers.

There are numerous sources of transaction-specific, idiosyncratic investments that generate value. A vendor might invest in specific tools or production technologies to produce a version of his product specifically adapted to the customer's needs. A customer might invest in employee training in techniques or procedures specific to the operation of a vendor's equipment (examples of this, of course, abound in the computer area). In another form of site-specific investment, customer and vendor people learn to communicate with and understand each other; one textbook on industrial marketing notes that customer engineers "normally prefer to work with companies with which smooth patterns of technical interchange have already been established."[19]

Perhaps the most pervasive investments are those in learning—the supplier learning about the special features of the customer's operation, and the customer learning the special features of the supplier's products and how best to use the equipment in a specific environment. What exactly is an investigator in the Customs Service really looking for in using a database to crack a case? What exactly is needed to make the work flow more smoothly at a secretary's desk in the specific environment of the Veterans Administration? How exactly should the mainframes be configured at the Internal Revenue Service to process data most efficiently, given the nature of the transactions to be processed? The supplier who has invested in learning answers to these questions is in a position to offer more value to the relationship with the customer than one who has not.

Buck Rodgers, the former IBM marketing chief, illustrates how this process occurs for IBM customers.

> For instance, a marketing rep sells a piece of IBM equipment to the chief financial officer of a manufacturing firm, to handle his payroll. Later, he meets with the company's engineering and manufacturing people, and finds that with the same equipment they can speed up the orders on the shop floor and improve the inventory turnover. And when he talks to the people in purchasing, he learns that it takes five days to process those purchase orders. The processing time might be cut dramatically with minor additions to the existing machine: another disk drive, or additional tapes, or maybe another printer. The point is, a good marketing rep makes an ongoing effort to find new applications for the customer's equipment. *The more problems uncovered and the more solutions, the greater the company's value to the customer.*[20]

The customer, of course, knows the specific features of his site as well as, or better than, the vendor. Nonetheless, the vendor who has learned about the customer's operation is still in a good position to make helpful suggestions. The vendor can bring to the relationship greater knowledge of his own products and suggest ways to apply them to the specific problems of the customer's operation. The vendor can also bring a fund of experience from other customers and knowledge derived from research (such as, in the computer area, capacity planning, mainframe usage optimization, or ways to use databases). IBM, for example, has developed sophisticated tools for doing customer capacity planning and mainframe usage efficiency studies.[21] Vendors might also notice things that customers do not, because customers are accustomed to them. Vendors can also serve as a sounding board for customer ideas, since they mix knowledgeability about the customer's operation with less of a commitment to existing ways.[22]

As a result, vendors can not only solve problems the customer knows he has, but also uncover better ways of doing things the customer would never have asked about. A computer vendor who has learned that some professors take copious notes on books or journal articles for later use could, for example, inform them how to adapt software for filing and key-word searches. A professor who used his computer only for word processing might not have been aware of this possibility. Such suggestions are part of technical assistance, which has been discussed as an important factor distinguishing well-performing from poorly performing vendors. The earlier discussions centered on information about the likelihood of getting good technical-assistance performance and establishing incentives for achieving such good performance. This discussion adds the observation that vendors who have made significant transaction-specific investments are more *capable* of rendering good technical assistance simply because those investments have made them more knowledgeable about the customer.

Central to Oliver Williamson's argument is that transaction-specific knowledge creates value, but such value can be realized only in the context of a continuing relationship between customer and supplier. This value creates, Williamson argues, a fundamental transformation of the customer-vendor relationship.

> Significant reliance investments in durable, transaction-specific assets introduces contractual asymmetry between the winning bidder on the one hand and nonwinners on the other. . . . [E]conomic values would be sacrificed if the ongoing supply relation were to be terminated. Faceless contracting is thereby supplanted by contracting in which the pairwise identity of the parties matters.[23]

Reaping the benefits of these transaction-specific investments, in other words, means modifying free and open competition. Williamson's argument tends to regard the presence or absence of pressures toward long-term rather than auctionlike relationships as inevitable in certain products and production technologies. Where standard products are used in standard ways and where the knowledge of those ways is accessible to any supplier, vendors need not know the specifics of a customer's operation. Where this situation does not obtain, transaction-specific knowledge adds value, pressures to invest in it will appear, and, once investments are made, the kind of competition embodied in auction markets disappears. In Williamson's analysis, product and technology characteristics determine the extensiveness of transaction-specific investments, and the extensiveness of those investments in turn determines the nature of competition. Transaction-specific investments are an independent variable, and the degree of competition is a dependent variable.

The situation with government procurement, however, suggests that this tone of inevitability ought to be abandoned. For when government regulation imposes free and open competition by fiat, it sets the film running in reverse. Lacking the ability to recoup transaction-specific investments through the assurance of repeat business, vendors fail to make investments that require conscious effort and expenditure of resources. The free and open competition requirement becomes the independent variable, and the degree of transaction-specific investment becomes the dependent variable. Free and open competition requirements cause a failure to invest in the creation of value for the customer. A mechanism that in Williamson's argument proceeded from technological imperatives to value-creating investment is short-circuited because the modifications of competition are prevented from emerging as they would if the system took its course. In the process, genuine value fails to be created. Although Williamson uses the terms investment and knowledge more or less synonymously, investments are typically regarded as voluntary and volitional, while knowledge is often acquired in a relatively passive manner through one's participation in a situation. Knowledge that vendors gain simply by being at the customer's site, without expenditure of additional resources, will, of course, be assimilated. (Such passively acquired knowledge is just the sort that incumbent vendors find useful in recompetitions of government contracts.) But vendors will do no more than that.

Note the connection between this argument and the one earlier in this chapter about preaward technical assistance. The kinds of site-specific investments in new ideas being discussed here are the same as the new ideas for applications referred to earlier as an example of preaward technical assistance. Vendors already on-site can provide this kind of preaward technical assistance better than vendors without the same knowledge of the customer can. But just as the failure to reward such preaward technical assistance causes it to dry up, so does this failure cause site-specific vendor investments in new ideas to dry up as well.

As is so often true of government procurement, the practice is almost certainly better than the theory. Vendors with long-term formal contracts may get change orders that reflect transaction-specific knowledge they have gained. Change orders are of no help, however, in encouraging investment in ideas outside the scope of the vendor's existing contract, since under procurement laws, such changes must be recompeted. If one's contract involves a financial accounting system, suggestions about computer applications that, say, could make data entering for the accounting system more productive do a vendor little good. Furthermore, uncertainty whether the ideas the vendor suggests are within the scope of the existing contract limit the likely investments even in areas arguably within its scope. Vendors also have incentives to invest in site-specific knowledge when they have indefinite-quantity task-order contracts with agencies for, say, custom software development. These are contracts of an indefinite substantive scope under which the agency and vendor agree on minicontracts for specific tasks.[24] Third, even if a competition must be held for the completion of a vendor's idea, that vendor will often have an advantage, especially if the idea grew out of the vendor's capabilities. Finally, as has been suggested earlier, even if vendors fail to make conscious investments in developing knowledge, the presence on-site can, for instance, make communication easier.

Despite all this the results of the Government Computer Managers Survey and the Private-Sector Computer Managers Survey show significant differences in vendor investments in transaction-specific knowledge and in the results of such investments for the customer. Managers in both surveys were asked the dollar value of their investment with their most important vendor and how many persons the vendor had working full time on site. For the private firms, vendors had one full-time employee on site for every $3.9 million of customer investment with the vendor. For the government, vendors had one employee on-site for every $6.4 million—and two of the thirty-one agencies skewed these numbers in favor of the government with an unusually large number of vendor employees.[25] No full-time vendor personnel were present on 32 percent of the government sites; but only on 20 percent of the private-sector sites. Clearly, vendors invest considerably more to generate transaction-specific knowledge in a private-sector than in a public-sector context.

Large private-sector firms normally have resident marketing, technical assistance, and systems engineering staff working full time on-site from their leading vendors, whose basic job it is to solve problems and develop ideas. Such on-site support staff is not provided in connection with any specific contract, nor is it paid for separately. Most vendors give their marketing managers a budget for such support, which becomes a negotiating item between customer and vendor. Such support is an investment by vendors, not in some specific contract, but in their total relationship with the customer. A federal marketing manager for a leading computer vendor told me specifically that his company committed far less on-site support to federal customers than to large private-sector ones, because the ideas an on-site support staff developed could be appropriated by the government and placed into a competitive RFP. In its proposal to the Immigration and Naturalization Service on the local office computerization contract, IBM attempted to bring the consulting service approach it uses with private-sector customers into the federal world by offering at no extra charge to the customer $1 million worth of advice on improving INS operations. This offer was essentially given no credit by the government because it could not be fit into any evaluation criteria in the RFP.

Those absent people deprive the government of something. The survey questions of managers about the most recent major computer contract asked to what extent vendors took "the initiative in identifying the needs or the applications that were eventually addressed in this procurement." Advice about problems the customer had not even known about is potentially the most valuable a vendor can give the customer, since the customer would be unlikely to produce the idea by his own efforts. Again, the results were striking. Respondents were asked to rate the role of current vendors in identifying the needs or applications on a seven-point scale. Table 4–1 displays the results. The government managers indicated that current vendors played essentially no role in generating the ideas that led to the agency's most recent procurement. Sixty-seven percent placed themselves at the extreme position that there was no vendor involvement in needs identification. The pattern for the private-sector managers was strikingly different. Only 20 percent of the private-sector managers placed themselves at the extreme position of no vendor involvement. And 29 percent of private-sector managers, compared to 12 percent of government ones, placed vendor involvement at somewhere from the vendor having taken the lead over to the midpoint of the seven-point scale.[26]

Both groups of managers were asked whether any vendor with

whom the organization had had no prior experience had played any similar role in identifying needs or applications. The responses were interesting. The mean values on a seven-point scale in the Private-Sector Computer Managers Survey was 5.1 for incumbent vendors and 5.8 for vendors with whom the firm had had no prior experience—reinforcing the point that incumbent vendors are in a better position than others to give preaward technical assistance. But the mean for nonincumbent vendors in the private sector (5.8) was higher than the mean for incumbent vendors in the Government Computer Managers Survey (which was 6.3). This suggests the importance of the ability to reward any vendor for preaward technical assistance, including a vendor who has no previous experience with the firm.[27]

It should be remembered that respondents were asked here about contracts that had actually been signed, so that unnecessary or self-serving vendor suggestions would probably not have passed internal review to proceed to contract award. And the respondents were asked about a major contract, so that the vendor suggestions in question should not be considered trivial or marginal. These results suggest that the site-specific investments of current vendors in learning about the customer's business do add value for the customer.

These results also suggest that the worst part of the government procurement system may be that public managers do not know what they are missing in the value that vendors can bring to their organizations. A customer will never know that he missed the opportunity to

TABLE 4–1

MANAGERS' RATINGS OF VENDOR INITIATIVE IN IDENTIFYING NEEDS
FOR MOST RECENT MAJOR COMPUTER-RELATED ACQUISITION
(percent of managers making evaluations)

		Government[a]	Industry[b]
Took the Lead	1	0	3
	2	6	5
	3	6	12
	4	0	9
	5	9	22
	6	12	29
No Role	7	67	20

a. $(N = 33)$
b. $(N = 153)$
SOURCE: Government Computer Managers Survey and Private-Sector Computer Managers Survey.

get a solution from a vendor to a problem he did not realize he even had. In measuring the costs of the current procurement system in government, therefore, we must consider not only the costs that agencies themselves perceive in dissatisfaction with vendor performance but also the costs agencies do not detect—of missed solutions to unaddressed problems. Those are costs we as citizens bear in government performance that is less than it could be. In particular, as a monopoly provider of goods or services, government agencies may have less incentive than firms in a competitive market to invest their own resources in innovation and new ideas. In such an environment, new ideas coming from outside sources such as suppliers acquire special importance. Because of the procurement system, the government may get less of something—innovative ideas—that it needs more.

The government has ways of getting around the lack of vendor suggestions. Agencies can separately purchase facilities management contracts with third-party vendors who specialize in this sort of help, often specifically for the federal marketplace. Such contracts are often used within the federal government for maintenance and systems-engineering support, typically for mainframe data centers. Such contracts do provide the government with some of what it might get through long-term informal relationships with regular vendors, but they are far from a full substitute. These facilities-management vendors provide less backup service than the equipment vendors do to answer questions, and they are probably less familiar with the equipment the government is using. Since they are in the dark about the equipment vendor's future technology and capabilities, they have a more difficult time crafting solutions that will create the fewest disruptions when the new technology comes out. Nor can they suggest new applications for equipment they are not responsible for. Finally, and perhaps most important, facilities management contracts are negotiated on either a fixed-price or a labor-hour basis, neither of which rewards the vendor for suggesting good ideas.

The government has tried another way of making up for the lack of vendor commitment to new ideas, mostly in the Department of Defense. A vendor can submit a "value engineering change order proposal" suggesting ways to meet a contract's requirements more cheaply, either by substituting materials, by redesigning equipment, or by reorganizing production. If it is accepted by the government, the vendor will share in savings the government realizes.[28] These efforts have generally foundered, however, partly because of contractor skepticism that the government will pay the vendor any significant amount, but mainly because of lack of enthusiasm by those who administer the program. To the government official, value engineering increases the already prodigious paperwork of the procurement process and raises the possibility of contract disputes with the vendor over the size of the monetary award. Officials tend therefore to shrug when the latest value engineering drive is mentioned and to regard it as just another program. Awarding new business to vendors in recognition of their suggestions requires far less documentation and bureaucratic hassle. Even when value engineering programs do function, they include cost savings only for existing requirements and not suggestions for solutions to new problems.

Managing the Problems of Long-term Informal Relationships

The pressures against "full and open competition" carry with them not only potential for value creation but also dangers and pitfalls. The development of site-specific investments and of performance incentives create value that would otherwise not have been brought into existence. Indeed, if these features of long-term informal relationships did not create more value than competitively bid contracts do, such relationships would never have developed.

But long-term informal relationships can also deprive the parties to the relationship of the protection that full and open competition provides against exploitation. How can individual workers in a competitive market, for example, avoid being exploited by employers, since an individual worker is in a much weaker position than the employer? The answer in a competitive market is other employers. If one employer tries to exploit workers by offering them less than the value they produce, another employer has an incentive to offer them a slightly higher wage. A bidding process among employers tends to raise the wage. If only one employer bids for the workers' services, they are indeed subject to being exploited because of their weak bargaining position.

Informal long-term relationships can put customers and vendors in a one-on-one negotiating relationship with each other and result in inequities in the division of the value created by the customer-vendor interaction. A vendor can exploit a customer in a long-term relationship in ways discussed in the last chapter or by demanding an excessive price when the contract is renegotiated. Vendors might claim so much of the value created by the relationship that the customers fare worse than they would in competitive bidding that would have created less total value but would have allowed the customer to appropriate more of the value that was created.[29] There is also a danger that in situations with high site-specific investments the vendor might become lazy and, in effect, appropriate some of the value created by the long-term relationship in the form of a quieter life (the best of all monopoly profits, the economist J. R. Hicks once suggested). Furthermore, there is a tension between the amount of site-specific investment and the ability to grant or withhold continued business based on the quality of past performance. If performance is bad, extensive site-specific investmens make a cutoff difficult.

If site-specific investments are high, the activity can be brought in house to eliminate the motivation for one party to profit at the expense of another. Indeed, Oliver Williamson argues that significant site-specific investment increases the likelihood that transactions will be organized within a single organization rather than between organizations dealing in the marketplace.[30] One study showed that automobile companies are more likely to manufacture components in house if they require significant firm-specific engineering investment.[31]

Assuring the in-house supplier of the business, however, eliminates the incentive for good performance that a relationship with a vendor creates. Moreover, in many industries, including computers, the organization that can spread large fixed costs for plant and equipment and for research and development among many customers is in a better position than an in-house supplier that would have merely a single customer.

In the computer business customers and vendors thus continue to be separate parties. A cautious strategy is to forswear informal long-term relationships and rely instead on full and open competition. This strategy lowers the total value created by the interaction but reduces the risk to the customer of egregious exploitation by the vendor. The bolder strategy is to accept a situation of being blessed by—or condemned to—informal long-term relationships and to manage those relationships so that the new value they create is divided fairly. This strategy implies greater risks and potentially greater rewards.

From the point of view of the argument underlying this book regarding judgment and discretion in public management, the cautious and bold strategies have different implications. Free and open competition relies on the operation of impersonal market forces in regulating customer-vendor interactions and requires little from the managers. But it lowers the chances for excellence. Managing informal long-term relationships, by contrast, requires skill and good managerial judgment—exactly the kind of discretion we worry about giving officials in the public sector. Yet the wise exercise of judgment creates the potential for best value.

Private-sector managers whose companies have informal long-term relationships with important vendors devote significant attention to seeing that the benefits flow in appropriate measure to the customer and that dependence does not create vendor laziness. The most important strategy is to have such relationships with more than one vendor on site, although if the number is large, the ability to create value from the relationship declines. Even two or three significant vendors can provide internal competition and encourage honesty. For this reason, many customers favor the development of multivendor or industrywide standards in the computer industry, which reduces a customer's dependence on the proprietary architecture or software of a single vendor. Managers sometimes award a contract to one vendor rather than another to keep the losing vendor on his toes.

Some areas do not allow for the presence of multiple vendors. Customers with mainframe computers not compatible with IBM are wedded to the vendor in which they have placed their huge investments in applications software and training. Even if several vendors are available, customers often choose to stay with one supplier because of the possibilities for value-creation.

Customers in one-on-one arrangements can guard against being exploited by periodically testing the market through formal competitive bidding or by asking others what prices they pay.[32] Private-sector computer managers use services, such as the Gartner Group, that provide information about prices big customers obtain for computers. "My IBM account manager knows," one told me, "that I had better never read anything in Gartner about another company who got a better deal on IBM equipment than I got. I don't want to find any 'whoops' down the road." Computer managers also told me about their interactions with colleagues at other companies, both at trade shows and over the telephone. Information about vendor exploitation of a customer or poor performance spreads quickly. Such a network mitigates the problems of a single firm in punishing poor performance.[33] Many of these techniques would be difficult for government computer managers to apply: for example, they would run afoul of rules limiting evaluation criteria to agency requirements if they awarded one contract to a certain vendor in order to keep the losing vendor from getting lazy on a different contract.

Successful informal long-term relationships are based on the realization that exploitation will destroy the relationship. The situation of vendors and customers in informal long-term relationships resembles that described in prisoner's dilemma game.[34] The best outcome is for the vendor and the customer to cooperate and not try to exploit each other. Each may be tempted, however, to reap a unilateral advantage that the other party will put up with. But a cycle of mutual exploitation and recrimination will destroy the relationship and the value it creates.

The research by Robert Axelrod on the evolution of cooperation among egoists sheds light on avoiding such destructive results.[35] Key to cooperation, Axelrod argues, is a relationship in which one can signal by cooperative behavior in the present the wish to continue to cooperate in the future. Computer simulations of repeated rounds of the prisoner's dilemma game using strategies developed by game-theory experts showed that a simple strategy called tit-for-tat produced the most successful, cooperative results. In this strategy, a player cooperates in the first round and then proceeds to cooperate each time the other player has cooperated and to retaliate each time the other player seeks to exploit him. The other player is therefore rewarded for cooperation (no effort is made to take advantage of it) but punished for attempts at exploitation. The most direct way to encourage cooperation, Axelrod concludes, is to make "interactions more durable."

Tit-for-tat in a computer tournament closely resembles the approach of those managing successful informal long-term relationships. Thomas Palay examined relationships between producers and the railroads that carried their products in situations where site-specific investments were significant.[36] Palay found among participants in these relationships a tit-for-tat-like mixture of trust and a big stick:

> When asked to describe what it was that held the informal contractual relations together, [one rail carrier] equivocated. In one breath it clearly mentioned and talked about trust and realized mutuality of interest. "We've been dealing with [this shipper] from the beginning. When they located and designed their plant they knew we'd be one of their primary carriers. I believe what they tell us. They know how we operate; that we're an honest bunch of people. Neither one of us plays games. I like dealing with them." Nevertheless, in the next breath [the rail carrier] was careful to point out its potential market alternatives. . . . "I guarantee you that [this shipper] knows that if he pushes me once too often he'll find himself sitting around with a lot of aluminum sheet and no cars. Alternatively, we could stop investing money in new equipment for him."[37]

This attitude matches those of computer managers with whom I spoke—expressions of good feelings and phrases about partnerships regarding their major vendors, combined with tough talk of "don't tread on me."

Competition Requirements and Vendor Assistance with Specifications

In government procurement, the government develops specifications for what it wants, and contractors then bid a solution and a price for meeting those specifications. Vendors, however, could be an important source of ideas and suggestions on what the specifications should be in the first place. Their importance is indicated by the trend in private-sector purchasing toward "early supplier involvement" and the selection of vendors prior to product or component design, so that the vendor can be involved in the design effort.

The problems in the government system with rewarding contractors for technical assistance have been discussed earlier. Here the issue is one step removed from reward. Recognizing the limitations in their own unaided ability to write specifications, customers might want to require that vendors provide such help as a condition for competing for the contract. Or they might want to ask vendors questions while working on specifications.

Yet vendor input into developing government specifications raises the most dreaded specter that haunts government procurement—the "wired" contract. Except for "sole source," no adjective in government procurement occasions such opprobrium.

Vendor involvement in the development of government specifications is supposed to take certain constrained forms. At the beginning of the process of defining needs, vendor involvement is considered not only acceptable but advisable. The *Federal Acquisition Regulations* require that agencies do a market survey to see what features and applications are available from vendors.[38] Vendors are free at this stage to come in and leave literature, make presentations or demonstrations, and confer with government officials in a relatively unconstrained manner. During this carefree time, vendors provide information to persuade program people that the vendor's capabilities mesh with the government's needs.

Later, however, such informality disappears. In about half the case studies, contacts with vendors ceased when work on an RFP began. Once the doors are shut, program staff may talk with vendors only at meetings to which all vendors have been invited and only with a contracting officer present. Otherwise contacts with specific vendors might produce biased specifications that will place other vendors at a disadvantage.

The problem is that contact between customers and vendors is cut off just as the rubber is hitting the road. It is one thing, as noted in a somewhat different context in the last chapter, for people to be cogitating in some general way about what their needs are in an upcoming procurement. And surely program people learn a great deal from discussions with vendors during and prior to the market survey phase. But most of us have certainly experienced the fact that, often, many crucial questions and many points that one thought one understood but perhaps doesn't as well as one would wish don't get dealt with until one actually sits down, pen to paper, to put one's general ideas into final form. When, for example, I was interviewing people to gather information for the case studies for this book, I asked all the questions I thought were important. Invariably, however, when I sat down actually to write a case study I discovered major gaps in my understanding and had to go back to ask for more information. What would have happened had I been forbidden to interview after I had started writing? We are inclined to delay serious thought about a problem until we actually confront it—in these cases, this is not generally, I would suspect, when one jaunts through a general presentation by vendors on what they have available, but rather when the specifications must actually be written.[39] The cutoff in contacts with vendors makes way for missed ideas and for defective specifications. Beyond this a fear of accusations of wiring contracts casts a pall over many managers who might otherwise obtain valuable help from vendors. "Most [government computer] managers don't understand that it's a good idea to do a market survey in depth," suggested one respondent in the Government Computer Managers Survey. "We carry around with us this problem about talking with vendors." Government managers also express fear of asking vendors questions during the market survey phase that are too detailed, lest they give some vendors an advantage in preparing for the RFP. Because of all this, government gets less value from vendors than it otherwise would. Competition requirements discourage the government from being able to get the most out of its relationships with vendors.

By contrast, some private-sector vendors issue no RFPs, but let the vendors explain their capabilities within a broad problem area. Firms achieve greater vendor participation in developing specifications by leaving requirements vague throughout the procurement process, even in the context of a formal RFP. In an RFP for selecting electronic component distributors discussed in one textbook, Raytheon Corporation asked bidders to "please surface three or four specific ideas on how we can improve our business relationship."[40] Computer managers at firms I visited indicated that bidders on their contracts were free to take exception to requirements stated in RFPs or to propose new ones. An RFP for an electronic mail system, developed mostly by users from the administrative side of the firm rather than by the firm's engineers, did not include any provision for transfer of engineering designs by electronic mail. "So a vendor came back to us in his proposal and said, 'By the way, you didn't mention the need for file transfer. We're finding that many of our customers need file transfer capabilities for their engineers.' " When I asked the chief computer manager at this firm how often vendors came up with ideas not in the company's specifications, he answered, "Almost always. You learn as you go along. You learn as you listen to their presentations."

These approaches would probably not be permitted in government. To ask bidders to make suggestions about something as vague as improving a business relationship suggests a lack of clarity in requirements that opens the door to unbridled discretion. To allow a contractor to take exception to a specification or to propose an alternative runs afoul of the edict that proposals must be "responsive" (that is, meet all the government's specifications) even to be considered. The idea is that unless all vendors bid on the same package, they are not competing on a level playing field.

The government tries to circumvent these difficulties by hiring consulting firms, especially nonprofit firms that specialize in government business, to help develop specifications. These firms are supposed to play a role simliar to the one that vendors might play and to compensate for lack of knowledge among government employees. To avoid the favoritism that the limitations on contacts with vendors is meant to prevent, however, firms that help with specification development are not allowed to bid on the contract for the work. The consultants therefore lack the vendor's incentive to develop solutions that are actually workable. Government managers also complain that things get lost in the indirect communication that third-party consultants broker between themselves and the actual computer vendors. One may also question whether these consultants have the same detailed knowledge of product capabilities that individual vendors possess about their own lines.

Conclusions

A conceptual failure that links many of the problems created by the model of full and open competition for government procurement is the treatment of contracts as discrete events, rather than as parts of a larger web of dealings. "It is necessary," one textbook on purchasing management reminds its readers, "to consider the selection decision as part of a chain of events, rather than as an isolated instance."[41] One of the federal marketing managers interviewed stated that, in contrast to the private sector, procurements in government are organized around a "chunk of events," rather than as part of an ongoing stream of interactions. Instead of a seamless web, government contracts are distinct threads. The threads may be long ones, but they are threads, nonetheless. To reward or punish past performance, and to take advantage of the stream of suggestions arising from transaction-specific investments by vendors, means to become involved in relationships, with a past and future as well as a present, more than simply in contracts. Furthermore, treating the customer's dealings with vendors as a relationship also provides keys to minimizing the dangers of exploitation that the limitations on competition could engender.

An underlying theme in this chapter has been how customers can best get a chance to learn from vendors. Vendors have much to teach customers. Failing to put oneself in a position to learn as much as possible means failing to get all one can out of vendors. Free and open competition requirements decrease the ability to learn from vendors because it reduces rewards to them for teaching and for investing in developing useful things to teach.

Margins computer vendors make on their government business are generally lower than those in sales to commercial customers.[42] Some will find this quite a surprise for they believe that government managers have little incentive to obtain good prices and therefore assume that contractors take bureaucrats (and taxpayers) to the cleaners. Others might regard these findings as confirmation that the procurement system gives the government a good deal on what it buys—although it would certainly be hard to make a convincing argument for why they should do a better job than their private-sector brethren.

In fact, I think that higher vendor margins in the private sector tell a story that is less immediately obvious but still not particularly happy for the effectiveness of government procurement. Modifications of the model of free and open competition create value for customers by increasing the incentive for vendors to perform well and by increasing their ability to provide technical assistance to customers. The division of that newly created value is then subject to negotiation between vendor and customer. Because long-term relationships discourage shopping around for the lowest price, some of the value is likely to be captured by vendors. This explains, I think, the high vendor margins observed in commercial transactions. But some of the value accrues as well to the customers, who gain higher "margins," so to speak, from their interaction with the vendor. Lower margins suggest that the government procurement system annihilates value that could have been created. Such losses are borne not only by government but by vendors as well.

Customers value the ability to reward or punish past performance and the transaction-specific investments that vendors undertake because the process makes practical sense, even at the sacrifice of full and open competition. The comparisons with private-sector practice suggest how public managers might behave if they were left to their own devices and were allowed to use their own good judgment. Indeed, public managers frequently try to behave in these ways, but the system limits them. They are not trusted to use their judgment.

5
Conclusions
and Recommendations

Successfully acquiring high technology such as computer systems is not easy. The technology itself is often new and therefore risky. Discovering interesting applications for the technology, beyond the most obvious ones, requires ingenuity and creativity. Introducing the technology into an organization often requires wrenching changes in the behavior of the people who use it. Computers are often not used to their full potential.

This book suggests that an important reason for problems in the performance of new computer technology in government is the way computers are procured. The problems with vendor performance presented in the introduction included the abandonment of a computer language that the vendor had promised to support, the disproportionate increase in equipment to be purchased to meet new traffic-load estimates, and the charges for managers who turned out to be not needed. Public-sector managers are significantly more likely to believe that computer vendors overpromise than did their private-sector counterparts. And the surveys of computer managers showed greater dissatisfaction with vendor performance among public-sector computer managers.

The specific problems observed in the case studies have something important in common—some feature of performance that was not covered in the commitment the vendor made in the original contract or that involved an ambiguity in the nature of that commitment. In each case, the behavior would count against a vendor if performance on earlier contracts with the organization were used as a source of information about vendor performance and as an incentive to reward or punish such performance. In each case, the government has difficulty considering such behavior in contract awards. The greater perception of overpromising in the public sector fits into this pattern as well. If the government accepts words proffered before contract award in disproportionate measure relative to an actual record of deeds, it should come as no surprise that those seeking the government's business will be tempted to say almost anything.

Observable problems with contractor performance may, unfortunately, not tell the entire story. No one can guess how many innovations were never developed and how many suggestions were never made, because full-and-open-competition requirements discourage contractors from cultivating the knowledge they develop working in government organizations. Public-sector computer managers credited vendors with identifying the needs or suggesting the applications embodied in their most recent major acquisition significantly less than their private-sector brethren did. As computer applications become less obvious and more critical, the need becomes greater for ideas from as many sources as possible. In such an environment, vendors must be allowed to apply their expertise and ingenuity to identifying new approaches for the public sector.

There is, finally, one more problem for the success of government computer systems, not discussed earlier in this book, to which the procurement system contributes. It is not an obstacle the system creates to achieving good vendor performance, but rather a problem the system encourages in how the government goes about the business of computerization efforts. The current system encourages the government to try to describe in advance too many of the features and applications of the system that is to be developed, rather than realizing that it is foolish to believe one can understand all the potentials and pitfalls of a brand new system in advance of its implementation— an insight suggesting that an incremental, learn-by-doing, iterative approach is in order. Trying to implement everything at once increases the risk of failure on a grand scale if the technology fails to work as expected or if the original idea was misconceived. Both in the specific literature on computer applications and in the general literature on planning in organizations, those doing something new and different are advised to get something (of a pilot nature, for example) into the organization, let users work with it, and develop system applications further based on the experience gained. Grand designs are at best a recipe for not getting all one can from a new computerization project and at worst an invitation to costly disaster.[1]

Nothing in the procurement system prohibits an incremental approach. Incremental improvements and alterations can be made through change orders. The extensiveness of such orders is limited and regulated, however, because they occur in a sole-source environment and can illegitimately be used to stifle competition. Some kinds of contracts, such as general-purpose software development contracts that do not specify the specific applications in advance, are also suited to an incremental approach.

Nonetheless, government computer acquisitions have tended toward grand design projects that lay out too many details in advance. Although nothing in the system requires such an approach, such grand designs fit the spirit of the current procurement system. The philosophy of reining in discretion establishes an elaborate process of relating specifications and evaluation criteria to government requirements and encourages a structured effort to set down requirements in advance, often with a view that more detail is better. In addition, the time and pain that the current procurement process creates provides a powerful incentive for people to reduce the number of procurements they undertake by bundling requirements into huge all-encompassing efforts.

Rule-boundedness and Government Performance

In an environment too complex to be reducible to simple rules or in one that changes more rapidly than the rules can be changed, a decision-making system that depends on rules invites disaster. The material presented here may be seen as the way this general observation plays itself out in one domain of public management. Some of the problems occur within the frame of reference the rules are intended to encompass. In many examples, following the procurement rules discouraged vendors from offering the government good prices (because information about postaward exploitation could not be considered in future contract awards). In such cases the procurement regulations themselves interfered with the goal of economy. In addition, the cases are also full of incidents bizarrely anomalous enough to risk classification as "horror stories"—such as the inability of the Immigration and Naturalization Service to give credit to a vendor's offer to provide free consulting services to the agency because the offer fit none of the criteria set out in advance. "Horror-story" anomalies of this type are standard features both of the literature on bureaucracy and of popular frustration with bureaucrats.

A deeper set of problems, however, goes beyond the values the rules are intended to foster and is only hinted at by the horror stories. When the world changes, overwhelming problems are created for our procurement system in particular and for our way of managing in the public sector in general. When most government procurement involved simple, standard products such as paper to write on or coal to heat the buildings—and when most government action involved straightforward tasks such as accurately collecting statistics or correctly determining veterans' pensions—it is understandable that the quality of performance was not considered as problematic as it might be today. Either good quality performance was easily seen as more or less coterminous with the observance of rules to ensure equity, economy, and integrity or else it was easily seen as something that substantive rules in the form of organizational standard operating procedures could achieve.

In procurement, more of what the government now buys is complex and hence ill-suited to the kind of complete specifications in contractual language that the original system used as the way to achieve good substantive performance by vendors. Vendors can serve more and more as sources of ideas, not merely as instruments to satisfy simple wants that government has determined. Similar stories could be told about other public activities, from collecting garbage to reducing poverty. The complex or experimental nature of what is being undertaken or the new expectations of citizens from government increase the difficulty of attaining excellence.

Existing rules become inappropriate as the world changes. Rules about full and open competition produce inappropriate results if vendor performance suffers because of the complexities of postaward contract performance and the importance of site-specific vendor investments in developing ideas for customers. Yet despite their inappropriateness to changed circumstance, rules are difficult to change. To achieve good substantive performance in a changing world, an organizational design relying heavily on rules of any sort becomes increasingly inappropriate. Many of the judgments that public officials must make about computer vendors (such as judgments whether a vendor's past performance was good) are too specific to the situation to be put into rules. In a changed world, it is not merely that old rules need to be changed. The old reliance on rules needs to be changed as well.[2]

Focusing on equity, integrity, and economy, the existing procurement rules serve as a clear signpost about what we value in the management of the public sector. The rules signal no analogous concern over excellence in substantive performance and therefore inhibit the ability to focus on goals other than those served by the rules. The connection of the rules to a certain vision of the goals of public management thus inhibits the transformation of that vision.

This book has been both about a way of managing in the public sector (that is, management based on rules rather than discretion) and about a vision of the goals of public-sector management (the goal of excellence in the substance of public performance as well as the goals of equity, integrity, and economy). Although there is not a necessary connection between approaches to these two questions, there is none-theless a good approximate fit. Rule-boundedness in the manage-ment of the public sector fits well with goals for public management that are limited to equity, integrity, and economy. In a complex and changing world, goals that give important place to the quality of government's substantive performance are likely to require that we give public officials more discretion.

Suggestions for Change

What is to be done about the problems the current system creates? The basic principle, I believe, should be to increase dramatically the freedom we give public officials to use their judgment in the procure-ment process. Behind such a conclusion lie two premises. One is a perception of public officials somewhat less dour than the prevailing notion, one that sees not only the risks of official sloth and venality but also the potential for achievement of many dedicated people yearning to breathe free. It is, I should add, a perception that comes closer to the impression I got of most of the people encountered in this research than the prevailing view.

The other premise, somewhat less dependent simply on one's view of the character of public officials, is that the current system is indeed broken. The failure to grant public officials more room for judgment and common sense has exacted a terrible cost in the poorer performance of contractors selling computer systems to the govern-ment (and in other areas of public-sector performance as well). The suggestion is not simply that government officials might, with more safety than some think, be given more freedom, but also that freedom is important in creating public value and not simply a luxury we might magnanimously grant if we conclude that they won't abuse it.

Some observers worry about the substantive performance of the procurement system but cynically believe that lazy or corrupt govern-ment officials allow vendors to perform poorly and cheat the govern-ment. They would presumably want the government to be tough against poorly performing vendors—wielding a big stick of withheld payments, lawsuits, or even prison. But while the injunctions to be honest, fair, and economical can easily be translated into rules, deci-sions about when and how to be tough with vendors require consid-erable judgment and discretion on the part of government officials. If the cynical observer does not trust government officials with discre-tion, then the proposal to "get tough" cannot improve vendor per-formance, since getting tough requires exercising discretion. He is simply reduced to ill-tempered bureaucrat bashing. If more discretion is given to government officials, the kinds of discretion outlined in this book appear the way to get more value out of vendors (particularly in government technical assistance and customer coddling) than a big stick approach.

The grant of more freedom to public managers that I propose should not be unconditional. Much greater freedom should be given in decisions that affect a manager's ability to accomplish his mission. Then the manager should be held responsible for how well he does in accomplishing that mission. In other words, there should be greater freedom to select the means to realize agreed-upon ends. Evaluation of performance in the computer area is not easy; because of the uncertainty of new technology, a manager who never fails is likely behaving too cautiously. But the energy that now goes into the development of rules to restrict public officials should be redirected toward thinking about how to develop results-based performance evaluation in this and other areas of public-sector management.

It would also certainly not hurt as well to accompany the grant of increased discretion with efforts to raise the quality of the federal work force in the computer area. Federal salaries for computer specialists become uncompetitive as one moves above the journeyman level. Under the evocative name of the "Trail Boss" program, the General Services Administration has begun to train government officials to take responsibility for major computer procurements.[3] Most of the increments in the ability to use judgment I am proposing (increments, that is, over the judgment officials already must exercise in evaluating vendor technical proposals) involve management and people skills, however, not computer wizardry. I therefore do not accept the criticism that my proposals for greater discretion would require a more technically distinguished computer work force than is required under the current system.

I favor experimenting with bold changes in the system to increase the judgment that public managers may exercise. I would urge statutory authorization for experiments in eliminating most procurement rules in favor of a regime with only two broad procedural requirements—written justification for each procurement decision, and multiple-member evaluation panels to reach decisions.[4] The written justification would, within the constraints that nonrevelation of proprietary information impose, explain why one vendor was selected over another or why only a single bid was solicited. It would be a publicly available document, like (although not necessarily so prolix as) the statements of reasons government agencies currently provide for administrative rule-making decisions.

On balance, furthermore, I believe that retaining multimember evaluation panels is a good requirement, although it does dilute the responsibility individual participants feel for their decisions. The reason is that panels such as these tend to encourage standards of excellence. Standards for excellence constitute our publicly stated ideals; sloth is a guilty private vice, and poor judgment is a source of embarrassment. Institutions that make us act in the view of others whose opinion we value encourage behavior more like our ideals.[5] The notion of justifying oneself to a group also argues in favor of efforts at reaching group consensus rather than simply tabulating opinions (as was done in only three of the eight technical evaluation panels in the case studies) since it is the effort to reach consensus that calls forth the group discussion where such justification occurs. Furthermore, it argues for selecting members of evaluation panels who know each other (as was true in five of the nine technical evaluation panels in the case studies; in another three, about half the members knew each other), since people are likely to value more highly the good opinion of others they already know. A consistent record of poor judgment is also more likely to become apparent among members who know each other and serve as a source of embarrassment. The administrative law system in Sweden (and perhaps in other countries with which I am less familiar) puts heavy emphasis on assuring that a group of officials deliberate together in making a decision, rather than allowing one official to make the decision alone; this serves as a substitute for many of the rules of American administrative law.[6]

The Civil Service Reform Act of 1978 authorized a series of experiments in personnel management that allowed departures from civil-service rules. Similar experiments in procurement would show whether management improvements would produce real performance benefits. Since volunteers for such experiments are likely to be the most adventurous, positive results in such experiments could not necessarily be extrapolated to the whole group. Nonetheless, the success of such experiments would encourage their extension.

A more cautious approach to reform would be to keep most present regulations but to look for ways to compensate for problems the system creates, usually by developing new contract clauses. Many efforts at compensation already occur, on an ad hoc basis, as participants experience problems and deal with them. Long-term contracts with technology refreshment clauses, for example, allow price exploitation by vendors who need not worry that such exploitation will damage them in future awards. Although technology refreshment clauses are recent developments, such exploitation has prompted the Environmental Protection Agency and the National Institutes of Health to develop a new contract clause. The upgrades must now be priced not at the price of the original bid but at the same percentage discount as in the original bid.[7]

Contracts to develop an indefinite quantity of custom software allow the government to gain some of the site-specific knowledge investment advantages of informal long-term relationships. If no specific decision has been made in advance about what the contractor will produce, the ideas the contractor develops on site need not be subjected to outside competition. This feature appears to be an unintended consequence of an arrangement developed for another reason—namely, the difficulty of specifying all of an agency's application requirements over a multiyear period in advance of contract award. This feature of these contracts is probably not consciously managed by the officials very often. The current procurement system tends to regard the development of requirements as the government's function and vendor-initiated ideas as vaguely sleazy, so it works against making effective use of such opportunities to get more value from contractors. One might imagine a conscious acknowledgment of this opportunity and an effort to take the best possible advantage of it.

Most important, "past performance in contracts within the agency" could be added as a formal evaluation factor and incorporated into the normal evaluation system. Firms that had done well in the past would get a good score; firms that had not would get a poor score. If good past performance suggests good performance on the contract to be awarded, then a vendor who performed well in the past should be favored over one without prior experience at the agency, although the barrier should not be insurmountable. One might imagine a scoring range between $+10$ and -10—and a firm with no past experience with an agency might be given a zero. Firms that had worked for the agency before would have the potential to gain because of their performance or to be punished more than a firm that had never worked for the agency in the past.[8]

It might be well argued that a newly established firm does not have any control over the fact that it has never done business with the government in the past and that putting such a newly established firm at a disadvantage thus constitutes unfair discrimination. Newly established firms, of course, already face that disadvantage in the private sector. New firms have advantages in innovativeness and ability to react more quickly, compared with older firms that tend to be set in their ways. These are facts of organizational life favoring new firms over old ones that are not particularly under the control of established firms either. A higher score for a firm that has done well should be seen as no more inequitable than the higher score a vendor gets for a better technical proposal.

93

The more the scoring on this new evaluation factor depends on quantitative measures, the less radical the departure from the current system would be. I believe strongly that scores on this factor should be based on more than objective performance measures (such as meeting contracted delivery schedules), since so many dimensions of good performance are difficult to quantify. Officials should be allowed to use their judgment in rating performance. They should not be arbitrarily constrained nor should they have to state their criteria in advance. Judgments about past performance *should* be influenced by the vendor project manager's having come to the customer's site at three o'clock in the morning to figure out why the system was not working right. An argument against using past performance is that a firm might be good today and turn bad tomorrow, when all its best people resign. The answer to this argument is that this is why past performance scores cannot be mechanical but must indeed be judgments. The agency should only be required to provide an account of the basis of its judgment. Judgment rather than formulas will be needed especially during the transition period to a new system, because records of good or bad vendor performance under the present system would differ from those in a world where past performance is rewarded or punished.[9]

Cautious efforts are far better than nothing, but they have important limitations. Although the government has attempted to remedy problems arising from the current system through new contractual clauses, such efforts have generally not solved the problems. And I believe it is no coincidence that agencies do little consciously to take advantage of the potential for vendor innovativeness in general-purpose software development contracts because this potential violates the spirit of the procurement system. If counterproductive assumptions of that system are not confronted, participants in the system have difficulty even imagining a different world. Furthermore, until those assumptions are so attacked, serendipitous sources of potential value run the risk of being stamped out as ugly weeds rather than being nurtured as beautiful flowers.

Still, if no more than cautious reform is feasible, we should attempt to realize as much as possible from it by systematically relating it to an analysis of why the procurement system goes wrong and where problems are most likely to occur.

Possible Objections

What about the effect of these changes on equity and integrity in the procurement system? Will grants of discretion return us to the days of

Boss Tweed and the shame of the cities, of sweetheart deals and payoffs? One way to read the argument of this book might be that I am suggesting that too much weight is currently placed on equity and integrity at the expense of other values, such as the substantive quality of procurement performance. Herbert Kaufman's book *Red Tape* argues that bureaucratic rules grow from the desire to promote goals such as equity or integrity and that we should not simply damn the rules but recognize the trade-offs.[10] My critique might be then seen as a variant of the economist's concept of an optimal level of corruption, in which not more than a dollar in detection costs is spent to uncover a dollar's worth of fraud.[11] "Resources" here might be seen both as direct resources expended in combating corruption and as the forgone benefits of higher quality performance.

I should state at the outset that certainly in principle it might be the case—indeed, it is plausible to suggest—that such trade-offs between substantive procurement performance and equity or integrity might exist.[12] I also, however, take the equity and integrity goals of the current system more seriously than at least the economist's notion of the "optimal amount of fraud" suggests. I am happy there remains enough pride in our institutions of government to hold them to especially high standards of probity.

And I have also concluded that, in fact, one need not sacrifice equity and integrity to obtain better substantive procurement performance.

Let us take the equity goal of the procurement system first, the goal that vendors not arbitrarily be excluded from government business. One must here consider more deeply exactly what we mean by treatment that is arbitrary and hence inequitable.

I do not suggest that vendors arbitrarily be excluded from government business. Arbitrary exclusion is exclusion for no good reason, so if there are good reasons not to choose a vendor, the exclusion is not arbitrary. I suggest only that public officials be given more room for judgment in deciding not to give work to a vendor. No defender of the current system would suggest that vendors have a right to receive government business, only that they not be arbitrarily excluded.

Why might a public official choose one vendor over another for other than good reasons—that is, reasons related to how well the manager believes the vendor will do the work? The official might do so because he is lazy and is taking the path of least resistance. This problem should be dealt with by measuring results, not by procurement regulation. Or the official might do so because he has been bribed (a topic to be dealt with below). Public managers might arbitrarily stay with vendors they know because they feel more comfortable with them. Insofar as this is more than a variant of the suggestion that the official is lazy, it must be noted that such "comfort" frequently constitutes genuine value to the government that has been obtained through ongoing customer-vendor relationships—and hence are not arbitrary at all.

Vendors may complain that as taxpayers they have the right to bid for government business. Taxpayers in general have a right, however, to expect dollars spent on procurement to maximize the value the government receives. We must be willing to state that much of what some vendors might perceive as arbitrary or inequitable is not that at all. If equity is properly understood, a change in the system need not imply that government will treat citizens inequitably.

I take very seriously the goal of keeping the level of corruption in government low. The costs of government corruption are far greater than the monetary or performance losses to the government that result from corrupt bargains. Public corruption can devastate the ethical tone of society as a whole and decrease the inclination of citizens to behave ethically in their everyday lives. I am happy there remains enough pride in our institutions of government to hold them to especially high standards of probity. Thus, even the economist Arthur Okun has written that government "*should* spend $20 to prevent the theft of $1 of public funds."[13]

It is important to note the perception gap between a general public that perceives corruption to be a major problem in government procurement (and indeed in government in general) and government officials who generally perceive it to be only of minute proportions (in computer acquisition, at least). I believe the public tends to exaggerate the problem more than practitioners within government tend to underestimate it. Nonetheless, the recurrent corruption in municipal procurement, the occasional scandals at the federal level, and the anecdotal evidence suggesting that payoffs are an endemic problem in private-sector purchasing all reinforce concerns about the possibilities of corruption in government procurement.

The current procurement system exacts such an enormous toll on the quality of performance, however, that we are obliged to seek other ways of reaching the goal of keeping corruption down. And, indeed, combating procurement corruption through regulation turns out to be a terrible idea for many reasons, even beyond the toll it exacts on the quality of government performance. It is of dubious effectiveness. It unjustly punishes the many for the crimes of a few. And alternatives are likely to be at least as effective.

Earlier I held the view that the current system was at least effective in lowering corruption and that therefore procurement effectiveness was being traded for a reduction of corruption.

The 1988 defense procurement scandal persuaded me that the current system does little to reduce corruption. The scandal suggested that the procurement regulatory system functions as a sort of Maginot line, an imposing defense reduced to impotence because it simply redirects dishonesty into other forms. Almost unnoticed in discussion of the scandal is that the procurement regulatory system seems to have worked, at least on its own terms. Nobody could throw a contract directly. Instead, some contractors seem to have bought inside information that allowed them to prepare better proposals. Once they had this information, they could present proposals that "legitimately" made it through the formal procurement process and won because they were indeed the best proposals, however corruptly designed.[14]

Equally important, the elaborate oversight apparatus failed to generate the paper trail to catch those who misused it. According to press accounts, the trail began instead with a tip to government fraud investigators from an employee of a defense contractor who had been approached by a defense consultant selling inside information from the Defense Department. Government investigators then probed further with standard investigative techniques, such as wiretaps, and used those implicated to provide information about other perpetrators. Procurement fraud has become easier to uncover because of investigative techniques such as these, previously used almost exclusively in narcotics and similar cases.[15] By contrast procurement system records were not helpful in uncovering the scandal.[16] A former inspector-general at the General Services Administration, who tried to uncover fraud by examining procurement records, concluded that no matter how gross the corruption, one would still find the paperwork in order. "You won't find anything in the documents."[17]

Although the current system may do less to reduce corruption than we think, another hypothetical system in which nobody looked and nobody cared might indeed display levels of corruption higher than the current one. The current system may increase the effort required for corruption and hence serve as a disincentive; even the Maginot line made France somewhat more of a challenge to conquer. But the current system is less effective at corruption-reduction than many believe.

Combating procurement corruption through regulation also unjustly punishes many for the crimes of a few. The demands of justice suggest that we punish the guilty and spare the innocent. The current system, by contrast, places too much of the burden of combating corruption on honest government officials who are trying to accomplish a mission and on citizens who are the victims of poorer-quality government performance. From the point of view of justice, it would be better if the cost of efforts against procurement corruption could be better targeted on the corrupt than on all of us.

Finally, procurement corruption can be fought in other ways. Modern investigative techniques are the main way procurement corruption is uncovered now. The important business of fighting procurement corruption should be removed from the procurement regulatory system. The technology of corruption investigation—using tips, undercover agents, wiretaps, and perpetrators who can be made to "turn"—has advanced in the past decade far beyond where it was when the procurement system was developed. Some loosening of the procurement system itself to deter corruption might be compensated for by these improvements in criminal investigation.

Any loosening of the procurement regulatory straightjacket should be accompanied by, and linked to, increased resources for public corruption investigations to investigative units both outside the line agencies responsible for procurement and within those agencies. This latter would be so that no agency administrator need stand naked against the criticism that their operations were so mired in scandal a team of outsiders had to expose it. Currently, if a scandal breaks, administrators can point to the system of rules and regulations and say that the agency had done everything it could; extensive in-house investigative capability would allow these administrators to make the same claim in a deregulated world.

Deregulation of the procurement system should also be accompanied by an increase in criminal penalties for procurement corruption. The corrupt do not bear the full social costs of their corruption, since that corruption has costs not only in terms of the particular procurement that was "thrown" but also through the pressure that instances of corruption create for new and value-destroying procurement controls.[18] Our notion of the fitting punishment for such crimes should therefore be increased to reflect not only a view of the seriousness of the crime in the individual situation, or even the crime's effect on social standards of morality, but also a judgment of the effect of individual instances of corruption on the pressures for onerousness of the procurement regulatory regime. It should be noted that criminology research suggests that the likelihood of punishment is a more important deterrent than the severity of punishment, so the increase in penalties is no substitute for keeping up the investigative pressure.[19]

These moves regarding corruption would probably be at least as effective as the current system has been. Moreover, the focus on resources for investigation and on increased punishment for the guilty is more just than the current system, because it focuses the burdens on the guilty. A public announcement of increased resources devoted to investigation and of increased penalties would allow elected officials who might otherwise be worried that procurement deregulation signaled a withering of concern over public integrity, to display a visible signal of continuing concern over such issues and show that changes in the system in no way implied any lessening of attention to integrity in procurement.

A more subtle phenomenon that the procurement system seeks to minimize is intervention by elected officials who wish awards to go to contractors in their districts. Such intervention did not appear to be a problem in the computer-related case studies I examined. For the vast majority of vendors, business with the government may not be significant enough to call forth such intervention. Nonetheless, such intervention is said frequently to occur in defense contract awards (which of course are the lifeblood of a defense contractor's business) and one can certainly imagine many individual situations of smaller companies for whom government business might be sufficiently important so that political intervention becomes a possibility.

The present system may have the same difficulty detecting political intervention as it has with outright corruption. The current system's main (and not inconsiderable) virtue in this regard is that it provides government officials with an easy, unthreatening way to say to elected officials: "I'd like to help, but I have to follow the rules."[20] Changes in procurement regulations should therefore be accompanied by a requirement that contacts between elected officials or their staffs and an agency regarding a procurement decision be made part of the published record of the procurement. The media could then enforce limits on political intervention. Such a strategy would seek to influence the demand for political invervention by elected officials, rather than acting, as the current system does, on the supply of favors government officials are willing to offer.

The evaluation panel system should also be retained as an anti-corruption measure because a panel is far more difficult to bribe than an individual. Consensus scores on evaluation panels discourage corruption by making it more difficult for a bribed individual to skew scores. Finally, the same system of results-based performance evaluation that is key to the move to a procurement system that gives public officials greater ability to use their judgment is also an important part of the struggle against procurement corruption. The best inhibitor of corruption or politicization is the need to have competent vendors to get an organization's work done. When the spoils system was flourishing in the nineteenth century, agencies such as the Patent Office and the Department of Agriculture (then primarily a scientific research organization) had complex technical tasks that could not have been accomplished by unqualified spoilsmen. These agencies introduced their own merit system free of outside legislation or rules.[21]

It is fair to ask how federal managers who buy and use computers might react to any new freedom they might be granted. Classic accounts of problems created by adherence to bureaucratic rules, such as Robert Merton's "Bureaucratic Structure and Personality," suggest that bureaucracies become rule-bound from devotion to rules by the bureaucrats themselves. To be successful, Merton argues, a bureaucracy must obtain a high level of reliability and must undertake routine activities methodically; these means to effective performance then become the goals of the organization.[22] Others argue that if bad behavior provides an easy target for journalists and elected officials, and if good behavior is harder to discern, a natural pressure exists to follow the rules cautiously, so that one can deny having ventured away from the straight and narrow.[23] Deregulating the system, it can be argued, will do nothing to prevent reporters from continuing the focus on scandal that drives government officials to seek shelter in rules. If either of these arguments is correct, then setting government officials free will not improve performance because it will not change behavior. Indeed, if the worst features of the procurement system stem from the procurement culture and not from the regulations themselves, don't the bad features of the system go deeper than rules imposed on unwilling official victims?

Another argument might also support the conclusion that changing the system would not change behavior. An important problem with the free and open competition model is that it fails to gain the government some advantages of long-term relationships with vendors. But what incentive is there for government officials to worry about the long term when their politically appointed bosses stay in office such a short time?[24]

Certainly these objections cannot be dismissed out of hand. One can hardly be sure how government officials would behave under a changed regime. An experiment with a deregulated procurement environment would allow us to see what effect such an environment would have.

Descriptions of bureaucrats enjoying the rule-boundedness seem to fit, by and large, the behavior of the *contracting* officials encountered in this research. These officials gain standing through their status as experts on the rules. Since they lack any substantive responsibility for the missions furthered by the products or services being acquired, they also lack any countervailing pressures against sticking to the rules. Contracting offices thus fall victim to all the forces favoring rule veneration and become the source of the negative features of the procurement culture, which they present to unsuspecting technical or program people as if they were the law.

But the evidence regarding the technical and program people who actually have responsibility for accomplishing something in the computer area is not nearly as dreary. Their answers in the Government Computer Managers Survey suggest that they chafe under the current system, and the case studies suggest similar conclusions. Furthermore, surveys of senior government managers suggest considerable dissatisfaction with the rules and clearances in procurement, personnel, and similar systems.[25] And it should be kept in mind that just as powerful in the organization theory literature as the image of the rule-obsessed bureaucrat is the image of the autonomy-seeker, particularly the autonomy-seeking professional. "Autonomy is the prize sought by virtually all occupational groups," writes the medical sociologist Eliot Freidson, "for it represents freedom from direction from others, freedom to perform one's work the way one desires."[26] The close supervision that rule-boundedness embodies is normally thought to engender resentment from those subject to it, not the willing submission of escapees from freedom.[27] Finally, most accounts indicate that career officials do not hesitate to raise issues of long-term institutional capacity when political appointees offer quick fixes.[28]

The results-based performance standards that must accompany procurement deregulation can provide officials who are subject to criticism with something they can point to other than having followed the rules. Developing such standards is less of a political challenge than, say, developing standards for a welfare program because the evaluation of performance in computer management is less controversial. The concern over the quality of government performance that would allow a change in the procurement system would also provide some cover to officials who were criticized.

Additionally, some serendipitous direct evidence shows how government officials who acquire computers might behave in a different environment. Two federal agencies—the Federal Reserve Board and the Federal Deposit Insurance Corporation—are not subject to federal procurement regulations. The Federal Reserve Board, the larger and more visible, tries to follow the regulations fairly closely so as not to be put under their sway, but the FDIC buys computers largely as it sees fit. The experience at these two agencies, then, provides something of a natural experiment.

And—behold!—free of the procurement regulatory system, the FDIC and to a lesser extent the Federal Reserve Board do tend to buy computers along the lines recommended in this book.[29] At the FDIC, past performance of vendors at the agency is "absolutely" taken into account and is given "considerable weight." Computer managers there feel free to call customers they know personally for judgments about performance at other organizations; they do not limit themselves to vendor-provided reference lists, which they take with "a grain of salt."

The top computer manager at FDIC described one decision:

> We have both IBM and non-IBM peripheral equipment in our data center. We asked IBM at an oral presentation what they would do if a disk drive went down and it wasn't IBM equipment. They said that if they established that it was non-IBM equipment involved, they would take no responsibility. By contrast, the Amdahl people have shown us over the years that a problem at an Amdahl site is an Amdahl problem. They will work with peripheral vendors until the problem is solved.

This difference between the two vendors, according to the manager, "was a major consideration in not selecting IBM." In the rest of the government, this factor would have an insignificant weight since service capability as a whole seldom accounts for more than 5 percent. Such cut-to-the-point directness, as well as the reliance on an oral presentation rather than a written proposal resembled the approach of private-sector computer managers.

The differences at the Federal Reserve System were less dramatic. Since the agency's claim to be exempt from the procurement regulations had been challenged, it seeks to act in their "spirit" to "keep out of the limelight." Nevertheless, the board does take past performance at the agency into account, though modestly ("just because you have a vendor, you don't want to give them an unreasonable advantage"), and it talks with customers in addition to ones that vendors themselves provide. The Federal Reserve takes considerably less time to buy computers than most of the government does.

Reform is not possible as long as people believe that the current system minimizes corruption, provides all Americans a fair opportunity to bid for government business, and gets the good products or services for a good price. People must realize that the current system exacts a significant cost in performance—in quality, innovativeness, and even prices. Many perceive problems with the quality of performance of government contractors, problems that loom larger as more government operations are contracted out. But few relate those performance problems to the procurement system except, ironically, those who believe that current rules are not applied strictly enough or do not go far enough, and who wish to see more "competition" of the kind the system currently prescribes and less "favoritism." We must be willing to pound over and over again the point that the current system represents an affront to our common sense. We constantly make judgments about the future based on our experience in the past and could not function effectively if we did not do so. If we like a particular ice cream, we buy it again; if an auto repair shop has cheated us, we do not return. Yet the procurement system tells those who work in government that they cannot do the same in making government purchasing decisions.

Surprisingly many bad practices grow out of procurement custom rather than the requirements of law or regulation. Customs, of course, may be just as difficult to overturn as laws, but changes in customs need not await governmentwide edict. A few organizations can make the effort to change. The information that such practices are not required by law or regulation can also serve to liberate program managers who might otherwise assume that the edicts of their own contracting offices are equivalent to applicable law. Positive results from a few organizations that have departed from custom can inspire others to do likewise.

That intellectual effort succeeding, my predisposition to pollyannish optimism takes hold. That predisposition toward optimism is reinforced by the progress made during the past ten years in removing some of the most counterproductive features of the procurement regulatory system for computers.[30] For years, when agencies prepared to buy new generations of mainframes for their data centers—the major computer purchases many agencies made—they expected major battles. Concerned with the traumas of converting operating software for mainframes, the agencies wanted to exclude from the bidding operating systems incompatible with their existing equipment. Such exclusions, however, severely restricted competition—often to only the incumbent vendor. The guardians of the free-and-open-competition ideals in the congressional committees opposed any limitation of competition based on software conversion costs. And the regulations gave no consideration to the tremendous costs of software conversion in the acquisition of new mainframes. Agencies had to fight this issue case by case. Sometimes they won, sometimes they lost, usually at a great cost of time and effort. Here, certainly, was an example of requirements for competition that had no counterpart in the private sector from which the competition goal was purportedly being taken.

In the early 1980s, through the leadership of a new team running the computer oversight operation at the General Services Administration, this policy was changed. Agencies are now directed to perform software conversion studies that detail the costs and either limit bids to machines with compatible software or add the costs of software conversion to the bids of noncompatible machines.[31] These studies leave out some of the costs of software conversion, such as training costs and lost productivity during the learning period, and they often consume considerable energy strictly for the various overseers. Nevertheless, the policy change regarding software conversion was a major step forward. One hears little about software conversion problems anymore.

Another important change in the 1980s has been the technology refreshment clauses in big computer contracts. Given the length and complexity of the procurement process, the government has always favored long contracts with vendors, to avoid the nightmare of frequent recompetitions. During the lives of these contracts, however, as the fast-paced world of high technology kept moving, the equipment in the original contract competition became out of date before the end of the contract. Competition requirements were traditionally interpreted, however, to preclude delivery of any equipment other than that the vendor had bid. Since the competition had taken place on this equipment, delivery of new equipment would constitute a sole-source acquisition. Vendors therefore delivered what had become ancient equipment at the end of a long contract, at the prices it had bid when the equipment was new. This foolish policy, undertaken in the name of competition, bore a significant part of the responsibility for the antiquated state of much of the government's computer stock. It also cost the government unnecessarily, since the hoary equipment sold to the government toward the end of a contract had only a nominal market value by the time it was delivered. This policy, too, was swept away with the development of technology refreshment clauses authorizing agencies to receive newer equipment as long as the price was no higher. Since the General Services Administration now urges agencies to include such clauses in contracts, their use is universal.

During this same period, oversight and second-guessing of agency managers has also diminished. For much of the 1970s the House Committee on Government Operations maintained the informal authority to review agency computer procurements, because the General Services Administration passed procurement requests to the committee before approving them.[32] Procurements regarded as insufficiently competitive could be placed on hold for months or even years. Such holds were particularly frustrating because this review took place late in the process. By the time the agency went to the General Services Administration for a delegation of procurement authority, the requirements analysis was complete and the RFP was often ready.[33] During the 1980s, this practice has been eliminated. Furthermore, the General Services Administration has become less meddlesome in its reviews in connection with delegations of procurement authority. In none of the case studies I examined did the GSA review constitute a problem either in substance or in delays, although it had during much of the 1970s. In particular, GSA no longer pushes an overwhelming evaluation weight for price.[34] Indeed, GSA has encouraged a reduction of the time it takes to complete major acquisitions; its "Go for 12" program seeks to complete major procurements within a single year. This initiative responds to one of the major complaints of computer managers about the current system, although it does not address what I believe to be more fundamental problems. The effort emphasizes classic project management techniques, such as doing reviews in parallel rather than sequentially, but it does nothing about the basic features of the system.[35] These efforts have focused on agencies that are self-motivated to change; they chip away at the procurement culture through enthusiastic innovators who set an example, rather than using all their energy on a total assault that could fail.

I have on a number of occasions in this book stated that it is almost certainly true that the procurement system works better in practice than it does in theory. The most conscientious and devoted public officials seek—and at least sometimes find—ways to apply their common sense and good judgment to the procurement process. The problem is that, rather than encouraging an environment of excellence, the system keeps it the province of the heroic few. To quote again a manager in one of the case studies who kept a contract reaward from a firm that had done a poor job, "It was uphill. The system doesn't make it natural or easy. But you can either be victimized by the system or say, 'I'm a thinking human being.'" Simply to display common sense, such as by favoring a vendor because he is good, is to court questioning, disgrace, or even prison. Unfortunately, this is the pattern for far too much of the public sector. We owe public officials—and we owe all those affected by the quality of their performance—more than that.

APPENDIX A:
Research Methodology

For each case, I read available documentation about the procurement, such as the request for proposals, and interviewed relevant government officials (computer people, contracting officers, and, in some cases, end-users) involved in the decision as well as (when they were willing to be interviewed, which, unfortunately, was not always the case) vendor personnel. I also spoke with congressional staffers and General Accounting Office officials who might be familiar with the procurements. In all cases, I attempted to form a picture of the history of the procurement from the early stages of needs identification, through the development of the request for proposals, to evaluation and contract award, and, finally, to experience since contract award.

The Government Computer Managers Survey was an in-person interview with a mixture of fixed-format and open-ended questions soliciting both information and personal opinions regarding various features of the computer procurement process in the federal government.[1] The survey began with a series of questions where the respondent was asked to think about the most recent major acquisition of computer hardware, software, and services (for which there was enough experience with the contract to have formed an opinion about how well the vendor was doing) and then to respond to a series of questions about contract award and about contractor performance.[2] From these questions, the survey proceeded to a series of questions about aspects of the operation of the procurement system for computers. At the end of the survey, respondents were asked a number of fixed-format attitude questions as well as a question about how frequently they were dissatisfied with the performance of their computer vendors. Interviews generally lasted about one hour, sometimes more. Those interviewed were technical people whose job is computers, but who are key participants in (and customers of, so to speak) the procurement system, not contracting officials (who are part of other units within the organization) whose job is procurement per se.

Respondents were identified from a list of senior government officials appearing in the Office of Personnel Management, *U.S. Government Manual* (1986). Officials from the cabinet agencies and major independent agencies were selected and contacted. In addition, a listing of members in an interagency committee on information resources management organized by the General Services Administration was consulted for additional names. All members of this committee from civilian agencies whose names had not already been uncovered, except for those from very small agencies that were presumed to have extremely small computer budgets, were also contacted. (This listing provided names of a number of officials in subcabinet agencies, such as the Federal Aviation Administration in the Department of Transportation, and in smaller independent agencies, such as the Nuclear Regulatory Commission.) Finally, in a few cases where I knew that subcabinet agencies within a larger organization were major acquirers of computers—such as the Census Bureau and the National Weather Service in the Department of Commerce—I requested from the cabinet-level computer managers names of the senior computer managers at those subcabinet agencies. The General Services Administration has, since the survey was organized, published a printed directory of senior government information resources managers, but this directory was unfortunately unavailable at the time the list of managers to be interviewed was assembled. In all, thirty-six respondents were interviewed by a research assistant and me. Nobody refused to be interviewed, although in two cases it was impossible to schedule interviews because the managers were on travel during all the occasions the interviews were being held, and in a number of cases (no exact figures were kept, but I would estimate it at about one-fourth) the most senior managers referred us to someone else in the office for the interview. With a very few exceptions, the more junior people appeared to be knowledgeable and authoritative. Although this is not literally true, I believe it is accurate to regard these respondents as constituting the universe, rather than simply a sample, of the senior government technical managers or their designees involved in purchasing computers.

The Private-Sector Computer Managers Survey was a much briefer mail survey with fixed-format questions only. Most of the questions were identical to ones asked in the Government Computer Managers Survey (occasionally with small changes owing to differences in jargon between the two worlds), but only a fraction of the questions asked of the government managers were asked of their private-sector counterparts. These included the questions about experience with their most recent major computer acquisition, a number of general attitude questions, and the question about how frequently they were dissatisfied with the performance of their computer vendors.

Respondents were selected from the largest *Business Week* companies rather than the top *Fortune* companies because the former listing includes banks, utilities, and service companies as well as the manufacturing companies on the *Fortune* list. Companies that were themselves computer manufacturers, such as IBM or Digital Equipment, were excluded from the universe. Respondents were identified by writing letters to the public relations departments of the firms in question requesting names and addresses of the senior information technology/computer manager at the firms. Of the 340 firms to whose public relations departments requests were sent, 242 replied. The individuals so identified were sent the survey, together with a cover letter. A follow-up letter was sent to those who had not responded already. In all, 155 people responded, representing a response rate of 62 percent, an extremely high figure for a mail survey.

APPENDIX B: The Case Studies

CASE STUDY 1:
U.S. Department of Agriculture
Local Office Computerization

Ever since its establishment in 1862 as the "people's department," the United States Department of Agriculture (USDA) has been one of the least Washington-based and most field-oriented agencies of the government, providing technical assistance and other help to farmers directly on the farms where they live rather than from an office in Washington.

Two of the best contemporary embodiments of the traditional field-orientation of the USDA are the Soil Conservation Service (SCS) and the Farmers Home Administration (FmHA).[1] The mission of the Soil Conservation Service is to provide technical assistance to farmers and ranchers on dealing with soil erosion and the wise use of water resources.[2] This technical assistance is provided directly to farmers on a one-on-one basis; the local SCS agent actually visits farm sites. Agents give advice to farmers and also design engineering solutions for erosion or similar problems. SCS has approximately 2,700 local offices in the agricultural counties of the country, typically with only one or two professionals at each.[3] The FmHA is a dustbowl-era organization that initially made loans to farmers to allow them to buy or keep a home.[4] During the 1970s the mission of the agency became dramatically expanded into including support for a broad range of rural development projects such as multifamily housing industrial parks and sewer projects in rural areas. FmHA has more than 2,000 local offices—generally a bit bigger than SCS offices.

In 1985 USDA let a contract—the contract with the largest dollar value of any of those being examined here—for computerizing the local operations of these 5,000 field offices. This was an ambitious task, both because of the large number of offices involved and the extensiveness of the changes that would occur in their operations.

Professional employees of local SCS offices generally have degrees in agricultural science.[5] At their offices, the professional work they do that is appropriate for computerization generally involves engineering computations to prepare the design for a terracing system or what-if computations to observe the impact of varying a farmer's crop rotation on soil quality. At state-level SCS offices, where the more complicated problems are referred and where there are staff specialists in engineering or soil science, people might also use computers for the computer-aided design of simple dam structures or for computer-aided mapping of soil patterns. For all of SCS's professional work, computers are enormous timesavers.

Prior to this procurement, there had been little use of computers at SCS. Some of the state offices (but none of the county ones) had access to USDA mainframes for engineering calculations sent off to them in a batch mode. Most county-level offices used only programmable calculators.

Between 1981 and 1983 approximately 10 percent of the field offices bought computers on their own. The proliferation of different brands was one reason SCS launched a nationwide procurement. But the local experimentation with microcomputers did provide the agency with valuable experience about possible applications. This was helpful in developing requirements for the large procurement: SCS brought computer users from the field to Washington to help develop its specifications, and the agency also developed an inventory of available application programs (mostly written locally in-house or at state agricultural colleges) that grew out of the experimentation period.

FmHA people at local offices made and tracked loans, and provided borrowers with advice about the financial implications of choosing various crop mixtures. A master file of loan applicants and information about them was kept on USDA mainframes in Kansas City. But local offices were pencil-and-paper operations. In the existing environment, FmHA suffered both from the lack of communications capability between the mainframe and local offices, and also from the lack of local computing capability in the offices.[6] Because all information about loans was contained on the mainframe in Kansas City, any interaction regarding a loan—to request funds, to determine payoff schedules, to reschedule payments—had to be initiated by a mail request to the Kansas City office, followed by a printout generated by a batch run, which was then mailed back from Kansas City to the local office. The typical total turnaround time was one month or more. If there were any errors, the process needed to be repeated, doubling the turnaround time. "Meanwhile the farmer didn't have this check, and the planting season might have gone by."[7] Local offices received batch reports on delinquent loans that were two months old. Because it is common knowledge within the loan-servicing industry that quick action on delinquencies is a key to dealing with them, the delays significantly interfered with the government's ability to get back money it had loaned. The big increase in loan volume during the 1970s exacerbated the delays.

Major problems for the functioning of the operation also resulted from the lack of local computing capability in the county offices. The loan decision-making process was completely manual, requiring adding-machine calculations based on the forms the farmer requesting a loan had filled out. The manual process was very error-prone. In addition, in terms of service to FmHA customers, it had no ability to provide a farmer with advice by performing "what-if" sensitivity analyses that would try out different crop mixes or strategies and see their effect on farmer revenue. The lack of word-processing and automated tickler file capability also made it very difficult to follow up on delinquent loans.

There was widespread acknowledgment of these problems. A modernization effort began in 1974. Yet change was slow in coming. An important problem was that during the 1970s the number of FmHA programs, and the procedures for these programs, were changing so rapidly that it was difficult for the agency to settle on a definition of its requirements that would allow it to proceed with an RFP.

> Any program was supposed to meet "user requirements."
> The problem was that user requirements were changing all
> the time. It was tough to put your arms around something
> that was constantly in motion.[8]

Lynn Furman of FmHA believes that a more appropriate strategy would have been to buy some hardware and have the software developed by a task-order style contract with a broad statement of work. But this strategy was never adopted; instead, the agency waited until it had all its requirements in place so it could proceed by grand design.

The slowdown in the pace of change, combined with the climate of growing concern about high default rates on federal loan programs, encouraged the new Reagan-era management of the Department to put computerization efforts at FmHA on a faster track. It still took, however, about two further years of study before FmHA was ready, at the beginning of 1984, with a draft RFP.

Around the same time, and separately, SCS was proceeding with its own automation efforts. It was a bit further behind FmHA, but both organizations were just about ready to move when the Office of Management and Budget (OMB) intervened. As part of general efforts to improve efficiency in government operations, OMB was now advocating a merger of local SCS and FmHA office locations to save on rent, utilities, and clerical help. They also believed that if two agencies bought their computers in one big buy for one standard office configuration, the government could save money by getting volume discounts and cheaper maintenance.

In early 1984, therefore, the OMB ordered SCS and FmHA to merge their requirements and proceed on one consolidated procurement. Dutifully complying with the orders of USDA top management, the technical people at the two organizations stopped what they were doing and proceeded to develop a joint RFP, which was issued at the end of 1984.

When this procurement was completed, USDA ultimately had purchased an extremely unusual (probably existing nowhere in the world outside USDA), expensive computer architecture. This architecture turned out to be necessary to meet the requirements stated in the RFP. In essence, the architecture involved a microcomputer at each desk that was part of a multiuser system linked to a small minicomputer. The computers at each desk needed to communicate with a remote mainframe. To do so, they needed a terminal emulator card that would make the microcomputer appear to the mainframe to be a dumb terminal, since most mainframes are not able to communicate directly with microcomputers.

This configuration is extremely odd, to put it mildly, because if one goes to the expense of buying a small minicomputer for a multiuser system, the whole purpose of doing so is to have the mini take over processing responsibility, thus allowing each desk to get by with a much less expensive dumb terminal. To buy a processor that has the capability to do computing for a number of terminals and then also to buy microcomputers for each desk, which also can do the same computing on a desk-by-desk basis, is to purchase duplicate functionality. To require then each desk to be able to communicate with a mainframe, meaning that something that is or looks to the mainframe like a dumb terminal is necessary at each desk, entails that one also purchase a terminal emulator to override the microcomputer that has been placed at each desk. This adds insult to injury. For if there had been no microcomputers at each desk in the first place (a redundant capability, since processors for a multiuser system had already been bought), it would never have been necessary to spend the additional money to override the microcomputers and make them seem like the dumb terminals they normally should have been anyway.

The problem was not just that the solution for USDA was so expensive. The organization ultimately was saddled with software for basic word processing and financial applications (spreadsheets and database uses) that was written using the UNIX operating system at a time when UNIX software for the basic commercial applications of word processing, spreadsheets, and database management was still very primitive. It had bugs. It was not very easy to use. And it was not really integrated very well.[9] This result was particularly frustrating since there existed at the time countless well-developed software packages for these mainstream commercial applications, including integrated packages.

Because of this extremely strange result, it is important to look with more detail than in most of these case studies at the technical issues relating to the requirements and their implications for computer architecture.

FmHA had as its ultimate goal to download to each local office the files on borrowers serviced out of that office and then to do the computing work there.[10] Although such downloading of files to the local offices was still some time away when the requirements were developed, and the initial configuration of the system would involve local terminals accessing data off the mainframe in Kansas City, the requirements for the RFP were developed with this eventual shift into a downloaded environment in mind. Technically, there would be two ways one might organize local-office computing. One might place personal computers at each desk, connected to each other by a local area network and to a file server that would store the data (such as the files on each borrower) that people could then access to their desks for computing. Alternatively, one might have the data storage and the computing done by a small multiuser minicomputer acting as a processor, which would then be linked to dumb terminals at each desk that would then simply display results for people needing them.

The nature of FmHA's requirements, however, would have driven the organization toward the second approach of a multiuser processor with dumb terminals. One reason is that FmHA wanted it to be possible for more than one employee at an office independently to access different parts of a borrower's file simultaneously—so that, say, one employee could change an address on the file while another employee was entering a payment transaction. The alternative would have been for one user to have to wait until another user was finished, which would lower user productivity. At the same time, the system had to make sure that if two users were making changes on a borrower's file at the same time, both changes were made to the file—not just the one made last, as might otherwise happen.[11] The ability to allow this kind of simultaneous multiuser access to a single file is not available with a local area network/microcomputer solution, only with a multiuser processor/dumb terminal solution. In addition, a second

113

reason FmHA would have gone the multiuser processor/dumb terminal approach was that over an intermediate period of time they would still have all the data on the mainframe, not downloaded to the local offices, and mainframes communicate most naturally and least expensively with dumb terminals rather than with microcomputers.

FmHA had rather demanding data communications requirements for the years when its local offices would still be communicating directly with the Kansas City mainframe. Since it needed on-line, real-time communication with the mainframe and a fairly quick response time, FmHA needed high-speed modems, which would allow data to be transmitted quickly, and synchronous transmission, because it is a more accurate way to send data—an expensive combination driven by the agency's data communications needs.

SCS had a quite different set of computing requirements.[12] Basically, SCS needed stand-alone microcomputers. They would use them, of course, for standard word processing. But the most important computer-related work SCS does is scientific, such as doing calculations based on data from soil samples or crop yields. State-level SCS offices would also use computer-aided design programs. Because SCS was already using programs written in the MS/DOS operating language in the locations that already had microcomputers, it wanted the microcomputers it would buy under this procurement to use MS/DOS. (This meant IBM or any of its clones, a requirement that would have excluded only Apple Computer from competing.)

SCS had only modest data communications requirements. They would need to send in periodic reports from local offices to the USDA headquarters mainframe. And they would need occasional access to the database of soil characteristics at the USDA mainframe in Fort Collins, Colorado. These requirements were not particularly sophisticated. SCS had no need for on-line communications capability. Their simple, time-insensitive communications requirements could have been solved by less expensive, slow, asynchronous modems. For its offices with more than one computer, SCS also wanted a very simple local area network to allow the computers to share data, probably involving one of the microcomputers doubling as a file storage device for the office.

The origin of what was to become the anomalous configuration USDA eventually got was the merging of the FmHA and SCS requirements.[13]

Generally, merging the requirements simply involved agglomerating the two sets of agency demands. There was one important exception, however. When SCS learned that FmHA required a multiuser system (to achieve record-level locking of a borrower's file), it demanded that the RFP specify a UNIX operating system for the multiuser system, on the grounds that SCS had lots of software written in UNIX as well as MS/DOS, but little in other operating systems. FmHA had not in its requirements specified any particular operating system for its multiuser environment and actually had been looking at vendors such as Digital Equipment and Convergent Technologies with shared processors using proprietary operating systems specific to the vendors. The contracts office was a bit reluctant about the UNIX requirement, but gave its approval based on the fact that (as with MS/DOS) many different vendors offered UNIX and that it would therefore encourage competition compared with various proprietary operating systems.

As it turned out, the mixture of MS/DOS and UNIX requirements imposed the strange configuration that the agencies ended up receiving. It turned out there was no small minicomputer that could run MS/DOS as well as UNIX. *So USDA ended up getting a minicomputer to do UNIX and microcomputers (instead of dumb terminals) to do MS/DOS.* The microcomputers would then need to be overridden by terminal emulators to communicate with a mainframe. And since the office automation software such as word processing was intended to be located on the shared processor so that people, particularly at FmHA, would have access to standard form letters and other shared work, the agencies got stuck with poor-quality UNIX office automation software rather than better developed packages.

The evaluation criteria in the RFP gave the most points on the technical evaluation to "management factors," followed by software, followed by hardware.[14] Management factors counted 40 percent of the total nonprice part of the evaluation. The RFP listed five subfactors under management factors, "in descending order of importance," of which "corporate experience" was the third of five. (The two most important were training and "operational support," both involving plans that vendors presented in their proposals.) While the RFP did not state how these factors were to be evaluated, the instructions to bidders gave some clues about what USDA was looking for in proposals. Vendors were asked, for example, to provide manuals or other instructional material that would be used in training as well as training class schedules. They were also asked to provide descriptions of five recent projects and a list of all "relevant contracts on which work has been performed during the last three years," including names and telephone numbers of contact people.[15]

The RFP did not establish the relative weights of technical and price considerations, nor did USDA have any internal weights.[16] Some people within USDA believe that the purpose of this was to

115

encourage award to the low-price bidder if the technical scores were anything even close to each other. But Clem Munno, contracting officer on the procurement, denies this. Munno—of all the contracting officers encountered for these case studies the most flexible and least bound by a narrow interpretation of the procurement regulations—states:

> I told industry that technical and management criteria would be much more important than price. Of course, as technical scores get closer, price becomes more important. But we were installing computers in thousands of locations where computers had never been used before. So technical had to be important.[17]

At another point, Munno added: "I didn't want to make a decision based on just adding up points. I wanted to make a business decision."[18]

After the RFP was issued, USDA ran a bidders' conference and a request for comments, which produced a voluminous number of questions to which USDA formally replied. USDA issued over an eight-month period eight solicitation amendments changing specifications in the RFP in response to vendor questions or suggestions.[19] But in all of this plethora of communication from vendors, *no vendor ever pointed out to USDA that the only way to meet the requirements it had established would be to use an expensive configuration with redundant computing power and other strange features.* Everyone bid a set of requirements that would allow them to sell more hardware to USDA than they would have been able to sell had the requirements been different.

Six bids came in, of which only three (from EDS, Sperry, and Planning Research Corporation [PRC]) survived the initial evaluation and participated in the live test demonstration the RFP had announced. The configurations that were bid were somewhat different. But all were complex, custom-designed to meet USDA requirements, and expensive.

It is a bit unclear to what extent people at USDA were surprised. It would seem that a few were not, but most were.[20] People at SCS and FmHA were worried enough about whether vendors could meet the merged requirements that they asked a consultant, before the final RFP was issued, to survey the vendor community and find out whether vendors could meet the new requirements. Many vendors said both that they could do so and that they would be interested in bidding on the contract.[21] The problem was that USDA asked the wrong question: the right question was not whether bidders could meet the requirements, but what kind of configuration it would take to do so. They got an answer only to the question they asked. Most of the active participants in the process were surprised by what finally came in as the proposals.

Most people at the agencies were also surprised at how immature and user-unfriendly the UNIX commercial software application packages turned out to be.[22] Few of the technical people had much experience with UNIX. Some of those expressed skepticism about UNIX packages to higher-level management, but their warnings were discounted because they were felt to reflect simply hostility owing to unfamiliarity. People assumed that the general language in the RFP requiring that software be off-the-shelf production and user-friendly would protect them. "I would have thought that when you said 'off-the-shelf' you would be having significant numbers of customers on the products already," says Lynn Furman.[23] In fact, some of the UNIX packages had been "announced" just prior to vendor proposals and had no previous customers. (Many in the vendor community believe that "off-the shelf" means simply commercially available.)

Once the bids came in, stopping the process would have required returning to the drawing boards and redoing the entire solicitation, setting USDA back perhaps a year or more. The process therefore rolled along into evaluation. Three separate technical evaluation teams were established, one for management, one for hardware, and one for software.[24]

The three teams went off for a two-week meeting to go over the proposals. Most members of the evaluation teams knew the other members of the team who were from their own agency. Members did individual evaluations, and then the team met together to discuss discrepancies. Although people had to give explanations for discrepancies, no attempt was made to achieve consensus ratings if an individual wished to stick with his original scores. Instead, individual ratings were averaged to obtain overall results. To discourage any effort to "throw" the evaluation toward a preferred vendor, members of the teams were not told the relative weights of each of the evaluation subfactors within their overall evaluation area. They were also told not to communicate with members of the other evaluation teams, although they were all off-site at the same location.

USDA had significant experience with only one of the vendors bidding on the contract—Sperry. Sperry ran the large USDA mainframe data center at Fort Collins, Colorado, which was used extensively by SCS and which was one of the largest Sperry installations in the world.[25] USDA also had some experience with Sperry minicomputers. People around the organization were generally very satisfied with Sperry's record at the agency. "There were some people around who would have liked to see Sperry win this contract," according to

John Okay of SCS.[26] Erlend Warnick of FmHA described Sperry as the "sentimental favorite." But he added, "there was no way to justify" any extra points for Sperry, since Sperry's past performance at Fort Collins "wasn't included in the rating factors."[27] "We were definitely not allowed to favor Sperry just because we had had good experience with them," states Dan Stoltz of the hardware evaluation team. "When you're on an evaluation team, you look at the paper only."[28] According to Warren Lee, chairman of the management evaluation team, none of the members of that team had had any personal experience with Sperry at Fort Collins.[29]

Members of the management evaluation team did call the references that vendors provided. According to the chairman of the management evaluation panel, "We did learn something from calling them. One reference was very negative, and that influenced our scoring."[30]

The live test demonstration played an important role in influencing who won the contract. It consisted of timed exercises to see how long it would take to accomplish certain tasks outlined in a live test demonstration manual, "stress tests" of demands put on the processing ability of a local office configuration to handle various operations simultaneously, and tests of data communications capabilities that required actual accessing of the Kansas City FmHA database. Prior to the live test demonstration, Sperry had come in first place in the hardware evaluation, EDS first place in the software evaluation, and PRC first place in the management evaluation. These orderings switched after the live test demonstration because there were significant differences in how the three bidders did.[31]

All three vendors had problems at the live test demonstration. In particular, it was at the live test demonstration that USDA learned just how user-unfriendly and how unintegrated the software being proposed indeed was. In addition, it became apparent in the live test demonstration that although the proposals had each claimed to meet the RFP requirement for record locking that was important to FmHA, in fact none of them provided true record locking. Instead, they provided only for locking out some fixed number of bytes in a borrower's file, which did not really meet FmHA needs since the number of bytes that different records in a file took up was variable (the borrower's address would be allocated a different number of bytes than the date of last loan repayment, for instance) and thus the fixed number made record locking impossible.[32] The RFP had simply stated in general terms that "individual records should be protected from updating by two or more programs at the same time by a record locking technique. (Locking an entire file is not an acceptable technique to achieve record locking.)"[33] The irony of this was that the original FmHA demand for a multiuser system rather than personal computers with a local area network—which had landed USDA in the situation of getting both a shared processor and personal computers—was now not being met by the bidders. But it was too late to do much about it.

By a strict definition, none of the vendors would have passed the live test. To preserve competition, the contracting officer determined that all three had passed.

EDS did best at the live test demonstration, in significant measure (in the opinion of USDA officials) because they had prepared for it better than the other two bidders in terms of the organization of their demonstration rather than necessarily in terms of their actual computer configuration. The EDS people had clearly rehearsed to a far greater extent than the others. PRC had the worst problems. For a number of the exercises in the live test demonstration, the company simply could not get its configuration to work. "They just sat there and couldn't get their stuff to work," according to someone who was present. "It was very embarrassing."[34] The company was also plagued with some defective equipment that was brought for the demonstration. Sperry also had significant problems, although in the opinion of some at USDA, the problems had more to do with how well they had organized the live test demonstration than with any relative inferiority of their products. In particular, Sperry did poorly in the timed trials, but much of this had to do with the apparent inexperience of the data entry personnel the company had brought for the demonstration. Once the data had been entered, the configuration worked as well as that of EDS. After the live test demonstration, the software and hardware panels went back and redid their scoring. EDS replaced Sperry as the hardware winner, and PRC lost significant points both for hardware and software. The scores of each of the three evaluation teams were added up to produce an overall technical evaluation score.

Clem Munno, the contracting officer, believes that the performance of the vendors during the live test demonstration revealed something about their ability as managers.

> The live test showed us something about management commitment. The way you managed the live test shows me your planning. One of the vendors at the live test had a defective board. That tells me something.[35]

Munno went on to state that he "insisted on using this information" in the management evaluation scores for the vendors. "The proof of the pudding is in the eating, not in what they write," he states.[36] Yet Warren Lee says the management evaluation team was not even present at the live test demonstration and told me that no information about vendor performance at the live test was incorporated into the management evaluation.[37]

Munno also commented to panel members at the live test that he was concerned about EDS because of what many regarded as their reputation for pursuing contracts for every last dime and about the customer-responsiveness of an AT&T that was just coming out of a monopoly environment (EDS was bidding AT&T equipment). Such information, too, Munno believes should have gone into the evaluation process.[38] But Dan Stoltz, who heard Munno make these remarks, believes that he was not authorized to take account of them in any of his evaluation, assuming instead they would come in, if at all, later on when a final recommendation was discussed by the Source Selection Board.[39] Warren Lee of the management evaluation panel was unaware of the Munno comment when I mentioned it to him, and he stated that even if he had heard the comment, he would not have taken it into account. "That's pure speculation," he stated in an interview. "It has no value."[40]

Of the three vendors in the competitive range, PRC had bid the lowest price on the contract (by a fairly wide margin), followed by EDS, followed (in a fairly distant third) by Sperry. The final choice was seen as being between EDS, which won overall on the technical evaluation, and PRC, which had the lowest price. Because Sperry was highest on neither, it was eliminated. And with PRC having done so poorly in the live test demonstration, it did not appear to be a viable choice. To Clem Munno, the decision for EDS was a fairly clear one, and that is what he recommended to the Source Selection Board, which included the administrators of FmHA and SCS and which, pretty much as pro forma matter, gave the selection its approval. According to a number of people at USDA, had Sperry gotten its price below that of EDS, it might well have been awarded the contract, even though it had done somewhat more poorly on the technical evaluation.[41]

One important thing, it turned out later, that helped EDS bid what appeared to be a lower price than Sperry was the way the company chose to price one of the major items in the procurement, an item the RFP referred to as "basic system" for various office configurations.[42] The language in the pricing worksheet USDA provided was somewhat ambiguous, and EDS did not ask for a clarification, instead choosing to bid as "basic systems" hardware that lacked hard disks, software, and some other peripherals necessary to allow the system actually to function. EDS people involved in preparing the proposal state that they assumed that since there was a separate line item in the RFP for hard disks, they should not price hard disks as part of their basic system hardware bid as well. In support of their assumption, they note that the stylized purchasing assumptions in the RFP provided for equal numbers of basic systems and hard disks, leading them to believe that the hard disks were to be purchased for the basic systems. USDA people say that their intention was to create this separate line item for hard disks in case the agency needed to buy additional hard disk capacity into the contract. What is clear is that the price EDS bid was clearly much too low for providing functioning systems, something that a person knowledgeable about computers could have seen. The problem was that the technical people did not see price information from bidders. The contracting person doing this part of the cost evaluation did not know enough about computers to notice the problem. Meanwhile, the price difference per workstation between EDS and Sperry was magnified significantly in the overall cost evaluation because of the large number of systems to be purchased. After the contract was signed, USDA discovered that a functioning basic system would cost them far more than what EDS had bid.

There were no protests of the decision. "Usually, when the low-price vendor doesn't win, there's a protest," observes Clem Munno, and indeed PRC did ask for the decision to be reviewed by several management layers within USDA. "We tried to give them a very exhaustive de-briefing. We pointed out to them that we could have thrown them out after the live test demonstration. We tried to tell them how they could do a better job next time."[43]

In looking at EDS's performance since the contract was signed, it is somewhat artificial to separate some of their behavior prior to the contract award, such as bidding a very expensive configuration without warning USDA, from performance after the contract. Looking strictly at EDS's performance after the contract was signed, the general consensus within USDA is that EDS got off to a very poor start and then improved considerably.[44] For the first nine months of the contract, EDS fell terribly behind on the contracted delivery schedules. What was coming in often came in piecemeal, hardware but not software or vice versa. People working on the contract complained to the appropriate managers at EDS and then up the USDA hierarchy. Nothing much happened. There was talk of terminating the contract. Finally, one person involved in the contract saw an EDS ad featuring Paul Chiapparone, an EDS vice president who had been one of the EDS managers kidnapped in Iran and rescued in the Ross Perot operation dramatized in the book *On Wings of Eagles*. Chiapparone said in the ad that if a customer was ever having problems with EDS, he should call him. Going around channels—and causing a bit of consternation among some at USDA—an FmHA official initiated contact with Chiapparone. The contact made a difference in the view of USDA officials. (EDS people state that changes were under way prior to Chiapparone's intervention.) EDS put a new manager on the contract and threw in additional people. Deliveries began to improve dramatically. EDS met the overall installation schedule in the contract, and the equipment worked.

Unrelated to EDS's delivery problem, the UNIX software continues to produce persistent grumbling from users.

> We were having lots of problems—and we still have some problems—with core dumps, where all of a sudden you lose entire documents. When the Administrator is doing a speech in two hours and suddenly you've lost the document, you look like a nerd.[45]

People also have complained about the user-unfriendliness of the software and about the slowness of running database programs compared to other software packages.[46] There also persist problems with the service provided by AT&T, according to people at USDA. Some of the complaints involve poorly trained repair people. ("They sometimes use people who essentially are telephone repairers," according to one source.) The more persistent complaint involves the bureaucratic requirements that AT&T imposes regarding machine repairs. According to USDA officials, the AT&T repair hotline requires serial numbers for computers before they will come to repair them. However, USDA personnel discover when they call that frequently the serial numbers on computers that have been replaced because of earlier malfunctions have not been entered into the AT&T database—and that AT&T then refuses (or delays authorization) to repair them.

There have recently been developed shared processors that run both UNIX and MS/DOS, so that in future purchases under the contract, the redundant mini-micro-terminal emulator configuration will be avoided. "On a scale of one to ten, at the beginning I would have rated EDS a zero, today I'd rate them a seven," Lynn Furman of FmHA stated in 1988.[47] Furman's successor at the job has been impressed by EDS's willingness to help FmHA with advice about contract issues.[48]

CASE STUDY 2:
U.S. Customs Service
Local Office Computerization

The United States Customs Service has two broad areas of responsibility. The older one is the mission to collect, where required, duties on goods that commercial importers bring into the United States that are subject to tariffs. A second mission, initially growing out of the task of interdicting goods whose import is prohibited, involves enforcing laws against smuggling (such as drug smuggling) and money laundering. The "customs agent" a tourist encounters on returning to the United States from a trip abroad works for an inspection service within Customs that is separate from these big commercial and law-enforcement activities.

The Customs Service keeps large databases on centralized mainframe computers to support these commercial and law enforcement missions. The commercial database contains records of all import transactions coming into the country. The law-enforcement database contains information about people who have had legal problems of interest to the Customs Service. As of the early 1980s, there was some on-line availability of information from these mainframe databases at some local offices and field operations, but it was limited. And it allowed only access to these databases, not data processing using data on them. In addition, at local offices during the first part of the 1980s there began to be purchased, in fits and starts, personal computers and dedicated word-processing equipment (from a wide variety of vendors) for local office automation applications, mainly word processing.

In 1984 the Customs Service began two procurements to modernize and coordinate systems for computer use at Customs headquarters and field offices. One procurement (the Field Delivery System to be discussed in this case) would establish standard systems for office automation and local computing, as well as database access and data processing involving mainframe data bases. The other procurement would be for a communications network (the Customs Data Network) to provide a communications link between local Customs offices and the centralized mainframes.[1] The arguments for equipment standardization were that it would economize on training costs when people moved from one office to another and that it would, by consolidating purchases into a big contract, lower the cost of buying the computers. Furthermore, the easier access to the mainframe databases would allow their greater use in fraud or criminal investigations where information about past behavior (for example, the nature and value of a given import broker's imports) would be helpful in locating suspicious patterns or in providing evidence. And the belief as well was that individual local offices would use personal computers to develop their own local databases and data-processing programs for the offices' individualized needs.

Before developing the RFP, the people at the Customs Service involved in the contract (headed by Ken Malley, who was in charge of the project) spent a good deal of time, both at Customs offices and at the vendor sites, talking with vendor representatives about what products they had available. This was necessary because the Customs people were familiar mostly with a mainframe environment and knew little about distributed computing.[2] When visiting vendors, Customs officials were given "futures" presentations by top vendor management about where the firms were going over the next years, although the information from those presentations was not usable under the evaluation criteria in the final RFP. They also made a comprehensive survey of what Customs field offices wanted from computers, responses from which emphasized office automation applications.

The final specifications embodied in the RFP, which was issued in December 1984, called for what a number of people in Customs described as "the ultimate system," whereby Customs offices would be transformed from the dark ages to the cutting edge in one massive effort. Every desk at Customs would have a terminal that could be used to access data off the law-enforcement and commercial mainframes. Every desk at Customs would have access to word-processing, spreadsheet, and database programs, integrated so that people could easily move from one to another. In addition, Customs would establish a standardized computer configuration for offices of various sizes.[3] The smallest offices (those with fewer than twenty-five people) would use personal computers connected to the central databases via dialup lines. Large offices would have multiuser systems with dumb terminals connected to minicomputers of various sizes that were in turn linked to mainframe databases through the Customs Data Network.[4] "The whole philosophy was that we would tell each local office what they were going to get and what they were going to do."[5]

The RFP included no desirable features, only mandatory ones.[6] This apparently occurred in response to the philosophy of the contracting office at Customs. Barbara Lasky, the contracting officer on computer procurements, expresses her views on the use of desirables as follows:

You have to be careful about desirables. Your mandatory requirements are your minimum requirements. Desirable is something more than what is required. But the *FAR* is explicit about saying that the government should only satisfy its minimum needs. If it's so important but the technical people are still saying it's not really part of our minimum requirements, they're saying it's a luxury item with big benefits. I discourage people by telling them they've got to get it approved by a higher authority and really show that it's justified in terms of benefits to Customs.[7]

Ken Malley did not raise any particular objections to this. He did not have any "wide breadth of experience with desirables and mandatories," he recalls, and he did not push Lasky on the issue.

The evaluation criteria gave a maximum of 50 points (out of a total of 100) to the price the vendor proposed and up to 50 points for various categories of technical merit.[8] The RFP stated that the award would be made to the offer or with the highest number of points and that points would be calculated two decimal places.[9] Ken Malley had originally pushed for 70 points for technical and only 30 for price.[10] Barbara Lasky expresses her philosophy on the role of price in awarding contracts as follows:

I will always start off by saying these things should be 100% cost. GSA says that if the equipment is off-the-shelf and you have only mandatory requirements, it should be 100% cost. Now the technical guy says, "What about ease of use?" That's one of the true and only differences if you have mandatory requirements. That should be evaluated. The technical guys also talk about reliability. My opinion is that if you have an availability requirement in the contract, you can default them for not meeting it because they're not meeting specs. So they'll try to convince you that if you have a minimum requirement of 98%, if somebody does better than that, they should get extra points. They want to do that, and I fight them all the time, because it can be protested. Whenever somebody who's not the low cost bidder wins, he will scream and bitch and probably protest. So beyond ease of use, it's hard to see any case for anything but price.[11]

Lasky felt she had compromised a great deal to be willing to accept 50 points for technical merit. She was willing to live with such a high figure, she says, because the procurement was so central to meeting Custom's computing and office automation requirements. Clearly, however, she did not believe that anything close to 50 technical points out of 100 was really justified.

125

The evaluation criteria included no weight at all for management capability. Barbara Lasky argues that "we are buying equipment from these people, not their management," adding, "Management evaluation is where you go to court. If somebody loses because of those points, that's where you get a protest." She continues:

All my technical people want to give lots of points for management. I always say it's not necessary. If you get a negative report, how do you know how reliable it is? Let's get away from subjective things like that. If timeliness is important, put a liquidated damages clause in the contract. Remember, this is a contract. You've got legal coverage for their stuff not performing, or breaking down, or not being right.[12]

Ken Malley did not raise any objection to this:

We were technical people. We didn't have business acumen. The contract people had the responsibility to look at the business aspects. In looking at management capability, the contracts people had to determine whether vendors were viable or whether they were going to go bankrupt tomorrow.[13]

Bidders were required to give references to other users, and these references were in fact contracted, but only for use by the contracting officer in the determination of whether the vendor met the responsibility test required to be considered for a government contract.[14]

Four vendors bid on the contract. Customs had had no significant prior experience with any of them. About half the members of the technical evaluation team knew each other before the evaluation process. The team did not seek to achieve consensus on its ratings. "We were heavily instructed by contracts not to do that," says Ken Malley. Team members scored proposals individually, and then all the points were added up. "If you have teams of people getting together in a pack to get a consensus, that's an altogether different environment, where prejudices can be imposed."[15] Except for one vendor who had real problems with the live test demonstration, the bids were about equal on technical merit. EDS was, however, much lower on price and it won the contract for that reason. It bid AT&T equipment using the UNIX operating system. There were no bid protests on the contract.[16]

The contract at Customs got underway in September 1985 with what Customs officials describe as a prolonged bout of disaster. The biggest problem was simply that the computers frequently did not work. Sometimes local Customs officials, facing budget limitations, simply did not order enough computer horsepower to meet demands on their system, but there were other problems as well. The UNIX software to integrate the various individual software packages, as required in the RFP, had only just recently been introduced in the market and had many bugs. ("We were the first customer," notes Jim Ryan, director of the Office of Data Services. "And this was at a time where you could get office automation software *everywhere* that worked.")[17] The software for the printers often did not work well. There were some problems with how the systems were configured to the varying conditions of local offices as well. And AT&T and EDS, according to Customs officials, generally assigned extremely junior people, or people whose background was mainly in marketing, to work at the sites where the equipment was being installed. It should be noted that junior people were assigned because the customer had initially planned to use standard configurations at local offices rather than to customize them and that only junior people would have been needed to install them. It is hard for an outsider to judge how quickly one should have expected EDS to redeploy personnel as customer demands changed.

More serious than the configuration problems was the fact that Customs officials, believing what the vendor had told them, had assigned clerical employees (after training, to be sure) to manage and maintain the everyday operation of the minicomputers that were the brains of the multiuser systems at the field offices. Customs had no experience with UNIX and no basis on which to make an independent judgment at the time of contract award on the feasibility of having these systems maintained by clericals. Except for the very smallest of these minicomputers at the smallest of the offices with the multiuser systems, the notion that clerical people could take such responsibility turned out to be, in the view of Customs officials, simply a joke. The systems required people with considerably more computer background than secretaries who had taken a short course. Thus, at many sites printers did not print or the entire system crashed when demands on it were too heavy.

Users in the field also complained that the new equipment was not as user-friendly as the computers or word-processing equipment they had already been working with. Partly, this was simply a question of familiarity; people had gotten used to the commands and routines of their old equipment, and any change was bound to carry with it at least transitional difficulties. (For those users who were just doing word processing, of course, few general-purpose computers are as user-friendly as word processors dedicated only to that function.) Furthermore, the integration of the software packages that the

RFP had required added on the number of keystrokes needed to access any individual package. Beyond that, however, UNIX software is generally regarded as considerably less easy-to-use for the nonexpert than most other languages, although Customs officials say they had not known that at the time of the procurement (because they had had no experience with UNIX and little experience with environments other than mainframe ones at all). None of the vendors bidding UNIX informed them that it might be less user-friendly than what people accustomed to dedicated word processors or DOS-based personal computers would expect.[18]

One interesting question is why none of these problems had shown up during the live test demonstration. Vendors at the live test demonstration had to show that their hardware and software would work, and the evaluation criteria in the RFP placed significant weight on user-friendliness.

The answer is that the live test demonstration did not really reproduce the actual environment in the field.[19] Vendors needed only demonstrate a small number of standardized configurations, rather than the wider variety actually encountered in the field. Vendors had weeks to devote to getting these configurations to work, and they could assign their best people to the task. Furthermore, the volume and variety of the demands on the system in the live test demonstration was much less than what would actually occur in the field. Nor did the live test require that clericals—or anybody else at Customs for that matter—manage the operation of any minicomputers. That was done at the test by the vendors themselves. Finally, according to Ken Malley, the live test exercises did not give Customs people a very good idea of how user-friendly the equipment turned out to be in practice, because many of the user-friendliness difficulties turned out to involve operations such as underlining, superscripts, and footnotes that were not included in the production-type typing exercises of the RFP (since nobody had known in advance that such operations might be a source of problems).[20] And the clerical people who acted as users to evaluate the user-friendliness of the system were a self-selected group of volunteers whose computer-literacy and interest doubtless exceeded that of the typical clerical user.

People in the field had additional reasons for their hostility as well. They resented the idea of buying complex systems with more functionality (and attendant cost) than they felt they needed. Relatively few users, for example, had any need for integrated access to spreadsheets or databases, since many were using the system simply for word processing. Just at the time the contract was awarded, it had been decided, as a budget-cutting measure, to remove the line item in the Customs budget for the Field Data Service and to require local offices to finance purchases out of their own administrative appropriations (including savings from, for example, reduced maintenance charges for the out-of-date equipment they had been using). A fancy system with lots of functionality thus was no longer a free gift.

These problems were compounded by ways that EDS appeared, in the opinion of Customs officials, to be seeking to obtain as much money out of the contract as possible. When users were having trouble making their systems work, EDS initially tried to charge Customers at the contract's hourly rate for technical support. (It turned out that EDS had bid quite a high hourly rate for technical support.) Customs resisted paying, however. "We had some hard discussions with them," Ray Arnold recalls." I said to them, 'I'm not asking for tech support, I'm asking you to fix something you promised to deliver. I won't pay you to fix this, because it should have worked *originally*.' "[21]

Another money problem involved the local area network Customs had asked to be installed at headquarters. EDS has bid a price for the network, but then it turned out that to get any users actually hooked up onto the network, additional equipment would be necessary that dramatically increased the price of the network. According to Ray Arnold,

> They sort of said to us, "Oh, you want to hook somebody up to use the network. Well, in that case, here's what you've got to do if you want to hook people up." The problem is that they give you the answer to the question you ask, not to the question you should have asked but didn't know to ask.[22]

In the spring of 1986 Ken Malley was taken off responsibility for the Field Data System project. The contract was in trouble. Some Customs offices were refusing to pay for the equipment they had received. Many were refusing to place new orders. By the summer of 1986 the problem with the contract had escalated to the desk of William Von Raab, the colorful and highly regarded commissioner of the Customs Service. He had been hearing so many horror stories from the field—a Customs manager in California was loudly and continuously threatening to throw his equipment into the Pacific Ocean—that he asked the Office of Data Systems why they did not just kill the contract and start all over again. Von Raab's jolt turned out to be a turning point. Von Raab called in Ross Perot himself and told them that the government was close to terminating them for default— an action so extreme that it would certainly have pierced through into the management capability evaluations in proposals by EDS that other agencies would consider in the future—and that they had better make the system work, and quickly.

The upshot was that EDS took a hit on the contract. They assigned twenty-five people to work at Customs headquarters and in the field on the system's problems, and they ended up working for free. After a good deal of work, the software problems were (essentially) solved, and the multiuser system at headquarters, including the local area network, became established.

But the Customs people now in charge of the project had learned something from the agency's harsh experiences. They had come to the conclusion that the whole concept of the procurement was too ambitious. It was not merely that the integrated software packages did not work, it was also that few workers at Customs needed them. "Most of our word processing is done by clericals," Ray Arnold notes. "They don't need integrated access to databases and spreadsheets. We were going through all this hassle for little good reason." The local area network at headquarters had in fact been made to work, but Arnold believed it was an expensive luxury. "Now every terminal in headquarters can access every big database we have. But most people don't need to access them—and a lot of the databases are sensitive, so we don't *allow* most people to access them."[23] The people now in charge of the project decided in early 1987 that the entire strategy of acquiring multiuser systems with minis for the average Customs office was mistaken. It would cost too much for the benefits provided, and it would place unrealistic computer ability burdens on local clerical staff. Instead, the multiuser-with-mini strategy would be used only at headquarters and in the seven Customs regional offices. At local offices, people would be encouraged simply to do what they wanted to do anyway—namely, buy stand-alone DOS personal computers and terminal emulators (manufactured by Wyse Technologies, not AT&T).[24] Fortunately, earlier installation in the field had been such a disaster that few of the local offices had any of the equipment that was now being replaced by stand-alone personal computers.

This was a dramatic change in the acquisition. Such a dramatic change might normally have required a recompetition of the contract. But Customs, however, had several alternatives available that allowed them to buy the personal computers without recompetition. The original RFP had talked about buying stand-alone personal computers for the very smallest Customs installations. Therefore they were included as a line item in the indefinite quantity contract that vendors had bid on and hence could be bought off the contract— although in much larger volumes than the original strategy had called for. According to Stan Livingstone, director of the Contracts office at

Customs, had the original RFP called only for multiuser configurations, buying personal computers off the contract would have gone beyond the scope of the original contract and hence the change in strategy would not, under that contract, have been possible.[25]

There were other features of the requirements as presented in the procurement that turned out to be inappropriate, given what Customs learned after system installation had begun. There was something it turned out that was much in demand, which Customs had not realized when it established its requirements. In the pre-RFP surveys to establish requirements, users had emphasized simple office automation applications, doubtless because they did not know much about anything else. As people began to have access to data off the mainframe databases at their desks, they began to think up many ways they would want to be able to analyze some of that data for work they were doing. Some of that was possible for the mainframe to do, but some kinds of messaging were difficult or impossible using the application programs available on the mainframe, and it was almost always more difficult to have the messaging done on the mainframe rather than having the data downloaded to the local level. Yet not realizing the importance of those demands at the time of the RFP, Customs did not ask vendors to provide some of the capabilities required for accomplishing the downloading.[26]

Looking back on the history of the procurement, Ken Malley concludes:

> We went out and got the ultimate system. The users are now going through steps to eventually walk up to the system. Our approach might have been to get fundamental word processing and let that cook, then get local area networks, then another step. The biggest problem was the scope we attacked. That's what I would have done differently.[27]

CASE STUDY 3:
Immigration and Naturalization Service
Hardware Computerization

Of the procurements examined here, this was the one most tainted by the allegation of scandal. It generated first a loud protest by the losing vendor and later a General Accounting Office report alleging significant improprieties in the fairness of the decision to award the contract to IBM. The uproar itself led first to the replacement of the existing contract to one that was more costly to the government, then to a slowdown in contract implementation because of the high cost, and finally, after the General Accounting Office investigation, to a halt in congressional appropriations and a requirement that the Immigration and Naturalization Service start all over again. As for the actual nature of the scandalous behavior of which the agency stood accused, a closer examination appears to reveal lapses from the internal rules of the procurement system more than from any ethical code.

The Immigration and Naturalization Service (INS) in the Department of Justice has the dual mission of assisting people who are legally entering the United States and of preventing people from being in the United States illegally. The former mission includes many functions of a service nature such as processing people at the border and handling request for citizenship, visa extension, or changes in visa status. The latter mission includes functions of a law-enforcement nature: manning the Border Patrol; raiding workplaces believed to employ illegal aliens; and investigating and prosecuting deportation, fraud, and similar cases.[1]

The INS is an information-intensive environment. The agency keeps files on 20 million aliens living in the United States. It also maintains a "watch list" of people to look out for if they attempt to enter the United States and voluminous files relating to investigations of illegal activity. In addition, INS enforcement can be helped by access to information (such as information on past criminal records) held by other law-enforcement organizations.

The INS is decentralized into almost 900 local units of one sort or another—more than 600 ports of entry and more than 100 border patrol stations, as well as about 200 district offices and suboffices that handle claims for benefits (such as applications for citizenship) and investigation of enforcement cases.[2]

Although it is a highly information-intensive environment, the agency was, as of the beginning of the 1980s, computerized only to an insignificant extent. The INS "lookout" list used at ports of entry was on a mainframe but not on-line; INS enforcement agents got batch updates of the list periodically. Some information from the paper files kept on resident aliens was also on a mainframe, but very few local offices were connected on-line to that file in a way that allowed them to check, for example, if a person himself was a legal resident when he came to a local office to apply to get a relative admitted to the United States. Few offices had case-tracking systems; there were few files of employers with a history of employing illegal aliens; border patrol agents could not access information on criminal history or immigration status over the telephone. The agency was not in a good position to exchange data with the IRS or the Social Security Administration relevant to the missions of any of these agencies. Nor did the agency have a capability to allow employers to access any database on-line to check whether someone they were considering hiring was a legal resident of the United States—an important capability, given the new employer sanctions for hiring illegals.

An effort began to increase computerization at local offices in the late 1970s, buying a few minicomputers for case docketing and tracking at some local offices on a pilot basis.[3] The experiment worked well, but when INS tried to increase the number of computers it bought to expand to other offices, it was told by the General Services Administration that buying the additional computers went beyond the scope of the original contract and the project would need to be recompeted.

At this point INS began a planning process to lay out its requirements for computerization of its local offices, a process that went on for several years at the beginning of the 1980s and led to the conclusion that about forty different custom applications needed to be developed for the local offices and for central databases, combined with supporting hardware. The thought at this time was to do an A–109 process for this procurement.[4]

Some INS managers, meanwhile, were growing increasingly upset at the amount of time the planning process was taking, given the urgent computerization needs of the agency. The announcement of an A–109 process for procuring the computer systems, which would have added another two years to the process, was the last straw. The head of information resources management at the agency was pushed out and replaced in February 1983 by John Murray, who came to the agency from the Department of Energy and was believed to have been given the mandate in no uncertain terms to start moving faster.

Murray did move fast. He impressed top management by relocating an INS mainframe data center in one year. Then he broke up the computerization project from one massive project into separate software, hardware, and communications parts. The idea was that the software work could be competed relatively quickly by making it a task-order, requirements-type contract with a fairly general statement of work. In other words, the RFP would simply state that the software contractor would develop the forty-odd specific custom applications programs as discrete task orders, with specifications developed at the time of the task order rather than at the time of contract award. This meant the RFP itself did not need to give specifications for the software programs. Similarly, it was felt that the data-communications capacity to send data from mainframes to the field could be delayed until everything else was under control since INS already could use the existing INS contract with Tymnet for access to a public packet-switching network to transmit data. The software contract was awarded first and with amazing speed—mere months from start to finish. This left only the hardware contract with a relatively demanding set of specifications to be developed.

According to Murray, he used a number of techniques to shorten procurement cycle times so dramatically:

> I would make it clear to the various layers of review within INS that I expected a quick turnaround time. I would always have the documents hand-carried to them as a sign of how seriously we took getting it done fast. Vendors typically get 60–180 days to respond to RFPs. I gave them 30 days, maybe with a 15-day extension. The evaluation process inside the government usually takes several months. I tried to get it done within 30 days. You have to push people and give them strict deadlines.[5]

Flush with its software contract success, the Murray machine tore into the hardware contract. And there the trouble began. In October 1984 the INS put out for comment a draft RFP for a hardware configuration, and the non-IBM vendor community immediately cried foul. Four vendors formally complained, claiming that the technical specifications would be virtually impossible for anyone but IBM or IBM-compatibles to meet since they required (without naming any brand) IBM-compatible operating systems for much of the equipment. The cry of foul was justified. INS used Department of Justice mainframes that were IBM-compatible, and it is somewhat easier to communicate between mainframes and field locations if the field locations have the same systems. But it was hardly a necessity.

Murray agrees that the draft RFP unnecessarily favored IBM. He claims that INS simply picked up a draft RFP that had been written before his arrival and used it.[6] The RFP draft made it through the various layers of review within the INS and the Department of Justice because nobody reviewing it was technically knowledgeable enough to notice that the operating system requirements implied IBM-compatible products.[7]

The RFP was withdrawn, slowing down Murray's machine. And suspiciousness among vendors, and among those in Washington ever worried about alleged favoritism toward IBM, was raised.

Murray told Miller to withdraw the old RFP and develop a new set of specifications within one month, an incredibly quick turnaround time for the government. And, indeed, a new RFP appeared in January 1984. Murray essentially bypassed review by the procurement people at INS, presenting the furious contracts office the package as a fait accompli and saying it was necessary to meet the commissioner's demands for speed. "We said to them, 'This is just a draft. We're going to give you time to comment while the vendors comment.'"[8] In its comment on the procurement, the General Services Administration told INS that if the procurement was to be limited to IBM-compatibles, price would have to count at least 70 percent in the evaluation criteria. The new RFP was not compatibility limited as the previous one had been, but the General Services Administration comments suggest that the procurement's notoriety had spread beyond the agency itself.

The price for speed was presenting a set of requirements—for hardware, systems software, and systems integration—that was, by government standards, extremely vague. Says John Miller:

> Our basic problem was that we knew about how many transactions we would have to process, but we didn't really know how much computing power each transaction needed, and we didn't know what our custom software was going to be like yet because it was still being developed on the separate software contract. So we didn't really know how much horsepower we needed. To get those estimates, we would have had to do a simulation study, but that would have taken an additional year.[9]

The RFP provided vendors some numbers to use for estimating purposes (otherwise it would have been impossible to develop any specific configurations in their proposals). But it is not at all certain that those numbers corresponded very closely with what the transaction reality would have been.

INS had few computer people technically expert in issues involving the modeling for and establishment of systems as large and complicated as the one envisioned. Therefore, as one participant describes it:

> We didn't know what we wanted. We wanted to pay for smarts and creativity, for somebody to come up with a solution that was going to be expandable and flexible. We were babes. We wanted somebody to take us by the hand and walk us through the morass. We felt we needed someone we could count on and rely on.[10]

But Miller was afraid that the requirements were so vague that it would be difficult for the government to avoid making the award to a low-bidding vendor with an unworkable solution:

> You need to evaluate proposals against some set of requirements. Our problem was that our requirements weren't that specific. You're not allowed to throw in new evaluation criteria during the evaluation process. I had earlier had a major disagreement with Murray over the software RFP about getting a written evaluation plan before we received the proposals. Murray didn't want it. I was afraid of protests and of being accused of bias. For the hardware procurement, I was worried we'd have to make the award to somebody whom we intuitively knew couldn't work, somebody who underbid what we really needed, who would try to cut a lawn with scissors.[11]

The evaluation criteria gave price a 35 percent weight, a compromise between the wish of those working on the procurement that price count for only 25 percent and the initial demand by the Department of Justice computer oversight organization that it count 50 percent.[12] Corporate experience counted for less than 5 percent of the total.[13]

Only two vendors bid—IBM and EDS. This was itself something of a worrisome sign about perceptions of the procurement. Vendors may have been worried the procurement was "wired," or they may have been worried that it was too vague for a government procurement. The technical evaluation panel had eight members (Murray was not a member), of whom two had earlier served together on the technical evaluation panel for the previously awarded software contract and most of whom knew each other. Then the group met together; outliers were asked to explain unusual scores, but scores were averaged with no effort to enforce unanimity. According to both Miller, chairman of the technical evaluation panel, and Murray, Murray himself played no role on the technical evaluation.[14]

IBM's proposal had two extremely unusual features for bids on a government contract. INS, in the RFP, had defined its requirements as involving centralized mainframe location and processing of most of the data on its databases, which then would be accessed through terminals at local offices. The only applications that would be decentralized to the local offices themselves would be office automation and case tracking.[15] It was probably not wise to have been so specific in the first place, but that was the wording in the RFP. IBM did something very unusual. Rather than simply bidding what INS had specified, IBM did its own estimates of the likely INS workload for different kinds of applications—particularly of increases in workload that would occur if proposed immigration reform legislation were passed or in the unpredictable event of a sudden flood of refugees into the country—and determined that it would be more economical for INS to decentralize its data processing by storing much of the data, and doing much of the data processing, either in field offices themselves or in regional data centers with minicomputers rather than mainframes. Exploiting an ambiguity in the RFP that opened the way for a decentralized solution, IBM chose to make a case for (and bid an architecture encompassing) such a solution.[16]

The second unusual feature of IBM's bid was an offer to provide INS with $1 million worth of consulting services, not billed as a separate line item but included in the price of the package it was bidding, to do research and development on new computer applications for INS needs.

One interesting question is why IBM did any of this. Given the clear rules about evaluating proposals based only on criteria in the RFP, it is hard to see how IBM could have counted on getting any credit in the technical evaluation either for its $1 million consulting offer—although such an offer would have been typical for the way IBM markets itself in the private sector—or for its suggestion of a better solution that departed from the specifications in the RFP. IBM, unfortunately, declined a request to be interviewed on this matter.

Miller knew of no INS prior experience with either vendor. Miller says he does not know what kind of reputation the vendors, who had done work for other parts of the Department of Justice, had within the department "because I wasn't allowed to talk to anybody. Once we started, I wasn't even allowed to tell anybody who was bidding."[17]

The RFP had asked bidders to give references to work they had done at other sites, and the evaluation team did telephone those references. But Miller says:

> My experience on the previous software effort with calling people had been so poor, because we never got any negative information, that I didn't pay as much attention to it this time. It's really difficult if you haven't dealt with the contractor *yourself* to get an idea from talking with somebody else about how they did on a contract. I called the references to confirm that the contract had been completed as stated and that performance was acceptable. Points were awarded based on how close the other contracts were to what we needed, not on what people said about the contractor. If the company's not blacklisted, then what you're really interested in is pieces of work where the company has performed a similar level of effort and technical complexity.[18]

Interestingly, the evaluation panel did use some information from the live test demonstration in assigning management capability points. During the EDS demonstration, their terminals were improperly adjusted such that they did not provide the proper light-dark contrast, and one of the printers did not work at all. According to Miller: "You have to ask yourself, in terms of management capability, what kind of preparation did they put into the live test? This was their opportunity to shine, and they didn't." Since scoring of the live test itself was pass-fail, the panel subtracted some points from the management capability evaluation of EDS because of this. According to one participant: "I was a little uncomfortable about it. To tell you the truth, I don't know how kosher it was. But you run the risk of not being able to evaluate something you do want to evaluate, because it's not in the evaluation plan."[19]

As for the $1 million IBM promised to include for consulting services, it was hard to give it credit anywhere in the evaluation. According to Miller: "To the best possible extent, we tried to be flexible with the evaluation criteria. But there really wasn't any slot to give them credit for that offer they made, because there wasn't any specific evaluation criterion it fell under."[20]

IBM was, however, given credit in the technical evaluation for its decentralized solution, a solution that struck members of the evaluation team as sensible. They awarded points under the evaluation criterion "configuration expendability and flexibility" on the grounds that a decentralized solution was more adaptable than a centralized one.[21] All in all, IBM was the clear winner in the technical evaluation.

An event took place during the cost evaluation of the bids that later became the object of scrutiny by EDS when it filed its bid protest and after that by the General Accounting Office. Normally, people involved in the technical evaluation do not become involved in the cost evaluation or even see the cost numbers that vendors bid. In this case, however, John Miller "got a panicked call" from the contracts people in charge of the cost evaluation that they did not know how to interpret some of the cost information and needed help from somebody who knew more about computers. Miller asked one of the members of his technical evaluation team to finish up his work on the technical evaluation and then to help the contracts people; after the technical evaluation report was completed, Miller proceeded to help them himself.[22]

One problem that the technical people discovered while working on the cost evaluation was some confusion in the original RFP regarding the number of end-user terminals that bidders were to assume, for purposes of the cost evaluation, that INS would install. A bidding schedule in the RFP specified that for the purposes of the bids it was to be assumed that 8,517 terminals would be installed. If, however, one added together the number of terminals required for the four separate kinds of standard office configurations that INS asked vendors to bid on for evaluation purposes in another part of the RFP, the number of terminals was 12,416.[23] In their cost bid, IBM had bid a price for 12,416 terminals, and EDS had bid a price for 8,517.

According to a statement Miller later made:

> The IBM corporation recognized the potential for misinterpretation of the RFP on this issue, and on at least three occasions explicitly, and in writing, requested guidance from INS as to whether their interpretation was correct. . . . No one from INS Contracts asked me for an interpretation or ruling on this issue, and, since the Source Evaluation Panel had not been permitted to review the cost proposals, I had been unaware of the discrepancy.[24]

With the problem discovered, it might appear to have been an easy matter simply to adjust IBM's cost bid downward to reflect the different number of terminals. It was not quite that simple, however, because the RFP had required lifecycle cost bids for the terminals that could not simply be adjusted on a pro rata basis. Miller therefore explained the situation to the contracts people, and they agreed that the INS needed to meet with the IBM people to get information to do the bid adjustment. Because of the time pressures Murray was putting on everyone, Miller wanted to set the meeting as soon as possible, scheduling it after hours. The contracts people told Miller the ground rules for the meeting but said they would not be able to come. ("The people in Contracts always say they can't stay late because they'll miss their carpools," states Murray, with some contempt.)[25] IBM officials coming to the meeting signed the log at the INS office building, hardly suggesting, as some later were to imply, that the meeting was surreptitious. The meeting went on until 3:30 in the morning.[26] With the help of the information obtained at the meeting with IBM, INS could now determine that IBM had the lowest cost bid as well as the best technical proposal, making contract award certain.

EDS promptly filed a protest, alleging among other things that EDS had been unfairly downgraded in the technical evaluation for bidding the centralized solution that INS had stated in its requirements, while IBM was unfairly given credit for bidding a decentralized solution that was not responsive to the RFP. The EDS protest also alleged that at "a closed-door after-hours meeting from which all members of the INS Contracting Office were excluded, INS Source Evaluation Panel members improperly and unlawfully engaged in discussions with IBM after submission of best and final offers"—an event soon dubbed the "midnight meeting."[27] (Procurement regulations forbid the government from doing any further negotiations after it has received so-called best and final offers from bidders. If the government wishes to reopen negotiations after such receipt, it must reopen them for everyone.) The INS position was that the meeting with IBM did not constitute negotiations but merely a request for clarification, whereby IBM did not change its bid but merely clarified it.[28]

Following the EDS protest, the situation began to deteriorate rapidly.[29] When a judge issued a temporary injunction to enjoin INS from implementing the contract until the EDS protest could be heard, Murray panicked. The Department of Justice lawyers told him that the litigation could take over a year, and he saw his fast track mired in mud. He took the lead in negotiating an out-of-court settlement with EDS, whereby EDS was chosen as the vendor but would supply the solution (and the hardware) that IBM had bid. The settlement was reached in January 1985.

Murray thought at the time of the agreement that the out-of-court settlement would be no more expensive to INS than the IBM bid was.[30] IBM agreed to supply its products to EDS at prices even lower than they had bid in their proposal, and the price structure EDS offered appeared to be favorable. But once the agreement was implemented, INS technical people came to feel that INS had been misled; the prices INS ultimately paid for the IBM equipment were considerably highly than IBM would have charged, although EDS committed to keeping the total present value price of the contract unchanged, by lowering prices for hardware and maintenance in the contract's outyears. In fact, the prices were so high that implementation of the contract was very slow because INS could not afford the equipment. EDS also insisted on supplying various management personnel that had been stipulated in the original RFP but which, in INS's view, turned out to be unnecessary.

Soon the contract descended onto a death spiral. In March 1986 the General Accounting Office issued a report bluntly titled, "Immigration and Naturalization Service Should Terminate Its Contract and Recompete."[31] The report endorsed accusations of bias toward IBM in the original contract award. The report specifically criticized INS for giving credit to IBM for suggesting a decentralized rather than centralized solution:

> The panels's narrative comments gave IBM credit for suggesting "alternative methods and approaches" and for making "a case" for decentralizing the centralized programs. By deviating from the RFP requirements and agreeing to the superiority of decentralizing additional applications, INS improperly influenced the technical evaluation in favor of IBM's proposal. *If INS wanted to consider a decentralized approach, it should have amended the RFP and allowed EDS as well as IBM to submit an offer on the basis* [emphasis added].[32]

After issuance of the General Accounting Office report, Congress cut off all appropriations for the project for a year. The INS began the procurement over again, starting with a simulation study to determine exactly how much computing power they required. That study has been only recently completed—and has itself been questioned by the General Accounting Office.[33] Murray, meanwhile, had left the INS to work for a consulting company.

It is hard for an outsider to judge the broad question of the extent to which Murray was biased toward, and biased the evaluation process toward, IBM. Some people within the Department of Justice oversight bodies dealing with information technology accept the view that Murray was unfairly biased.[34] At least some features of the process suggest bias—the initial, and quickly withdrawn, IBM-oriented RFP and the decision of only two bidders to bid on the contract. Furthermore, the statement by one participant about being babes wanting somebody to take their hand sounds to an outsider much like the sentiment that frequently, in a private-sector context, drives customers to choose IBM.

At the same time, most of the specific allegations made to support the contention that the evaluation process was unfairly rigged to produce a victory for IBM do not appear to hold up particularly well.

141

The midnight meeting would seem innocuous to any but those caught up in the world of the procurement regulations themselves. Indeed, it would probably come as a pleasant surprise to some to learn that middle-level government career civil servants were engaged in such a long, late-night meeting. In any other context but government procurement, a useful suggestion from a vendor that an alternative solution made more sense than the original solution envisioned would be regarded more as a service than as an offense. (And the suggestion, made by the General Accounting Office, that if INS liked IBM's ideas it should have amended the RFP to allow everyone to bid on them seems hardly to provide an incentive for a vendor to develop such ideas.)

John Murray had promised to move the procurement forward quickly. Doing so involved shortcuts—dusting off another agency's RFP, meeting quickly with IBM on cost clarification even though the contracts people had to get home. His fancy footwork had worked before, but this time he stumbled and fell. The quick implementation of a new system he had hoped to see was delayed more than he ever could have imagined.

CASE STUDY 4:
Customs Service Consolidated Data Network

As noted in the earlier case study on the Customs Service local office computerization, the agency has mainframe data bases both for enforcement and tariff-collection purposes that field employees need to access on a real-time basis. Around the same time the Customs Service was buying office automation and data-processing hardware and software for field locations, it also bought a new infrastructural network to tie the mainframes in with the field locations.

The existing system involved two separate mainframe data centers (one using IBM, the other Burroughs equipment) for the enforcement and commercial systems, tied into field locations using a traditional data-communications configuration involving dedicated leased telephone lines and equipment such as concentrators to allow information from many terminals to pass through a smaller number of telephone lines.[1] The existing system had severe capacity and flexibility limitations that made difficult the expansion of traffic envisioned by new applications such as the automation of the paperwork flow between the Customs Service and import brokers bringing goods into the United States. Furthermore, existing communications links were not secure.

Newer technologies for data communication, such as packet switching, allowed both greater flexibility and greater operating economies, since they work on the principle of evening out systemwide peaks and valleys in data flows rather than requiring that dedicated leased lines be kept up whether traffic demands are high or low. The new technologies required significant initial fixed investments. These fixed costs could be more easily justified the greater the overall traffic load. Therefore, the decision was made within the Department of the Treasury to build one such network for the entire department, with the initial network to be procured by Customs. The addition of new sites by other agencies within Treasury would be an option under the original contract that could then proceed without separate procurements.

The Customs Service had two consultants prepare reports on possible ways of meeting their data-communications needs. During this phase, Customs people spoke with some vendors about what solutions were available to those needs. Such communication ceased, according to Customs procurement rules, when people sat down to begin to write the RFP. Roger Malatt, who was in charge of developing the RFP, expresses mixed views about the importance of contacts with vendors during the process. On the one hand, he notes that the RFP was written around a set of infrastructural requirements for the Customs Service, so that talking with vendors about the nature of possible solutions was not particularly necessary. He also notes that listening to vendors is "terribly time-consuming—you can spend your life listening to vendor presentations."[2] On the other hand, Malatt also notes that while sitting down to write the RFP, questions frequently arise that had not previously arisen and for which one would like to get answers in an effort to write a better RFP. But at that point it is too late to talk with them.[3]

The final RFP simply outlined the nature of the Service's requirements, noting the hardware (mainframes and local terminals) they had and specifying that the new network not require any modification of that equipment. Furthermore, the RFP stated that whatever system was proposed had to be expandable both within Customs and for a larger network for the entire Treasury Department.[4] The RFP specified that the system had to meet various response times (they were more rigorous for field enforcement locations such as airports and land border stations than for commercial applications and for local Customs Service offices).[5] The Customs Service could not estimate exactly what its traffic requirements were (how many terminals they would have sending and receiving how many messages) or how much traffic would increase during the five-year life of the contract. Therefore, the RFP simply established a set of assumptions about these crucial parameters and asked vendors to bid a configuration that would solve the problem given those traffic assumptions.

The RFP consisted essentially only of mandatory requirements. The only desirable feature was for a fast response time, for which the vendor would be awarded extra points in the evaluation.[6] As with the Customs Field Data Service procurement discussed earlier, the contracts office at the Customs Service opposed using desirables. Reflecting what he referred to as the "advice" he got from the contracting officer, Roger Malatt stated:

> You get into playing too many games with desirables, and it means you end up with a protest. You can use desirables to sole-source almost, and eliminate competition. That's when GSA starts taking a harder look and when the vendors start protesting. Remember that it costs only $100 to protest. If you don't keep it clean, good luck.[7]

144

The technical people wanted the evaluation criteria to be weighted 80–20 in favor of technical; the final compromise with the contracting people placed the weight at 60–40 technical.[8] Of the technical points, about one-fifth were assigned to corporate experience, none to the quality of the management team being bid for the project.[9] The RFP specifically stated that the bid with the highest total number of points would receive the award—and noted that points would be calculated "to two decimal places."[10]

Six vendors bid on the contract.[11] The technical approaches of the various bidders were basically similar. All bid packet-switching technology (although this was not required by the RFP). There was no significant difference in the degree of off-the-shelf equipment and software versus customized items. Some vendors bid smaller switches, which Customs felt were more easily expandable than the larger switches other vendors bid.

Because of the way the evaluation process works, Malatt approached it with some dread:

> You get into the evaluation stage, and you have lots of things locked in. You might see what a bidder has designed, and you see something that makes the functionality you want impossible, but it still meets the letter of the mandatories. You either leave them in and take your chances or you try to get them out and hope you can get away with it. If something is not in the categories described in the technical evaluation criteria, you can't take credit away from them.[12]

Fortunately, Malatt adds, this did not turn out to be a problem in this case.

The Customs Service had no prior experience with any of the bidders. The technical evaluation team did call the references the bidders listed in their proposals, but they were not given negative information about anybody.

The technical evaluation team consisted of four members—Malatt and an assistant, and two people from one of the Customs mainframe data centers. All knew each other prior to the technical evaluation process, and they sought to achieve consensus in their assignment of points. Malatt helped the contracting office make the cost evaluation after the technical evaluation was complete.

Computer Sciences Corporation (CSC), bidding packet-switching equipment made by Bolt, Beranek, and Newman, was the narrow winner of both the technical and price evaluations, and was hence awarded the contract.

The first phase of the contract was development of a pilot network for part of the system, which the RFP stated had to be successfully completed within six months or else, theoretically, the Customs Service could cancel the contract.[13] According to people at Customs, CSC did an excellent job on the pilot.[14]

Then, however, according to the Customs people, the situation began to deteriorate. The problems involved both performance and price. After the pilot project was completed, the vendor yanked off the project most of the management that had been working on it since development of the company's original proposal. Work on the rollout of the network then slackened. Meanwhile, CSC revealed a series of contractual and technical interpretations that generated charges to Customs far higher than the agency expected.

The most important issue of contractual interpretation centered around the meaning of the expression "site" in the line item in the cost section of the RFP that required each bidder to state how much they would charge for doing the design work to configure the network at each field site. The word "site" had not been defined in the RFP. Customs assumed that by site was meant each location where a Custom Service activity was located. After the contract was signed, CSC stated that their interpretation of the word was different: a site, they argued, was a discrete equipment configuration, and there might be several such sites at a given Customs location. They proceeded to bill the government for site implementation costs several times what Customs had assumed in interpreting the original bids.

The most important technical issue involved what happened in the transition from the "evaluated network configuration" of the RFP to the real world of Customs Service demands. As was true of many of the other procurements discussed here, the Customs Service was not certain at the time of the RFP of how many end-user workstations it would have, of all the variations in how workstations might be configured, or of how great the traffic would be between end-users and the mainframes. For an infrastructural network such as this, assumptions about the number of end-user workstations and about traffic are important, since they will affect the amount and exact configuration of equipment used to meet the requirements. As with the other procurements where these kinds of issues arose, Customs presented in its RFP a set of assumptions about the locations and number of workstations and the expected volume of traffic, which vendors were to use as a basis for their bids.[15] Bidders were to present, and price, a configuration that would meet the response time requirements the RFP laid out on the assumptions the RFP stated.

The solution CSC presented in its proposal, given those assumptions, was, however, never tested because the assumptions were actually far too conservative regarding the number of workstations and the amount of traffic. The problem was that, in view of Customs officials, the vendor took advantage after contract award of the revised level of demand to upgrade in a disproportionate way the quantity of equipment that the vendor claimed it needed to meet the response-time requirements of the RFP. "When the scenario changed, they used that to pad on extra equipment. What they would say to us was, 'I can't guarantee the response item unless you put all this extra stuff in.'" Looking back on the situation, Roger Malatt reflected, "If I had been smarter and asked them how would you price out different scenarios, I'd have had them." He added:

> From our experience under this contract, I've concluded that company experience is more important than I thought at the time. If I had it to do over again, I'd spend a week or two looking at those references. The problem is that the only way to get any real information is to take the reference and go out and talk with people at the site and then buy them a drink. But that's all off the record. And for the bid evalution, you can only use what's on the record. I would in no way, shape, or form give these folks a good recommendation. But I'd hesitate to put it on the record. I've been told by the company and by people in other agencies that this is defamation of character and they'll have a lawyer on us in thirty seconds.[16]

As the relationship between CSC and the Customs Service deteriorated, the company again put new management on the job. The basic philosophy of the new managers was to separate the contract disputes over dollars from the company's efforts to move the network forward, hoping that if they could get the network up and running, the dollar disputes would be easier to resolve.[17] That strategy appears basically to have worked. The Customs network got completed more or less on schedule. It has ended up costing considerably more than Customs originally anticipated; on many of the contractual disputes, the agency and the vendor essentially split the difference. The level of anger at Customs has declined considerably. Meanwhile, other agencies at Treasury have begun to exercise the contractual options for the CSC network. The alternative would have been lengthy new procurements and duplicated fixed costs.

CASE STUDY 5:
Veterans Administration Office
Automation Contract

As was true of numerous organizations both in and outside government, the many operating bureaus of the Veterans Administration (VA) began buying stand alone word-processing equipment and personal computers in the early 1980s.[1] In 1985 the agency awarded an indefinite quantity contract to Wang Laboratories to standardize its office-automation equipment. The arguments for doing so were the normal ones: the larger quantities that standardization allowed would give the VA lower prices, standardization would reduce training costs when people shifted jobs within the agency, and an agencywide system could gain economies from using minicomputers and dumb terminals rather than stand-alone machines.

The VA decided to pursue a plain vanilla strategy in this procurement, emphasizing workhorse basic office-automation functions rather than the state of the office-automation art or mixes of data processing and office automation.[2] The agency began by doing a market survey to learn what features were available on the equipment of various vendors. After the initial market survey was completed, VA rules required that a contracting officer be present at any one-on-one meetings with vendors, but apparently the VA people working on the RFP did schedule some such meetings and brought Contracts people along. Features that the VA decided to ask for were divided into mandatories and desirables, with the main candidates for mandatories being those that people at the VA were using already. The rule of thumb the people working on the RFP adopted was that no feature would be made mandatory unless at least three vendors had it available, although it might be made a desirable feature even if only one vendor had it.[3] The mandatory features the agency eventually asked for included, for example, capabilities to do scrolling, to move as many as 100 pages of text from one place in a manuscript to another, and automatically to center sections of a text; desirable features included cupped keys on the keyboard, right-margin justification capability, and the ability to be able to print in multiple fonts at a single pass.[4]

This was one of the first VA computer procurements that was not

148

completely price-based. According to Buddy Edwards, the contracting people were willing to accept a significant weight for nonprice considerations as long as it did not exceed 50 percent. The technical people were also able to get the Contracts people to accept the large number of desirable features listed in the RFP through the somewhat interesting technique of assigning each desirable feature a dollar value (rather than a point score). What the RFP did was to give an exact dollar price to each desirable feature. For example, right-margin justification was valued at $100,000. Any vendor who proposed to include the feature would then have $100,000 subtracted from the total cost of its proposal, while whatever price the vendor was asking for the feature would be incorporated into the vendor's total price. The idea was that if the vendor could provide right-margin justification for less than $100,000, it would pay the vendor to bid it.

Persuading the contracting people to allow so many desirables in addition to the mandatories was a relatively delicate task. According to Eliot Christian, who headed the technical evaluation team, "The problem with desirables is that the weight you give them is sometimes so loosy-goosy. We convinced the procurement people that we might increase our total productivity by spending extra money to get extra features."[5] The theory was to establish dollar values for the desirable features by estimating the amount of time each feature would save—a process that must have been inexact at best. "Since we were willing to identify up front the benefits to the government, the contracting officer trusted us that we weren't out to get a Cadillac," according to Buddy Edwards.[6]

In addition to the desirables, various other evaluation criteria—such as ease of use, training, and maintenance, and company experience—were also included, and also given dollar scores rather than points. Each bidder's total score then consisted of his price bid minus the dollar credits for desirable features, technical excellence, and management competence. The bidder with the lowest adjusted price would then be awarded the contract.[7]

"Company experience" counted for 20 percent of the overall technical score, or 10 percent of the overall evaluation formula. "The percentage is so small because that's all the contracting officer would accept," according to Buddy Edwards.[8] Under the corporate experience section, vendors were asked to provide references, and were also asked questions (such as questions about current production rates of the various items being offered) that were designed to tap whether equipment being offered was simply announced or whether it was actually currently being produced and sold.[9]

Three vendors bid on the contract—Wang, Digital Equipment,

and Honeywell. The VA had extensive prior experience with all three. Honeywell ran an interactive system with mainframes and terminals for the VA's Division of Veterans Benefits. Digital supplied both some office automation equipment and also the computers used by the Division of Medicine and Surgery. Wang supplied word processors bought off a General Services Administration schedule contract.[10] People around the VA were enthusiastic about Digital, quite happy with Honeywell, and dissatisfied with Wang. Wang had done a bad job of servicing equipment and of delivering things on time; the agency had also had problems with Wang-provided software.

The technical evaluation team was divided between people in the VA information-resources management office and computer people in the various user offices within the agency. Most knew each other. The team attempted to achieve a consensus in their ratings. The technical evaluation team did not speak with the references the companies provided in their proposals.

Wang won the contract. Bidders offered a remarkably similar menu of desirable options. The technical scores for all three vendors were similar, with a slight advantage for Digital. But Wang bid a much lower price than its two competitors; with that, the contract victor was clear.[11]

Given the agency's past experience with Wang, the decision to go with them was not popular among VA users. "When we announced that Wang had won, there were cries of agony within the building," recalls Buddy Edwards.[12] "Personally, I didn't feel good about Wang," stated another source at the agency. "But Wang had the numbers. At that point in time, I would have loved the numbers to have come out differently."[13] According to the contracting officer on the contract,

> The procurement people would have to caution the technical evaluation panel that when it gets into past performance, that's a matter of vendor responsibility, and that's determined by the contracting officer. Realistically, it's bound to come in. The technical evaluation people might give a point or two to a vendor if they've had good experience with them. The best you can do to prevent this is to have the panel meticulously identify the strengths and weaknesses of the proposal itself.[14]

One of the issues widely discussed among private-sector computer buyers around the time the VA made its award was whether Wang was in the future going to be successful in making the transition from a company producing dedicated word-processing equipment to a general-purpose computer supplier. Wang was losing many private-sector contracts because of a fear that it would not be big enough or adaptive enough to advance technologically with progress in the industry.

Although Buddy Edwards recalls that there were questions in the RFP asking vendors to explain how they planned to keep up with future technological change, I could find none—the relevant questions all dealt with the past.[15] Even if such questions had been present, the VA would still have been limited in its consideration of this issue to what the vendors said in their proposals rather than including, for example, knowledge gained from reading the trade or general business press.

According to Jack Sharkey, head of information resources management at the VA:

> When Wang got the award, I told them they weren't starting at zero, they were starting subterranean. I said, "You'd better produce or we'll default." Dr. Wang himself came down to talk with me.[16]

Wang's performance began inadequately and then improved somewhat.[17] Initially, Wang had trouble meeting VA delivery schedules. There were also glitches in the network Wang set up at VA headquarters to link dumb terminals to minicomputers for office automation applications, although VA officials do concede that the network was an ambitious project (the largest Wang had ever installed) done under fairly unfavorable building conditions. There has also been continuing dissatisfaction within the VA about how Wang manages the debugging and upgrading processes with its packaged software. Wang established a separate maintenance organization to service the contract, and VA mumbling early on about defaulting the contract for late deliveries "got Wang's attention," according to Buddy Edwards.[18]

One of the problems the VA has had has been on prices for the equipment Wang has provided. Wang actually delivered very little of the equipment they initially had bid at very favorable prices to the VA, because it soon became obsolete. (The VA did buy Wang VS minicomputers that Wang bid in its proposal.) On newer generations of equipment supplied under the contract, Wang ended up getting close to General Services Administration (GSA) schedule prices, which were considerably above the price levels (compared with GSA schedule) they had bid on the original equipment. Nonetheless, because of price-performance improvements in computer technology, the newer generations of equipment could still be offered at prices equal to or less than those bid for the older equipment, thus keeping within the terms of Wang's contractual commitment.

Interestingly, one incentive for Wang to perform on this contract with the VA is that the contract is large enough to be visible to potential Wang customers outside government. The contract award at the VA came at a time when Wang was losing market share and when there was widespread concern over the company's ability to make a transition out of the era of dedicated word-processing equipment where it had made its mark. "Private-sector clients were looking at them here," Jack Sharkey said. "If they fail here, their whole company is in jeopardy."[19] At the same time, when asked whether Wang's performance on this contract was good enough to make him inclined to want to award the contract to Wang when the contract comes up for recompetition, Buddy Edwards responded, "That's immaterial. You can't judge Wang's performance in making the award the next time around."[20]

CASE STUDY 6:
Internal Revenue Service Center Mainframe Replacement System

During the 1985 fiscal year covered by these case studies, the Internal Revenue Service (IRS) decided to purchase eighteen mainframe computers to upgrade the capacity of the computers used at the agency's ten tax-processing service centers. This was a sole-source acquisition from the Sperry Corporation of computers to complement the existing computers that Sperry had at the service centers; the sole-source character of the procurement was justified on the grounds that only new Sperry machines were software-compatible with the existing ones and that the capacity upgrade had to be made quickly.

The reason for the urgency was that the IRS had just endured the operational and public-relations nightmare of the 1985 tax filing season, which was the year the new computers failed to work. It was the year of delayed refunds, of improper dunning notices, and of suggestions that overworked employees had chucked tax returns into the trash. The key story about the 1985 procurement of the equipment upgrade was the acquisition that had necessitated the upgrade in the first place, which is the story that will be told here.

The Internal Revenue Service (IRS) is one of the most computer-intensive agencies in the federal government. Salient information from taxpayer returns is entered into computer files and processed to generate results that include simple recalculations of taxes owed because of arithmetical errors by taxpayers, tax refund payments for those due a refund, and returns selected for audit. Both initial returns processing and much of this data manipulation take place at ten IRS regional service centers. (A large data file, the Individual Master File, which contains salient information from all tax returns filed over the previous five years, is kept at the IRS National Computer Center in Martinsburg, West Virginia.) Some of this work at the service centers (mainly returns processing) is done in a batch mode. This is done to a limited extent during the day, but mostly nights and weekends. For other work, IRS employees either at the service centers or in local IRS offices need immediate, real-time access to returns information. Such immediate access is needed, for instance, in connection with audits, in responding to taxpayer questions over the telephone, or in locating and correcting errors in a taxpayer's file. This work is done on-line, with employees at terminals having direct access to data from the files.

The information stored in files at the ten service centers is prodigious, as is the volume of transactions the system must handle. As of the beginning of the 1980s, the IRS was using mainframes dating from the early 1970s that had essentially gone out of production and software that likewise was the product of an earlier epoch.[1] For batch processing, the agency was using Honeywell equipment; for on-line transactions, it was using Control Data Corporation equipment. All the software consisted of custom code written in assembly language, rather than some higher-level programming language that would now almost universally be used for software.[2] By the late 1970s, it was clear that it made no sense to try to add to the capacity of the existing machines, even if the agency were able to keep upgrading them, because the technology was so obsolete. The decision was therefore made to buy new mainframes to run both the batch and on-line operations at the service centers. Because the software for the new mainframes would be written in higher-level programming language rather than assembly language, the IRS would have to undergo the trauma of software conversion for 1.5 million lines of code, a major undertaking. It also meant that the IRS could, from a technical point of view, start from scratch in terms of vendor selection, since a software conversion effort would be necessary in any case.

Initially, the IRS believed it made sense in conjunction with the purchase of new mainframes to expand the computer's capacity sufficiently to allow the automation of new functions. For budgetary reasons, however, Treasury and the Office of Management and Budget told the IRS that it would not be given money for the capacity to purchase any expanded applications, only to roll over existing applications to new equipment. Thus EREP (Equipment Replacement and *Enhancement* Program) became SCRS (Service Center *Replacement* Program).

The dominant issue during the development of the RFP—and, in the clear light of the events that were to follow, what came to be seen as a sort of Charge of the Light Brigade of the IRS contracts office—was the weight to be accorded price as an evaluation criterion in the procurement. The initial position of the Contracts people was that this was essentially a procurement of off-the-shelf hardware (the software conversion work would be done by the agency's own programmers in-house) and that therefore price should be weighted 90 percent. The technical people felt that much more weight needed to be given to the performance capabilities of the machines. One example they frequently cited was the differences among machines' upgradability. But beyond that,

> We couldn't predict what might be out there. There might be something out there we didn't know about, and it might be worth something to get extra performance. But the contracts people would say, "You can't document those needs for the government." They always took a very conservative viewpoint. They wanted to avoid giving the agency the opportunity to misuse additional discretion. They were afraid we would buy something just for the hell of it. We would respond, "Even though we don't know exactly now what our needs are, we can know that there will be new needs."[3]

According to another participant:

> The number of technical points was a contest from day one. Contracts thinks only about what's legally defensible. They bend over backwards to avoid appeals, and that leads to a big emphasis on cost.[4]

The RFP issued in February 1980 assigned 80 out of a possible 100 points to price. "It was," states Lou Kuttner, currently the hard-hitting director of the Hardware Division with characteristic bluntness, "a disgraceful number enforced on us by Contracting."[5] The evaluation of technical features (such as ease of use for operators and programmers, ease of upgrading, reliability, and privacy and security features) was given a total of 12 points. Management capability and service capability were together given 4 points.[6] "As far as looking at our past experience, in terms of how good are these people to work with, that's almost prohibited. It's too subjective," says Roger Howard, one of the evaluation team leaders.[7] According to RFP, "The award shall be made to the officer receiving the highest total number of evaluation points. Points will be calculated to two decimal places."[8]

The RFP established requirements in terms of transaction processing volumes (with an 8 percent annual growth in the number of transactions over the life of the system) and of interfaces with other elements of the existing IRS system. The RFP also required that the computers the vendors were bidding pass a bench-mark test according to which the machines needed to process a set of transactions that the IRS would provide on a bench-mark tape within a response time that met existing IRS response-time standards.[9]

Initially, three vendors responded to the RFP, Honeywell, Sperry Corporation, and Vion (the American agent for Hitachi, a Japanese manufacturer of IBM-compatible mainframes).[10] Control Data decided not to bid because its increasing emphasis since the early 1970s on the scientific market made their computers inappropriate for the kinds of business-oriented applications IRS needed. Honeywell withdrew from the competition after submitting a proposal, apparently because the company realized it would not be able to pass the bench-mark test with the machines it was bidding. Both these events perhaps should have suggested that the equipment being purchased was not as straightforward as some in contracting might have imagined. But at this point the evaluation weights, having been established in the RFP, could not be altered. IBM did not bid because it didn't feel it could successfully compete on price.

The Sperry and Vion proposals were very different.[11] To keep its price down, Sperry bid a minimalist solution, the smallest amount of hardware that would just barely meet the transaction-processing requirements in the RFP. Vion, by contrast, bid a capacious solution that exceeded the requirements of the RFP. Sperry's product line was less broad than Hitachi's, and Sperry was already bidding its biggest machine, which meant that the Sperry equipment was not as easy to upgrade as the Hitachi machines. The Hitachi equipment also did a better job at recovering from errors caused by power outages, equipment problems, or operator mistakes. Vion's machines, however, would cost $160 million. Sperry came in at a $103 million. At that point, for all intents and purposes, in a decision made 80 percent on price, the decision was made.

It was not completely made, however, because it was not certain that Sperry's minimalist solution could pass the bench-mark test.[12] The bench mark had two parts, one involving real-time applications only and the other a mix of real-time and batch operations. The number of transactions thrown at the computer was a peak-load volume based on projected transactions volumes that the computers would actually have to deal with a few years hence.

Vion and Sperry were each given the bench-mark tape in advance (to help them determine what kind of capacity they needed to bid). According to IRS officials, Sperry's strategy was to "tune" its machines so as to direct specific bench-mark transactions to specific disks, as well as to customize some of the software for their machines, to allow the machines just barely to deal, within the required response time, with the specific transactions in the specific order appearing on the bench-mark tape. "Every time we wanted to change the bench mark at all, Sperry would object," according to one participant. "Sperry was so tightly tuned that they couldn't do any changes. Vion was more cooperative, because they had enough horsepower to do the changes."[13]

However, the bench mark was a representation of IRS production reality, not production reality itself. The solution that Sperry crafted to allow its minimalist solution to pass the bench mark, IRS officials believed, would not necessarily pass under real production conditions, where the actual order of transactions would be different.

The RFP had been silent on machine "tuning" that involved giving the computer certain instructions based on existing code rather than changing any code. The agency was therefore unable to downgrade Sperry for "tuning" that allowed the machines to pass the bench mark, even though the tuning would have made it impossible to meet the required response times with transactions presented in another order, such as would occur in a real production environment. However, the RFP had directed bidders to inform IRS of any use of non-off-the-shelf code. While the bench mark was being run, IRS officials discovered the presence of problems with the bench-mark-customized code. "At that point the Sperry evaluation team all personally felt we should throw them out, that we can't live with people who don't tell us the truth."[14] With Honeywell having dropped out, however, there were only two competitors left. And, according to the technical people, the decision was made somewhere "higher up" in IRS to do everything possible to avoid failing Sperry on the bench mark (which would have left one competitor). Sperry eliminated the nonstandard software that was discovered and brought in top company engineers to tune the machines further. In many cases after several tries for part of the bench mark, Sperry was certified as having passed.

The IRS had had no prior experience either with Sperry or Vion. Sperry's behavior during the bench mark, and the general attitude of Sperry management that their behavior suggested to IRS officials, did not influence the score Sperry achieved for management capability.

> Their performance wasn't used in the management evaluation. The contracting officer does the management evaluation, and if you're talking about a major corporation there's no way you can downgrade one of them against another. They'll all get the same points.[15]

Overall, Sperry's score on the technical evaluation was far below Vion's. But Sperry, in June 1981, won the contract. "We got Sperry," states hardware chief Lou Kuttner succinctly, "although nobody preferred them."[16]

It is interesting to speculate, incidentally, why Vion behaved the way it did. Why bid capacity beyond that minimally required to meet the bench mark, when doing so raises one's price and makes contract award less likely?[17]

Indeed, Sperry officials and others note that there is no reason for a vendor to bid more than what the government asks for—bidding more will cost more money, and if the government wants more, it should ask for it in the RFP.[18] One account of Vion's behavior would simply be that the way its product line was organized, it had only the choice between bidding too little capacity to meet IRS requirements and too much. But then the question is why it bid on the job at all. It might not have completely understood the procurement system at this rather early stage of marketing to the federal government and hoped that it would get more credit for a better solution.

The problems that were hinted at prior to contract award continued after award. Only a few months after award, the IRS discovered—at a Sperry user meeting—that Sperry had decided to discontinue providing support for the system software it had bid for the contract and begin using a different system software code instead.[19] This shift concerned the IRS for several reasons. Sperry apparently was intending to leave the agency with the alternatives of paying for the new software or living with the older, now-unsupported software, which Sperry would no longer modernize or improve with new releases the way it does for current software. In addition, it appeared that the new software would be more capacity-intensive than the previous software, meaning that the computer power that Sperry had bid would now be even less sufficient for the IRS's tasks.

The contract had called on the winning vendor to continue to "support" software it bid under the contract, without further definition of that term. Sperry's position, apparently, was that support simply meant that the company would answer questions or solve problems as necessary, but that the concept of support did not include any commitment to provide new releases, updates, or improvements in the software, as IRS had assumed. There is, in fact, no commonly agreed upon definition of what it means for a vendor to support software. Sperry never asked for clarification before contract award, nor did it say anything to IRS about its plans to change its systems software, although this was clearly at least a possibility at the time of Sperry's bid.

The IRS began to huff and puff about terminating the contract, and in January 1982, a few months later, Sperry agreed to rerun the bench mark using the new software and to provide IRS with additional machines at no cost if necessary to meet the bench mark. The problems were still not over, however. Before the bench mark was supposed to be rerun in June 1982 and during that bench mark, IRS discovered, through a leak from a whistle-blower within Sperry, that yet additional nonstandard software—beyond the customized software that IRS had already discovered prior to contract award—had been used to modify the system Sperry had originally bid to allow those computers to pass the original benchmark tape. IRS technical people then declared that Sperry did not pass the June 1982 bench mark, and in July the IRS informed Sperry that it was imposing a moratorium on further contract deliveries.

According to the General Accounting Office report on the situation:

> IRS considered terminating the contract for default. However, IRS believed that it needed to move ahead with its modernization plans, particularly the software conversion. Terminating the contract would have caused a significant delay in IRS' plans because a recompetition of (the contract) would have had to take place.[20]

Sperry at this point agreed to provide an additional $12 million of computers free to the government to allow its hardware (barely) to pass the bench mark. The moratorium on purchases was lifted in September 1982.

The 1985 problems received wide attention in the press and on television. The bulk of the difficulties involved simple delays in posting tax returns and consequent tardiness in getting refunds back to taxpayers, caused by capacity insufficiency, mainly for weekend batch processing.[21] Specifically, the number of refund checks mailed so late that the IRS needed to pay taxpayers interest increased by almost 50 percent, or in actual numbers by about 700,000 (of approximately 70 million returns filed). Approximately 300,000 taxpayers needed to file duplicate returns to get their refunds, after waiting at least 16 weeks without having received one. There were also dramatic, if uncommon, incidents where a small number of data tapes were not entered into the system in a timely fashion (and in at least one case lost or erased), a situation resulting in the issuance of incorrect tax assessment notices and dunning letters. Furthermore, even this level of performance required significant increases in personnel overtime within the system.

IRS officials concede that the problems with Sperry were not the main causes of the difficulties during the 1985 filing season.[22] Instead, they came mostly from what IRS officials themselves regard as a poorly managed software conversion process. Some important applications programs were not ready in time for the 1985 filing season, and other programs were poorly written so that they required far more computer time than should have been needed to run, causing machine backlogs.[23] If there wasn't a problem with the capacity of the

Sperry machines, however, the reason was that the IRS in effect rewarded Sperry for its behavior by earlier-than-expected exercise of contract options to purchase new computer capacity that Sperry's original offer didn't provide.

One IRS official, who does not place any direct blame on Sperry for the 1985 events, nonetheless argues that the choice of Sperry did create two problems for 1985. One was that IRS programmers had more experience with programming IBM-compatible code and thus might have done a better job doing software conversion into the Hitachi machines. The second problem was more subtle. One of the responsibilities of a good vendor, this official argues, is to give management good—and hard—advice when the customer is making a mistake. "A good vendor," he says, "would not have let us mismanage the conversion process as badly as we did."[24]

Two other points on this story are of note. One is that the hostility toward the Contracts people generated by experience on the Sperry contract marked a turning point within IRS. Henceforth, the Contracts people had to accept lower weights for price than they had succeeded in imposing previously.[25] A second is that several years after all this Sperry was one of the bidders on a major IRS contract for communications front-end processing equipment. Sperry's behavior on the service center replacement contract was not taken into consideration in the decision about contract award on the front-end processors.[26]

CASE STUDY 7:
Federal Aviation Administration
Host Computer Replacement

Computers play a central role in operating the air traffic control system. Tremendous demands are placed on them in terms of processing intensity, response time, reliability, and availability. In the late 1960s the Federal Aviation Administration (FAA) in the Department of Transportation acquired from IBM a number of mainframe computers to manage one part of the system—the twenty so-called en route control centers that direct air traffic when it is in between airports. Around the same time the FAA had Sperry developing console processors to be used in control towers at airports. The computers bought from IBM for the en route system were IBM 360s, introduced in the mid-1960s, configured specially for FAA's needs. In 1975 Computer Sciences Corporation (CSC) took over software maintenance and facilities management for the computers, so IBM was no longer on-site at the FAA.

In 1981 the FAA announced the beginning of a major redesign and improvement of the entire air traffic control system, partly to reflect the need for new computing capacity because of increases in air traffic and, in significant measure, to improve the functionality of the system by developing new applications that would make air traffic safer (such as by allowing quicker detection of wind burst dangers) and also less subject to traffic-control-caused delays. The entire plan involves fifteen major projects (each a separate procurement) to be implemented over a twenty-year period at a total cost of more than $15 billion—the largest civilian procurement ever.[1]

Originally, the intention had been to keep the old computers in operation pending development of at least some of the new applications intended for the system.[2] However, with airline deregulation and the subsequent increase in air traffic, it was becoming increasingly apparent at the time the new plan was being developed that an interim measure pending final development of the new system would be needed to upgrade the capacity available in the older IBM computers. As it was, the computing system was straining under the load of insufficient capacity, especially when one part of the system was down and backup processing had to be used. In cases such as these, controllers responded by spacing planes farther apart to avoid compromising safety, resulting in traffic delays. In addition, maintaining these old computers was becoming increasingly expensive—and problematical altogether—since IBM was no longer even manufacturing spare parts for them. The FAA therefore decided to acquire new host computers for the en route centers, while leaving the applications to which the computers were put unchanged pending other parts of its modernization plan.

If the purchase of a new generation of mainframes had been all this procurement involved, it would have been simple (though still expensive, given the number of big boxes to be purchased). But that was not all that was involved. The systems software from the old computers needed to be converted for the new environment—a task involving rewrite of about 100,000 lines of code—so that air traffic controllers would notice no difference on their screens between the old and new host computers. And the new computers had to be put on-line without disrupting the operation of the already functioning system. The software conversion was itself a far more daunting task because the FAA had waited so long to get new computers. "If we were the private sector, we would probably have just sole sourced a computer upgrade to IBM 370s in the mid-1970s," according to Mike Perie. But that was impossible in a government context and not really even considered.[3]

Given the size of this program, the FAA had extensive discussions with the Office of Management and Budget (OMB) during development of the modernization plan. During these discussions, OMB pushed the idea that since they were undertaking a major systems acquisition, they ought to follow the principles laid down in OMB Circular A–109 on major systems procurement.[4] The main feature of that document is the division of the procurement into a design competition phase, where two vendors are selected (from those bidding) to develop, at the government's expense, a prototype of the system being acquired, and then an acquisition phase, where these contractors bid a price to supply the system they have prototyped. The notion is that the duplicated expenses (and time delays) the government incurs early in the project are more than compensated for by reducing the design risk—since no contract is awarded until successful prototypes have been developed—and also by reducing the final price by achieving price competition between two vendors for the production contract. Fairly early on, the FAA seemed to have accepted the A–109 approach for major elements of the modernization plan, including the new host computer acquisition, more or less as a given.

As daunting a task as the software conversion was likely to be, it nonetheless was significantly less daunting if the new computers at least continued to be IBM or IBM-compatible, since at the level of machine language software code in the core of the system, the old computers would then be the same as the newer machines. "The FAA didn't have too much difficulty getting approval from the General Services Administration for a competition for the new computers that would be limited to IBM-compatible mainframes."[5]

The only two teams that bid to participate in the design competition were a team headed by IBM and a team headed by Sperry. (The Sperry team did not, however, bid Sperry equipment, which was not IBM-compatible hardware, but, rather, hardware from Amdahl.) The design competition that the FAA proceeded to organize, starting in September 1983, essentially involved giving the contractors the most difficult portions of the software to redesign and telling them that approximately two years later, they would be asked to plug their software into the equipment they were bidding to see how it worked. The FAA would then proceed to bid the production contract. Contract award would take into account the contractors' performance during the design competition phase, their strategy for the remaining software conversion, their implementation plan for assuring an interruption-free transition from the old to the new computers, and their price. (The computers were to be offered at a fixed price, and the remaining software development at a cost-based price.)

According to people at the FAA, both vendors had advantages and disadvantages going into the design competition phase. IBM knew the original software it had developed for the old machines—and they brought back some people still at the company who had worked on developing it—but they had been out of the FAA since 1975, and the FAA had gone through several new releases of its software since IBM had left. Sperry was still around at the FAA and had up-to-date knowledge of the air traffic control system, but only at airports and not at the en route centers.[6]

Basically, IBM turned in a significantly better performance than Sperry during the design competition phase. Sperry had lots of trouble, especially at the beginning of the project, and they needed lots of hand-holding throughout. The FAA decided to help out, since they did not want there to be only one vendor who successfully passed the design competition test and hence could go on to bid unopposed for full production. According to the FAA official in charge of monitoring Sperry during the design contract competition:

> We wanted two guys at the end who could bid, but with Sperry it was touch and go. We were all over them, looking

over their shoulder. I wasn't impressed by Sperry's management skills. FAA did a lot of the management.[7]

In the end, both sets of software passed the design competition tests, with little differences in their performance scores. Sperry had, however, gone about 25 percent over their estimated budget, while IBM came in basically on budget.[8]

The FAA then proceeded to the award phase of the procurement, issuing an RFP for IBM and Sperry to bid on.[9] The evaluation criteria in the RFP stated that the "Technical and Business Management proposals are of principal importance. . . . It is not expected that the Cost and Price proposals will be as important . . . and will not necessarily be controlling. However, it is an important factor."[10] No specific breakdown between the weights assigned price and nonprice factors was mentioned in the RFP, nor did the FAA develop such figures internally.

There were significant debates between the technical and procurement people at FAA, and between FAA technical people and the Department of Transportation, about the weight to be given price. The Department of Transportation has a reputation for awarding contracts to the low bidder, even though this seems a bit anomalous for FAA, given the safety-sensitive nature of the equipment it procures for the air traffic control system.[11] There were apparently some procurement people within the FAA who believed that since the design competition had shown both contractors could do the work, the agency should simply proceed with a sealed-bid procurement and make the award on low price alone.[12] But with the argument that the safety of the public was at stake in selecting the right vendor, the technical people succeeded in getting higher management to accept the language in the RFP. Nonetheless, despite the victory, according to one of the technical people "we would have never gotten past the front office with choosing the higher bidder," since the design competition had shown that both contractors could in some sense do the job.[13]

The evaluation criteria stated that the technical proposal would be weighted four times as heavily as the business management proposal.[14] The technical evaluation criteria were themselves divided into four subparts. The highest weight was given the vendor's plan for accomplishing the details of implementing the actual transition from the old environment into the new—a task, it will be remembered, that needed to be accomplished without any interruption in air traffic control service.

Interestingly, *the lowest weight of the four technical evaluation criteria went to the vendor's performance during the design competition phase.*[15]

According to Mike Perie, the decision to weight the design competition phase performance so low

> was a political decision. There was a fear that since Sperry hadn't done well, you'd run into problems if you made it obvious that the decision was going to be based on the design competition phase. Sperry might refuse to bid or it might protest the RFP.[16]

Business management was given only one-fourth the weight of technical qualities in the evaluation criteria. The business management part of the evaluation included evaluation of each vendor's cost and schedule performance during the design competition phase, as well as evaluation of the quality of the key personnel vendors bid for the project. (This latter factor got the lowest weight in the business management evaluation criteria.) The RFP also required the bidders to provide information about work on similar air traffic control or command-and-control systems. But the RFP stated that company experience would simply be evaluated on a pass-fail basis, and not scored like the other evaluation criteria.[17] According to Mike Perie, "Department of Transportation rules say you're not allowed to score past company performance. The fear is that the company's reputation gets scored and not company performance."[18]

IBM had a better reputation for the work it had done designing the original en route system than did Sperry for the work it had done developing the consoles at the airport terminals. Sperry had done well on the original design of the terminal consoles, but they had subsequently had a series of problems, on more than one occasion, developing enhancements for the system.[19] "They were viewed with suspicion." However, "we were not allowed to take past experience on other contracts into account. People tried to keep it out of their minds."[20]

The business management portion of the evaluation criteria did allow the cost and schedule performance of the vendors during the design competition phase to be evaluated. But, although there was a clear feeling that IBM had done considerably better than Sperry in these regards, members of the evaluation team were worried that Sperry might protest any significant differences in the scores, on the grounds that their cost and schedule problems were the result of changes in the work that FAA had imposed during the design competition (even though IBM had to deal with the same changes). Because members of the evaluation team felt that they could not prove that Sperry's performance problems were Sperry's fault, the difference in

165

scores between IBM and Sperry on design competition performance ultimately were negligible.[21]

There were more than thirty people on four technical evaluation teams, divided about equally between people who worked together throughout the host project and field people who worked with the en route system but had had no experience with the design competition phase.[22] People could be on more than one team, but nobody was on all four teams. The teams discussed their ratings together, partly to ensure common interpretation of the language in contractor proposals. According to Mike Perie, no effort was made to require group consensus; however, those ending up with divergent ratings in an area were required to write a minority report.

Despite the fact that IBM got only marginal credit for many of the areas where they had earlier demonstrated superiority over Sperry, the company still came out ahead in the technical evaluation, largely because of what the evaluators believed was a markedly superior implementation plan for how they would accomplish the details of the transition from the old to the new machines.

> We were looking for familiarity with details of our buildings, our electrical systems, the details of our procedures. We had both IBM and Sperry visit our sites so they could learn as much as possible. Sperry said some silly things in their proposal. They thought the cable was the same at all sites. IBM knew that some cable needed to be replaced. Sperry didn't know the details. They wrote things that annoyed the field people who were doing the evaluation. There was too much of "Sperry's done it before, and we can do it again" instead of giving us real installation details.[23]

IBM's ability to show a good eye for details was not, in the opinion of Mike Perie, a result of their previous experience with the system, since IBM had not been around the en route centers for so long. However, this eye for detail did not, in Mike Perie's opinion, reveal anything about the company's ability or willingness to handle glitches or problems that were certain to arise one way or the other after the contract was awarded.[24]

According to people at FAA, it was still not at all clear that IBM would win the contract, despite all that had gone before, until the cost proposals were evaluated after the technical evaluation was completed. To the considerable surprise of the people at FAA, IBM came in with an extremely aggressive price bid, about $70 million under Sperry's—and also considerably under the $275 million budget estimate that the FAA had been working with (which in turn reflected an assumed 25 percent discount off General Services Administration multiple award schedule prices).[25] "People were stunned."[26] IBM's price made the final decision in July 1985 to go with IBM an easy one.

Officials at FAA make various guesses about why IBM bid so much more aggressively on price than anyone had expected. The air traffic control system has high visibility to the public. IBM was bidding against hardware manufactured by Amdahl, their major mainframe competitor in the United States, in an organization where their equipment was already installed. Although an American-founded company, a large part of Amdahl is today owned by the Japanese. And IBM was about to enter another design competition (this time against Hughes Aircraft) for design of the new applications software to be run on the new host computers.[27]

With some fairly insignificant delays and fairly insignificant cost overruns on the software designed since contract award, IBM has gotten the new host computers installed, without any glitches, at the twenty en route centers. Sources outside the FAA confirm the view that the host project has been a "success story."[28]

At the same time, other elements of the FAA modernization plan are not going as well, with some instances of fairly significant cost and schedule slippage. It is intriguing to speculate about the reasons. An important explanation, no doubt, is that some of the other projects are technically more complex than the host software conversion, since they involve writing code for entirely new applications. There is, as well, the fact that IBM's performance on this project is visible not just to the FAA but to the traveling public, a group that includes decision makers on computer acquisitions in the commercial world. As Jim Cain of the FAA notes: "IBM is still boasting in their marketing about how their systems are so good that they are being used for air traffic."[29]

CASE STUDY 8:
Environmental Protection Agency
Computer Operations and Maintenance Service

In 1981 the Environmental Protection Agency (EPA) awarded a contract to Computer Sciences Corporation (CSC) to provide assistance of various sorts in managing EPA computer operations and databases. Unlike the IRS computer services contract, to be discussed below, most of the services purchased under the contract involved ongoing work rather than one-shot projects. Thus, for example, the contractor was in charge of actually collecting data on toxic waste dumps submitted to the agency pursuant to various statutory requirements, coding and keypunching those data to create a large database, and performing data retrieval or computer analyses using the database. The contractor might also provide various ongoing software maintenance or other support services for one of EPA's computer operations in headquarters or in field offices and laboratories. The contract included some one-shot projects, such as developing software for EPA financial systems, but such projects constituted a minority of the activities under the contract. Much of the work is of a type that might very well have been performed in-house in a political environment less sympathetic to contracting out or less constrained by headcount ceilings. A number of the typical arguments for contracting out activities, such as requirements for special expertise or a temporary surge demand for certain services, do not really apply in this situation, and most of the people interviewed stated or suggested that in general the services bought off this contract were typically of a fairly uncomplicated, production-shop sort far removed from the high-tech state of the art. The contract is the largest computer service contract, in terms of dollar volume, at EPA. (EPA has similar umbrella service contracts for general software programming, application systems development, and scientific lab automation systems development.)[1]

In 1985 this contract was recompeted, with a scope of work essentially unchanged from the existing contract. The reviews CSC received for its performance on the previous contract were mixed to mildly positive.[2] Nobody thought it had done a terrible job; nobody thought it had done an outstanding one, either. Work such as this depends on the quality of people at the operating level and the quality of people and management systems (project organization, quality assurance procedures, ways of motivating employees) at the top. The CSC people at the operating and management levels generally did receive good marks for their enthusiasm and intelligence. But the contractor was criticized for assigning untrained, junior employees to the contract, for reassigning them too soon ("after getting on-the-job training at EPA"), and for not giving the contract the senior management attention it sometimes needed. According to one of the EPA officials interviewed:

> I get the impression that (they) have lots of good people someplace. We get the new people. They move people to private sector work once they get experience, because the company gets higher profits from private-sector work.

He went on to say that "we get lots of foreign nationals—we've had people who hardly speak English." According to another person interviewed, EPA has had problems, when difficulties develop in a project, gaining time or attention from higher-level management. In EPA locations outside Washington, where contractor turnover was lower and personnel developed an identification with local EPA operations, performance was generally good. The problems were greater at headquarters, where turnover was much higher. Poor performance was reflected in high error rates for documents being prepared, lots of rework required on documents because vendor personnel didn't understand agency operations well enough, and delivery delays that produced cost overruns (since the contract involved cost-reimbursement of labor hours rather than being done on a fixed-price basis).

According to John Hart, the technical manager for the contract at EPA, there has been ongoing interest among EPA technical people involved in this and other major computer service contracts in increasing the incentives for good contract performance by pitting vendors against each other not just for initial contract award but for tasks under the contract. The idea would be to make awards to several contractors for possible work on the contract and then to select one of those contractors for individual tasks. However, Hart says that the Contracts people have told them that the regulations preclude doing that unless a separate formal competition is arranged for each task, which would be a daunting prospect. "They ask us, 'What methodology are you going to use to select one contractor or another if you have three contractors you can choose among?' "[3]

Developing the requirements for the RFP was quite a straightforward process, since the scope of the contract was to be little changed from the previous time around. Once EPA began preparing the RFP,

169

the policy was and is to try to avoid speaking with any vendors. According to John Hart, "I try not to talk with people. I probably have talked with some on occasion, but in very general terms. That's a risk, a risk that you give somebody information you don't give others."[4]

The RFP did not specify the relative weight to be given technical scores and price in making the award. This is pursuant to general EPA procurement policy. In the opinion of John Hart, this is so that the Contracts people can award the contract "to the lowest price that's minimally qualified." Not specifying the weight given price, in Hart's opinion, increases the weight price eventually is given.[5]

Mark Walker, the contracting officer, disputes Hart's judgment about the reason for not specifying a price weight.

> The myth is rampant among some technical people that we are packed with people who only want to award to low price. That's not necessarily true. We don't have any weighting formula—even internally—so we can have maximum flexibility to exercise good business and management judgment when we make an award. We come out of NASA, and the concept is very big at NASA of not being tied to any authoritarian formula. But we constantly have very close technical scores and very big price differentials. Are 3 points better on technical really worth $10 million?[6]

Walker states, however, that the increasing frequency of bid protests from unsuccessful vendors is driving EPA in the direction of specifying all weights in the RFP.

> We had a protest recently on computer services where I don't think we would have had a protest if we had a formula. Given the great cost of preparing proposals, there's a real predisposition to protest. A formula is mechanistic, and if you lose, it seems more like fate. So you become more accepting.[7]

The Contracts and technical people each perceive the other as powerful and at least slightly malevolent. John Hart, the technical person, speaks of the Contracts people as being "very powerful here," adding "there isn't anybody in a position to challenge them on their arguments based on the regulations and on the legal advice they've gotten." Mark Walker, the Contracts person, says that "in these contracts, the pressures on us against an award to anyone but the best technical proposal are remarkable."[8]

Although the RFP specified no relative weights for price and technical, the RFP did specify the division of points among the various technical evaluation factors. The largest weight (90 points out of a possible 200) was given to the qualifications of "key project managers and key technical personnel." EPA was looking for a number of things in evaluating the qualifications of vendor personnel. They wanted to know whether the individual met certain minimum educational requirements. They wanted to know how many years of experience the individual had in work with varying levels of responsibility (such as number of people supervised). They wanted to know how experienced the individual was with various computer applications or technologies such as database management or local area networks. Out of 200 technical points, 20 were assigned to "corporate experience and capacity." Nothing in these evaluation criteria addressed the dimensions along which EPA was dissatisfied with CSC performance, such as employee turnover or degree of attention management gives a project that is having problems—both factors that are hard to capture in a proposal format.[9]

Because there was an incumbent vendor who was expected to be bidding on the contract again, at least some attention had to be given to the effect that the weights given various evaluation criteria might have on the likelihood that the incumbent would win the contract again. According to John Hart,

> If you talk about how well a contractor understands the agency and its requirements, an incumbent vendor can throw in a lot more boilerplate in their proposal that results from the fact they've been around here. Another firm would really have to do its homework and get their hands on relevant documents that describe EPA programs. And it's really hard to learn about our (computer) environment if you're not an incumbent, even if you did your homework. You'd probably have to get some documents under the Freedom of Information Act to get some feel for that.[10]

There was in the RFP no specific evaluation criterion such as "knowledge of the agency" that would directly favor an incumbent based simply on information the incumbent would inevitably pick up by having worked on the previous contract. There was credit given for "insight (into) technical problems expected to be encountered" and "insight (into) managerial problems expected to be encountered," both of which would be easier for an incumbent to answer. But these factors were given relatively few points. In addition, an incumbent would be more familiar with the procedures or styles that EPA management favored and hence in a better position to present a management plan in their proposal toward which EPA would likely react favorably.[11]

According to John Hart, the choice of technical evaluation criteria and the weights they are given was made based on what was required to perform the work, not on the impact of the criteria or weights on the degree of incumbent advantage. According to Mark Walker, conscious efforts have been made over the last several years to reduce the presence and weight given to evaluation criteria that favor incumbents.[12]

EPA received four responses to the RFP, including one from CSC. The people on the technical evaluation team, which was chaired by John Hart, generally knew each other, and Hart worked toward obtaining consensus evaluations through face-to-face meetings after the individual members of the team had read the proposals and individually scored them. "I've never failed to develop a consensus," reports Hart with pride.[13] The way contract award procedures work at EPA is that after the technical and cost evaluations have occurred, a Source Evaluation Panel is convened, which includes a technical person and a Contracts person as well as Ed Hanley, head of Information Resources Management at EPA. The contracting and technical people present reports, but they act only as advisors to the Source Evaluation Panel as a whole.[14]

The evaluation of the quality of the key personnel proposed by the different vendors, which received the largest weight in the technical evaluation, was done strictly on the basis of résumés the bidders submitted. EPA did not personally interview any of the proposed key personnel, nor did they call any previous employers. John Hart says that the Contracts people do not approve of personal interviews; Mark Walker disagrees, although he adds that such interviews are often not worth the time they take.[15] Basically, the evaluators toted up whether the résumés showed evidence of the individual meeting the various formal qualifications set out in the RFP. Thus, a person who had had experience working with both database management and local-area networks would, if being evaluated for a job where knowledge of both was helpful, get a higher rating than one who had worked with database management alone.

How would the evaluation score for the résumé of a person be affected, for example, if the technical evaluation team noted in reviewing a résumé that the individual in question had switched jobs ten times in ten years? Or would a person be rated higher for having graduated summa cum laude from Stanford in electrical engineering? According to Mark Walker, "Unless it's in a stated evaluation criterion in the RFP, you can't take it into consideration. You have to judge the résumés by the stated factors." Why are such factors so seldom placed into evaluation criteria? "These aren't the sorts of things you can sit down in advance and see all the potential permutations you can hit.

You only realize the problem when you see it in the résumé." In addition, Walker was worried about "intuitive" factors entering as evaluation criteria for résumés.

> We can't just put anything we want in evaluation criteria. They must have a clear logical relationship to performance. It may raise some eyebrows that an individual held ten jobs in ten years, but it doesn't mean he can't do a good job for us. Under our key personnel clause, after all, we only require a commitment to work for us for 90 days.

Walker noted that when his Contracts people review the evaluation scores for résumés of key personnel, they frequently observe what Walker referred to as "discrepancies" in the scores—differences in scores not explained by differences in the résumés as judged according to the stated evaluation criteria.

> Generally when we go back to the technical people and question them about it, it'll be something like your example of the guy who had ten jobs in ten years. They'll tell us, "We have this funny feeling about this person." Or worse, they'll say: "We know this person from another contract, and he's a deadbeat."

The Contracts people in such cases will question the differences in scores. "It's simple," says Walker, "We won't allow it."[16]

Although there was an incumbent vendor with whom EPA had had several years of experience on the very tasks being recompeted in the contract, the past performance of CSC on the previous contract could not be taken into consideration in the evaluation process, even in assigning scores for the twenty points granted "corporate experience and capacity." John Hart, responding to a question about whether the problems he perceived with CSC performance the previous time around would have any influence over the evaluation process on the recompetition, sighed and shook his head. "It wouldn't," he said. "That's the problem. Nowhere will your actual experience influence the score that they earn. An incumbent who has done a bad job can still win the next time around."[17]

In discussing this question, Mark Walker, the contracting officer, emphasized the danger of protests:

> The more there's any subjective judgment involved in the evaluation process, the more likely you are to get a protest. Sometimes a contractor says, "I know who's on the technical evaluation panel, and I know they don't like the work we've done, so they're prejudiced." That's a situation that is likely to lead to protests.[18]

In John Hart's view, "The regulations do us a disservice. We have to accept what's in that proposal they write. We can ask for clarification, but we can only go on what's between those covers."[19]

Ed Hanley, the head of the Office of Information Resources Management at EPA, discusses the case of the recompetition of another large computer service contract shortly after the recompetition of the operations and maintenance contract, where EPA was extremely dissatisfied with the performance of the incumbent vendor. Nonetheless, the evaluation of proposals when the contract was being recompeted showed the incumbent to be the winner. When the procurement arrived at the Source Evaluation Board, Hanley intervened. "Here I am basically suing these guys, and I'm about to give them a new contract." Hanley was able to get permission to address the incumbent vendor with formal interrogatories that forced the vendor to place damaging material about its performance into the contract proposal. Recalls Hanley:

> I said, "This time I'm going to rock the f—king boat." I ranted and raved. Everyone had to put their thinking caps on to come up with a way to deal with this because I was carrying on like a crazy person. It was uphill. The system doesn't make it natural or easy. But you can either be victimized by the system or say, "I'm a thinking human being."[20]

The level of dissatisfaction with the performance of CSC on the operations and maintenance contract was not nearly that great, however, and the process took its course. The technical scores of the various proposals were similar, and CSC got their price down far enough so they emerged fairly clearly as the winner.

One of the important ways CSC got its price down was, during their negotiations with EPA, to lower the hourly rates on various labor categories used under the contract, often to below the rates being charged the agency under the existing contract. Shortly after the contract was renewed, however, CSC people began asking the program managers at the various sites where they were working to upgrade the skill categories being used to do the work (from, say, "control clerk" to "senior control clerk") so that CSC would no longer be selling EPA services at these new, lower rates.[21] The rates for the higher labor categories were no higher than the previous rates for the lower labor categories, so the programs would not actually need to budget more money to get the work done. But an opportunity would be lost to achieve the cost savings that the CSC bid had suggested would occur. Whether it was because they had not been informed about the new lower labor rates for the existing labor categories, or because they were not particularly sensitive to the opportunity to save money as long as they did not have to spend more money, many of the EPA program managers who dealt with CSC began requesting changes in labor categories in conjunction with the switch to the new contract. According to John Hart,

> I started getting requests from many of our program people to change labor categories. The program managers are naive, they want to keep the contractor happy. I blew my stack and protested to Ed Hanley. We refused to issue the changes. But the contractor was persistent with the program people, and eventually, gradually, they got the changes.[22]

In general, according to Hart, the contractor's performance since the reaward of the contract has been about the same as the previous time around.

CASE STUDY 9:
Internal Revenue Service
Computer Support Services

In 1985 the Internal Revenue Service (IRS) let a contract to provide units within the organization with computer programming, training, and consulting services. In contrast to the support services EPA was buying under its operations and maintenance contract, none of the services under the IRS contract involved ongoing assistance from the contractor in performing any operating function. Instead, services purchased under this contract would be discrete task orders, specifying in advance what work would be accomplished and what specific deliverable the contractor would produce.[1] The services would be requested and paid for by individual units within the IRS. A contract administration unit would help to ensure that statements of work were clear and assist with price negotiations with the contractor. Each individual task order would be done on a fixed-price basis.

In effect, the IRS was purchasing individual work products the way a firm would from a consulting firm. The difference, however, was that this was a requirements contract with a length of up to five years and a maximum accumulated value of $50 million. The contractor would not be guaranteed any orders under the contract because decisions to order the services of the contractor would have to be made by the individual IRS units that would pay for them. But the fact that this was a "requirements" contract meant that the winner would be granted a monopoly over providing these kinds of services for any unit in the IRS that wanted them. In other words, units within the IRS did not have to use outside help at all if they chose not to. But if they did want outside help, they would have to use the vendor selected for this contract.[2]

The IRS had little practical alternative to this arrangement. The IRS might have separately competed each individual task order, but that would have been an incredibly time-consuming process. The IRS would not have been permitted to make awards to several vendors from whom IRS units could then have selected one for a given task order. The problem with such an approach, from the point of view of the procurement system, is that the selection for an individual task of one rather than another of the several approved vendors would be regarded as arbitrary without a separate competitive procurement in each individual case. Selecting one vendor over another from an approved group of vendors would therefore have to be the same as conducting a separate procurement process for each discrete task.

IRS was, prior to the contract, obtaining computer support services of the kind involved in this contract (mostly software programming) from an 8(a) firm provided IRS through an agreement with the General Services Administration.[3] The firm, according to Emory Miller of the IRS (at the time a senior analyst working on the computer support services program), generally did decent work but had great difficulty providing people in a timely manner to be available at the unpredictable times when demands for their services would appear from various IRS units. This experience produced a conclusion about the most important thing to look for on the procurement—namely, the ability of a company to manage the workload.[4]

In talking with Emory Miller and Sue Ensslen, the two people at IRS most involved in developing the RFP for this contract, it became clear that they were passionately concerned—indeed, preoccupied—with trying to get the procurement process to yield a contractor who would do good work. It is also clear that they struggled long and hard, and participated in numerous internal debates, about how to develop evaluation criteria for the RFP that would enable them to determine from the bids which vendors would perform well and which unsatisfactorily. "Our biggest problem," Miller states, "was to figure out how we could see that somebody could do the job. We went back and forth and back and forth thinking about how to structure the evaluation to get that result to come out of it."[5]

The result was an RFP where the dominant technical criterion, counting for almost half the technical points, was what was called the "management plan."[6] What the RFP meant by "management plan" was something quite specific and fairly narrow, namely the formal procedures the company proposed in its written documents to use for processing task orders, for assigning people to tasks, and for recruiting new people if necessary in the event of sudden increases in IRS demands for service. Thus, for example, the RFP required that bidders describe their "planning, estimating, scheduling, accounting, monitoring, and administrative procedures" for dealing with a task order received from an IRS unit from the time the task request was received until deliverable products were accepted by users.[7] Bidders were also asked to "indicate the estimated time required to start work after a task order has been issued," and to "describe how you would determine the skills and hours required for assigning the personnel necessary to satisfy user requirements."[8] In addition, the RFP required proposals to detail how they would handle a hypothetical situation involving extreme peaks and valleys of demand. In the hypothetical situation, the company is given one task on day one and then, around the time of completion of that task, given four new tasks. Then, in the middle of those tasks, one of the project managers becomes seriously ill and is placed on indefinite sick leave. At the end of the period, the company is given no new task orders for nine months.[9]

One of the most satisfying features of the RFP for Emory Miller and Sue Ensslen was their development, for the first time in government computer support services procurement to their knowledge, of what the RFP refers to as a "benchmark" test for bidders. In addition to the technical points awarded based on the aforementioned management plan presented in their proposals, another 20 percent of the total technical score was based on the bench mark. The bench mark required bidders to respond to a hypothetical task request from an IRS user organization that described a statement of work (for developing software to manage requests by taxpayers for filing deadline extensions) and the deliverables to go with it. The standard operating procedure under the contract was to be that when an IRS user organization issued a task request defining what it wanted done, the contractor would respond with a "task proposal" outlining the amount of time the contractor expected to spend, the skill levels they intended to assign, and a fixed price for the deliverables requested.[10] The bench mark in the RFP required that bidders present such a task proposal for the hypothetical task request. The bench mark thus required the bidders to discuss how they would perform the task. But, as the bench mark-materials stated in bold capital letters, "The 'benchmark' does *not* require the offer to perform the work of the task."[11]

What is fascinating about all these criteria is that none actually addressed itself to the question of the actual quality of the work product that contractors would produce on tasks they were presented. The various requirements for demonstrating a vendor's task-processing and staffing procedures would provide information about how good vendors might be at getting into various tasks in a timely manner, the requisite number of warm bodies who met the IRS formal requirements regarding educational attainments, number of years on the job, and types of past jobs held. One way of phrasing it is that the evaluation criteria reflected the potential of a vendor to do good work. The evaluation criteria, however, provided no information on whether the contractor was actually likely to produce work of brilliant, acceptable, or terrible quality.

The technical criteria that might address issues of likely work quality—which were the evaluation factors called "experience" and "personnel"—were given less weight in the technical evaluation. (Together they accounted for somewhat less than 40 percent of the technical points. Evaluation of the key people to be assigned to the contract counted for approximately 10 percent of the technical score.)[12] In addition, the way the evaluation criteria were written gave minimal consideration of how bidders and their key managers had actually performed in their earlier endeavors. Vendors were to present examples of past projects at other organizations they had worked on that involved similar demands, listing the number of people working on the previous contracts and the dollar volume of the contracts, the lead time the customer had given to assign personnel, and variances between planned and actual project completion dates.[13] The criteria did not specify that the quality of the work bidders actually did on these previous jobs would be considered, although bidders were required to give a name and telephone number for the customer and the RFP did state that "inquiries may be made of the customers indicated in the examples to determine the contractor's performance."[14] However, according to the evaluation criteria,

> project examples will be evaluated according to their size and complexity, their degree of similarity to anticipated contract tasks, and the degree to which they demonstrate the firm's experience in assembling large numbers of qualified personnel within stringent time frames.[15]

The criteria, then, called for looking into the nature of the firm's past experience, rather than how good a job they had done.

Evaluation of the people on the bidder's proposed management team occurred through an evaluation of résumés "for meeting minimum skill level requirements and for the degree of significant experience . . . (that) was of a level of responsibility appropriate to the skill level for which the résumé is offered."[16] The RFP stated that "previous employers may be contacted to verify experience and job performance," but the evaluation criteria for key management personnel did not specify previous job performance as a factor to be scored.[17]

Emory Miller defends the relative lack of weight given the evaluation of the quality of a company's key management people on the grounds that "there is no guarantee that the people who appear in the proposal will stay on." Past experience does not reveal much, because "a good company can become a mediocre company overnight. A company is no better than its last task."[18] Fred Martin, contracting officer on the contract, states, "These guys they bid leave immediately. We can't force contractors to bring in good people."[19]

The IRS developed its RFP essentially without talking with vendors.[20] The RFP stated that the winner would be the proposal with the highest score.[21] The main internal controversy on the RFP was the division between price and technical points in the evaluation. The Contracts people wanted a 90–10 weight in favor of price. According to Emory Miller:

> We felt very strongly that this was inappropriate. We had many discussions with Contracts about why price alone wouldn't give us the best vendor. We pushed for 50–50 and got it. We were the first people to ever get 50–50 with Contracts.[22]

According to Fred Martin, Contracts had been burned by the experience on the earlier IRS Service Center mainframe contract, where his office got blamed internally within IRS for imposing such heavily price-weighted evaluation criteria.[23]

Eight firms bid on the contract. Most of the members of the technical evaluation team were users who had little or no knowledge of the firms that were bidding. Few of them knew each other prior to their joint service on the technical evaluation panel.[24]

Panel members read and scored each proposal before the group met. No efforts were made to achieve unanimity in panel ratings. Emory Miller, chairman of the technical evaluation panel, asked members of the panel who had rated some part of the proposal much differently from the tendency of the group as a whole to discuss in front of the group the reason that they had rated the section of the proposal as they had, in an attempt to give the group an opportunity to see whether it was wrong or the outlying rates were wrong. Generally, there was significant convergence in the ratings even prior to the group discussions.[25]

The proposals that did poorly in the central "management plan" evaluation criterion were those that did not have procedures in place already for dealing with peak loads, but merely promised to develop procedures in the future. Proposals that emphasized dealing with peak loads through new recruitment were also downgraded, since it was feared that the new recruits might not be available in time. Nobody on the technical evaluation panel telephoned any of the company references or the past employer references for key management people. "Those features didn't have much point value anyway," states Emory Miller. "We asked for it in the RFP to keep them honest. The winning company was surprised when they learned we didn't call."[26]

The winning firm was a fairly small company called Vanguard Technologies, which had no experience doing work for IRS and was unknown to anyone at the agency. Vanguard found out about the procurement by reading about it in the *Commerce Business Daily*.[27] The IRS contract was by far the largest Vanguard had ever won.

Of course the easiest way to deal with the kinds of peak load staffing requirements IRS stressed in its technical evaluation criteria is to be a very large firm that can even out workflows at a companywide level by having many customers whose individual demand levels are variable over time. This is impossible for a small firm, and Vanguard dealt with this problem in its proposal by including Planning Research Corporation (PRC), a large systems integrator, as a subcontractor and a backup.[28]

It was clear to members of the technical evaluation panel that the Vanguard proposal was much superior to any of the others, including some by much bigger companies. It was also the lowest on price. "During the evaluation process," Miller states, "we went to the greatest extremes not to favor one vendor. The only thing we didn't want was a protest." Emory Miller expresses pride that the members of the technical evaluation panel were "unbiased" enough to choose Vanguard over a Big Eight accounting firm that also was bidding.[29] There were no bid protests over the award.

Were people apprehensive about awarding such a big contract to a relatively small company about which they had never heard anything before? Sue Ensslen answered a quick and confident, "No." Emory Miller confesses a bit more worry. "We felt very comfortable. We hoped they were as good as their proposal."[30]

Among the eight bidders were firms with which IRS had had previous experience. "Their past experience at IRS didn't come up in the panel discussion," Miller states. "Nobody within IRS outside the evaluation panel was allowed to know who the bidders were, so they couldn't try to influence the panel based on their experience." One of the firms that submitted a proposal was one with which IRS had previously had very bad experience. "Sue was the only one involved in the procurement who knew about it," Miller says. "She was careful not to tell anyone on the panel. The people evaluating proposals can only use the written proposal. You can't use any other information."[31]

IRS has had extremely positive experience with Vanguard under the contract.[32] "I've been in contract administration for years, and I've never seen a contractor so responsive," states Betsy Beckman, who is in charge of contract administration for the contract. When deliverables have not lived up to the expectations of the users who requested them, Vanguard has generally fixed them up without complaining and without trying to charge extra. When one deliverable was rejected by the user organization as unacceptable, Vanguard decided not only to redo the product but not to charge IRS for the project at all. Once when IRS changed a training program at the last moment so that the Vanguard speaker scheduled for the program was unable to do an appropriate job, Vanguard redid the presentation and did not charge for it, even though the problem was the fault of IRS. "They return calls very quickly. They will come to a meeting at a moment's notice," Betsy Beckman reports. In a survey done of IRS users of the Vanguard contract, 73 of the 76 respondents expressed satisfaction with the work Vanguard had done for them.[33]

It is unclear to what extent Vanguard's performance simply reflects the company's culture and to what extent it reflects incentives built into the situation. Vanguard seemed to hope, perhaps somewhat wishfully, that they might use their success at IRS, by far the firm's largest contract, as a reference for developing other business. And although IRS users are required to use Vanguard if they use computer consulting services, they at least have at the margin the alternative of doing the work in-house. "When they won the contract, I told them, 'You have only won an opportunity to provide service,' " notes Emory Miller. 'If you're not doing a good job, the work will dwindle.' "[34] While there is only so much work IRS is adequately staffed to do itself—and the notion that had the work been bad demand would have "dwindled" may therefore be a bit of poetic license—good work has indeed meant more IRS business for Vanguard. In 1988, halfway through the contract, IRS had depleted its procurement authority under the contract and had to go about prematurely, and hurriedly, preparing for a recompetition of the contract.

The upshot of the procurement, announced at the end of the summer of 1989, was a shocker. Vanguard lost the recompetition to a firm called OAO, with whom the IRS had never done business. Indeed, Vanguard's proposal was adjudged so inferior to that of OAO that the agency did not even include Vanguard in the "competitive range" of bidders with whom the government conducts further negotiations.[35] Vanguard's proposal lost out on two counts. The RFP for the recompetition, just like the one for the original contract, included a hypothetical situation to which vendors were supposed to reply. The response in Vanguard's proposal to this hypothetical situation was scored much lower than the response in OAO's proposal. Second (although not decisively, according to IRS officials), Vanguard bid higher labor hour rates for various categories of labor than did OAO.

The evaluation of vendors in the recompetition took place in a sort of organizational clean room, from which any evidence about Vanguard's actual performance under the existing contract had been

removed. Vanguard was downgraded for its response to a hypothetical situation, even though the agency had extensive evidence of
Vanguard's response to real situations. Hourly wage rates on different
labor categories were evaluated independently of any evidence about
the extent to which Vanguard had played fairly or unfairly in the
number of labor hours or the nature of the labor skill mix it bid on
work it had done for the agency. (To take an obvious example, Vanguard was given no credit for its not asking for more money to redo
work that customers weren't completely satisfied with.) Stated one
official involved in the procurement:

> According to the methodology used to evaluate the vendors,
> past performance was not used. Evaluating performance is
> something that's frowned upon. We have such an attitude
> toward maintaining full and open competition that just be-
> cause the contractor does work for the government and does
> a good job, it doesn't mean he can get the business again.
> I'm proud of the process. I take pride in the fact that we're so
> objective.[36]

Notes

1. Government jargon for computer-related technology is "automatic data processing" equipment, commonly abbreviated ADP. This phrase will not be used here, nor will the corresponding private-sector jargon term "information technology" or IT.

2. These figures are taken from Kevin Power, "IRM Budgets Still Rising," *Government Computer News*, 6 (November 20, 1987), p. 1.

3. Of course there are differences across procurement areas. Procurement of major weapons systems, for example, involves the special difficulties arising from procuring developmental items that go beyond the existing state of the art, as well as the problems that arise from political controversy over whether the items ought to be bought at all. The latter sorts of problems apply to procurement in any number of "contracting out" situations as well.

4. See U.S. Department of Commerce, *Survey of Current Business*, 68 (July 1988), p.60.

5. The *Federal Acquisition Regulation* is CFR 48, chap. 1. (The page length is as of the October 1985 edition.) The *Federal Information Resources Management Regulation* is CFR 41, chap. 201.

6. Subjects for the case studies were located by writing letters to the contracting offices of all the cabinet departments and the major independent agencies asking them to identify any contracts that fit the criteria I had established. I received responses from all the organizations to which I wrote. Most of the agencies had no contracts meeting the criteria for that year. All the agencies that did have a contract or contracts cooperated with the research, so the case studies represent the universe of contracts meeting the criteria.

7. The companies were Digital Equipment Corporation, Hewlett-Packard, IBM, Unisys, and Wang. These respondents were promised anonymity, and information from these interviews will not be attributed.

8. A number of alternative hypotheses to explain these results should be noted. One would be that private-sector computer managers are involved mostly in operating centralized mainframe data installations in the private sector, while their public-sector counterparts are more involved in end-user computing as well and hence exposed to more of the dissatisfaction created by such acquisitions. A question was asked on the Private-Sector Computer Managers Survey to see how involved these managers were in decision making on end-user computing acquisitions. Responses showed that they were overwhelmingly involved (82 percent said they had "a lot" of influence over such decision). Furthermore an analysis of the data showed no correlation between degree of involvement in end-user computing and degree of dissatisfaction with vendors among these managers. A second alternative hypothesis is that business firms develop far more of their custom software in-house than do government agencies, thus exposing government agencies to a greater extent to dissatisfaction-creating software development contracts.

Responses showed that, indeed, private firms are quite likely to develop software in-house (80 percent of the companies developed "all" or "a lot" of their custom software in-house). Yet analysis of the data showed no correlation at all between the tendency to develop software in-house and dissatisfaction with vendors—perhaps because dissatisfaction is measured against expectations (and expectations for custom software development are low) or perhaps because respondents did not think about software development when answering the question. Finally, one might argue that this lower satisfaction by government managers is accounted for simply by a message vendors receive of less-exacting expectations or standards to which government holds vendors compared with more-demanding standards in the private sector—a sort of "good-enough-for-government-work" situation. Frankly, I have no reason to believe such lower standards exist. If, however, government were less demanding, this would still be no reason to believe it should be more dissatisfied with vendor performance than the private sector. Since dissatisfaction is a subjective measure, the lower standards would produce a lower baseline against which satisfaction was measured. (Under such circumstances, the objective level of performance would be lower, but this was not measured in the survey.) Furthermore, dissatisfaction might be expected to be greater in the private sector because it is faster to experiment with new, cutting-edge computer applications than is the government (at least outside the Department of Defense, which was not included in this research). New applications are inherently more risky, more subject to the danger of vendor overpromising, and more likely to engender customer dissatisfaction.

9. Respondents were told in the questionnaire they could define "major" however they wished.

10. The private-sector responses on the most recent purchase had a significantly larger proportion of mainframe computers as the organization's most recent major purchase than was the case for the government respondents. A check, however, showed no correlation between the type of acquisition and overall satisfaction levels.

11. $N = 152$ and 31, respectively.

12. $N = 149$.

13. This material is calculated by the consulting firm Computer Intelligence and appears in the firm's publication *Federal Database* (November 1987).

14. "Top Postal Buyer Defends Sole-Source Contract Award," *Purchasing*, 105 (July 28, 1988), p. 29.

15. Quoted in Calvin Sims, "Postal Service Truncates Perot's Role," *New York Times* (August 11, 1988), p. D–1.

16. $N = 28$.

CHAPTER 2: PROCUREMENT REGULATION AND OFFICIAL DISCRETION

1. For a discussion, see Michael Barzelay and Babak J. Armajani, "Managing State Government Operations: Changing Visions of Overhead Agencies" (Cambridge: stencil, 1989). I am indebted to Michael Barzelay for helping me put my thinking about the goals of the procurement system into the context

of the development of the doctrine of American public administration. Mark Moore has written extensively on alternate conceptions of the task of public-sector management. See, for example, his "Small-Scale Statesmen: A Normative Conception of the Role and Function of Public Management in Contemporary American Government" (Cambridge: stencil, 1988).

2. Opening Statement of Congressman Jack Brooks, "Competition in Contracting Act of 1984," *Hearings Before a Subcommittee of the Committee on Government Operations*, U.S. House of Representatives, 98th Congress, 2nd session, March 27–29, 1984, p. 2.

3. See, for example, ibid., pp. 40, 45–46, 61.

4. Material in this section is adapted from Steven Kelman, *Making Public Policy: A Hopeful View of American Government* (New York: Basic Books, 1987), pp. 3–4, 195.

5. Gabriel Almond and Sidney Verba, *The Civic Culture* (Boston: Little Brown, abridged edition, 1963), pp. 64–65.

6. Cited in Seymour Martin Lipset & William Schneider, *The Confidence Gap*, (New York: The Free Press, 1983), p. 271.

7. See Leonard D. White, *The Jacksonians: A Study of Administrative History 1801–1829*, (New York: Macmillan, 1958), chap. 20.

8. Statement of Hon. Carter Manasco, *Federal Property Act of 1949*, Committee on Executive and Legislative Reorganization, Subcommittee on Expenditures, 81st Congress, 1st session, April 12, 1949, p. 147.

9. Much of the impetus for the procurement regulation has come from the Congress, which many regard as one source of the problems. In passing procurement laws designed to stamp out favoritism, Congress appears to be acting in the manner of the dieter who padlocks the refrigerator.

10. The material that follows is adapted from Kelman, *Making Public Policy*, pp. 195–96.

11. Those less interested in the details of how the procurement system functions, or who are already knowledgeable about this, may wish to skim the remainder of this chapter.

12. The contract award actually went to the lowest "responsible" bidder. The meaning of this term is discussed below.

13. Quoted from Stanley N. Sherman, *Procurement Management: The Federal System* (Bethesda, Md.: SL Communications, 1979), p. 79.

14. See Frank M. Alston et al., *Contracting with the Federal Government* (New York: Wiley, 1984), p. 1, and Sherman, *Procurement Management*, p. 82. See also *Report of the Commission on Government Procurement* (Washington, D.C.: Superintendent of Documents, 1972), vol. 1, pp. 21, 163–84.

15. Sherman, *Procurement Management*, p. 98.

16. Ralph C. Nash and John Cibinic, Jr., *Federal Procurement Law* (Washington, D.C.: George Washington University Press), vol. 1, p. 318.

17. The Armed Services Procurement Act is 10 U.S.C. 2301 et seq., and the Federal Property and Administrative Services Act is 41 U.S.C. 251 et seq.

18. Sherman, *Procurement Management*, p. 98.

19. Commission on Government Procurement, pp. 20–21.

20. This is a quotation from the Senate Report on the Competition in

Contracting Act, cited in Matthew Simchak et al., *The Competition Statutes* (Washington, D.C.: Federal Publications, 1987), pp. A-12–13.

21. Provisions for such procurements are discussed in *FAR*, Subpart 6.3. It might be noted that the term "sole-source procurement" has a different common meaning in the private-sector purchasing world; there "sole-source" refers to the number of suppliers who end up providing the organization's needs rather than the number of vendors bidding for the business in the first place. Thus "sole-sourcing" in the private sector means getting all one's requirements from one, rather than a multiplicity, of vendors. "Sole-sourcing" in this context contrasts to "dual" or "multiple" sourcing. In private-sector purchasing, the expression that corresponds to the government term "sole-source" is "single-source." Incidentally, the expression "sole-source procurement" appears nowhere in statutes or in the *FAR*. These kinds of procurements are referred to instead as procurements conducted by "other than full and open competition."

22. Simchak et al., *The Competition Statutes*, p. A-43.

23. Ibid.

24. For a full list of the requirements, see *FAR*, 6.303–2.

25. For a discussion of the various approval levels, see *FAR*, 6.304.

26. Simchak et al., *The Competition Statutes*, p. A–25.

27. *FAR*, 6.305.

28. *FAR*, 10.004(a)(1).

29. *FAR*, 10.002.

30. Ibid., 10.002(3)(ii). See also 10.0004.

31. Ibid., 15.605(b).

32. Alternatively, a stated sum of money, reflecting the "value of the feature to the government," will be added to the bid price of vendors who do not offer the feature.

33. General Services Administration, Information Resources Management Service, "Guidance the Standard Solicitation Document for ADP Equipment Systems" (Washington, D.C.: stencil, June 1987), p. 32.

34. Ibid., p. 19.

35. *FAR*, 15.608(a).

36. The *FAR* states only that the government must lay out evaluation criteria in advance; it says nothing about evaluating vendors based only on their proposals.

37. See for example, the General Accounting Office decision in *Lektron Inc.* (B–228600., January 25, 1988).

38. My personal impression, however, is that case law in procurement is less developed than in contract or administrative law.

39. Simchak et al., *The Competition Statutes*, A–28–31.

40. Joel R. Feidelman, *The Bid Protest* (Washington, D.C.: Federal Publications, 1987), p. 12.

41. See Simchak et al., *The Competition Statutes*, p. A–20.

42. Promulgated in *Federal Register* 52 (December 8, 1987), p. 46445; effective January 15, 1988.

43. Ibid., pp. 85–87.

44. Ibid., p. 103.

45. *FAR*, 1.602.2–(b).

46. One might argue that the significance of the procurement culture suggests that the system allows significant discretion—and that the culture reflects ways that discretion has been used by government officials, paradoxically to establish a system with less discretion than allowed. In fact, the procurement culture follows the spirit, though not the letter, of the procurement regulations. It has been developed by those people inside the system who embody and support the spirit of the regulatory system. Few program and technical people have any idea that many of the injunctions they are receiving do not have the force of law or regulatory requirement behind them. I am indebted to Michael Burack for raising the issue of the significance of the procurement culture.

47. Quoted from Victor H. Pooler, Jr., *The Purchasing Man and His Job* (New York: American Management Association, 1964), p. 22.

48. Michael R. Leenders et al., *Purchasing and Materials Management*, 8th ed. (Homewood, Ill: Richard D. Irwin, 1985), p. 280.

49. Max Weber, "Bureaucracy," in H. H. Gerth and C. Wright Mills, *From Max Weber: Essays in Sociology* (New York: Oxford University Press, 1946), p. 214. See also the discussion in Kelman, *Making Public Policy*, pp. 140–46.

50. The literature on this topic in organizational theory is huge. A good discussion of this problem in the context of government regulation of industry is Eugene Bardach and Robert A. Kagan, *Going by the Book: The Problem of Regulatory Unreasonableness* (Philadelphia: Temple University Press, 1982), particularly chaps. 2–3. A superb account of alternatives in organizational design is Henry Mintzberg, *The Structuring of Organizations* (Englewood Cliffs, N.J.: Prentice-Hall, 1979).

51. James Q. Wilson, *Varieties of Police Behavior* (Cambridge: Harvard University Press, 1968), pp. 96–97.

CHAPTER 3: THE TYRANNY OF THE PROPOSAL

1. It is largely rather than completely irrelevant since the same-price-or-better feature of the technology refreshment clauses means that if a contractor offered in his original proposal to supply equipment or software to the government for pennies, even improved price-performance characteristics would not save him since it would be hard to meet the prices that had been bid even with the new generations of equipment.

2. Donald P. Arnavas et al., *Managing Contract Changes* (McLean, Va.: National Contract Management Association, 1987), pp. 1–17, 20–21.

3. Buck Rodgers, *The IBM Way* (New York: Harper and Row, 1986), pp. 156–57.

4. Donald W. Dobler et al., *Purchasing and Materials Management*, 4th ed. (New York: McGraw-Hill, 1984), p. 664.

5. Stewart Macauley, "Non-Contractual Relations in Business: A Preliminary Study," *American Sociological Review*, 28 (February 1963), p. 61.

6. Dobler et al., *Purchasing*, p. 96.

7. E. Raymond Corey, *Procurement Management: Strategy, Organization, and Decision-Making* (Boston: CBI Publishing, 1977), pp. 28–29.

8. See, for example, the discussion of General Motors and its steel suppliers in ibid., p. 14.

9. William H. Davidow, *Marketing High Technology: An Insider's View* (New York: The Free Press, 1986), p. 48.

10. Ibid., pp. 34, 42.

11. Rodgers, *The IBM Way*, pp. 151–53.

12. Barbara Bund Jackson, *Winning and Keeping Industrial Customers* (Lexington, Mass.: Lexington Books, 1985), p. 52.

13. Rowland Moriarty, *Industrial Buying Behavior* (Lexington, Mass.: Lexington Books, 1983), p. 98.

14. This survey, by *Purchasing* magazine, is reported in Somerby R. Dowst, *More Basics for Buyers* (Boston: CBI Publishing, 1979), pp. 118–19.

15. On the distinction between search and experience as information sources, see Phillip Nelson, "Advertising as Information," *Journal of Political Economy,* 81 (July 1974).

16. W. Kip Viscusi, *Employment Hazards* (Cambridge, Mass.: Harvard University Press, 1979), chap. 13.

17. These views about adaptive expectations are carried to extreme by "rational expectations" macroeconomists, but a looser version is accepted by most macroeconomists. See, for example, Rudiger Dornbusch and Stanley Fischer, *Macroeconomics,* 2nd ed. (New York: McGraw-Hill, 1981), chap. 15. See also Robert E. Lucas, Jr., "Adaptive Behavior and Economic Theory," in Robin M. Hogarth and Melvin W. Reder, eds., *Rational Choice* (Chicago: University of Chicago Press, 1987), particularly pp. 217–18.

18. Government contracts can only be awarded to bidders determined by the *contracting officer* to be "responsible," a term of procurement art. "Responsibility" refers to the ability of the vendor to perform the work if it is awarded to him. Bidders may be declared nonresponsible because of worries about their integrity, their perseverance in completing the work they have agreed to do, or their financial or operational ability to perform the work. (See Nash and Cibinic, *Federal Procurement Law,* vol. 1, pp. 186–87.) In all cases, the contracting officer must look for objective evidence of problems. For example, indictments or convictions of a company or its officers for, say, tax evasion or violation of federal labor laws would provide evidence of a lack of integrity. Records of past contract terminations for poor performance, or "verifiable knowledge of personnel within the contracting office" of poor past contract performance, may show lack of perseverance or lack of ability to perform work. Contracting officers may seek evidence from other agencies, or (in particular when the question is over the ability of the company to perform the work in question) make a preaward survey of the firm's facilities before making determinations of responsibility. (Ibid.; *FAR,* 9.105.6. The quotation about "verifiable knowledge of personnel" appears in *FAR,* 9.105–1[c][2].) Protest bodies almost always uphold determinations of nonresponsibility by contracting officers, arguing that such judgments lie almost entirely within a contracting officer's discretion. (Nash and Cibinic, *Federal Procurement Law,*

vol. 1, pp. 180, 201.) Nonetheless, determinations of responsibility generally certify a bare-bones minimum standard of company ability. Contracting officers do not make declarations of nonresponsiveness casually, since such determinations exclude a potential competitor. More extreme than nonresponsibility is a decision to debar a contractor. Debarment decisions result from fraud or antitrust violations in connection with bidding on or performing government contracts or from a repeated history of bad performance. Debarment decisions, which require development of lots of evidence and provide vendors with many procedural safeguards, are usually government-wide and normally last for three years. See *FAR*, Subpart 9.4.

19. Incumbent vendors end up with advantages in gaining reaward when contracts are recompeted, but these advantages need not stem from good performance. This will be discussed below.

20. Corey, *Procurement Management*, p. 14.

21. Patrick J. Robinson et. al., *Industrial Buying and Creative Marketing* (Boston: Allyn & Bacon, 1987), p. 106 (emphasis in original).

22. Ibid., p. 128.

23. Inability of an agency to use information from past performance should be distinguished from incumbent advantage in contract reawards. This advantage generally exists independent of the quality of past performance and simply because of the vendor's past presence at the customer's site.

24. $N = 28$.

25. Brian O'Reilly, "How Tom Mitchell Lays Out the Competition," *Fortune*, 115 (March 30, 1987), p. 91.

26. Live test demonstrations are, as the case studies suggested, a poor test of a vendor's technical abilities. Some interviewed in the case studies believed that they show the quality of vendor management skills. Although this suggestion was meant disparagingly, it suggests that the points vendors receive may be surrogate management quality points. I regard this as an unintended positive result.

27. $N = 32$ and $N = 19$, respectively.

28. This use of references is suggested by a General Services Administration Board of Contract Appeals case. It was ruled legitimate to give a vendor a low score on some evaluation factors based on reports by references that the scope of the work performed for those references was much less than the scope required for the contract in question. See Consolidated Bell Inc. (GSBCA No. 9726–P, December 2, 1988).

29. General Services Administration, Information Resources Management Service, "Guidance the Standard Solicitation Document for ADP Equipment Systems" (Washington: stencil, June 1987), p. 37.

30. On the permissibility of surveys, see General Accounting Office, *Storage Technology Corporation* (B–215336, August 17, 1984). One decision questioning reliance on Reliability Plus data is Memorex Corp. (GSBCA 7927, 1985).

31. To arrive at these calculations for procurements where no price weight was specified, I assumed a 50 percent price weight for the EPA operation and

maintenance contract and a 25 percent price weight for the USDA local office computerization contract.

32. $N = 31$.

33. *FAR*, 15.605(e).

34. Ibid.

35. Eberhard Witte, "Field Research on Complex Decision Making Processes: The Phase Theorem," *International Studies of Management Organization*, 2 (1968), pp. 516-182.

36. Ibid., p. 170.

37. It may be noted that the tendency to write RFPs is lower in mainframe and sole-source acquisitions; only 31 percent and 22 percent of the cases, respectively, of those acquisitions used RFPs. $N = 151$.

38. For a summary and discussion, see A. W. Wicker, "Attitudes versus Actions: The Relationship of Verbal and Overt Behavioral Responses to Attitude Objects," *Journal of Social Issues*, 25 (August 1969).

39. This criticism is suggested, although not emphasized, by some of the classical criticism of the rational choice model, such as David Braybrooke and Charles E. Lindblom, *A Strategy of Decision* (New York: The Free Press, 1963).

40. Herbert C. Kelman, "Attitudes Are Alive and Well and Gainfully Employed in the Sphere of Action," *American Psychologist*, 29 (May 1974), p. 316.

41. Russell H. Fazio and Mark P. Zanna, "Direct Experience and Attitude-Behavior Consistency," *Advances in Experimental Social Psychology*, 14 (New York: Academic Press, 1981), p. 180.

42. Russell H. Fazio and Mark P. Zanna, "Attitudinal Qualities Relating to the Strength of the Attitude-Behavior Relationship," *Journal of Experimental Social Psychology*, 14 (July 1978), pp. 398–408. This finding is, of course, a natural extension of the notion that experience in the course of action influences one's attitudes.

43. Dennis T. Regan and Russell Fazio, "On the Consistency between Attitudes and Behavior: Look to the Method of Attitude Formation," *Journal of Experimental Social Psychology*, 13 (January 1977), pp. 33–34.

44. Contel Federal Systems Inc. (GSBCA No. 9743–P, December 14, 1988).

45. $N = 26$ for the government managers and 151 for the private ones.

46. The dependent variable was satisfaction rated on the 1–10 scale used in the survey. The questions about satisfaction and the winning vendor's price and technical scores were asked at different parts of the survey, with the question about the price and technical scores being asked first. Responses were recoded and rank-ordered with "best on price, not best on technical" coded lowest. A slightly different recoding produced a correlation of .47. $N = 28$.

CHAPTER 4: GETTING THE MOST OUT OF CONTRACTORS

1. Dobler *et al.*, *Purchasing and Materials Management*, 4th ed. (New York: McGraw-Hill, 1984), p. 657.

2. The first study is cited in George A. Luffman, "Industrial Buyer Be-

havior: Some Aspects of the Search Process," *European Journal of Marketing*, 8 (1975), p. 96. The second study is Yoram Wind, "Industrial Source Loyalty," *Journal of Marketing Research*, 7 (November 1970), p. 453.

3. This study is cited in Luffman, "Industrial Buyer Behavior," p. 96.

4. Government contract law sounds very tough on this score as well. In principle, contracts may be terminated not only for default (that is, bad performance), but also simply for the convenience of the government (because the government has changed its mind about wanting the work done in the first place). This latter is a provision that has no counterpart in private contract law. In reality, however, the same time and effort problems that drive the development of long-term contracts in the first place discourage contract termination, since terminated contracts must normally be recompeted.

5. Michael R. Leender et al., *Purchasing and Materials Management*, 8th ed. (Homewood, Ill.: Richard D. Irwin, 1985), p. 210.

6. Luffman, "Industrial Buyer Behavior," p. 99.

7. Wesley J. Johnston and Thomas V. Bonoma, "Purchase Process for Capital Equipment and Services," *Industrial Marketing Management*, 10 (1981), p. 260.

8. E. Raymond Corey, *Procurement Management: Strategy, Organization, and Decision-Making* (Boston: CBI Publishing, 1977), pp. 12, 36–37, 39.

9. "Vendor X" is substituted here for the name of an actual vendor named by the person being interviewed.

10. Johnston and Bonoma, "Purchase Process," p. 261.

11. See, for example, Somerby Dowst, "Early Supplier Involvement Gives Design Team the Winning Edge," *Purchasing*, 102 (March 12, 1987), pp. 52–60. See also John F. O'Connor, "Purchasing Outlook: How Your Job Is Changing and What It Means to You" (Boston: Cahners Publications, n.d.).

12. Somerby Dowst and Ernest Raiaa, "Design '88: Teaming Up," *Purchasing*, 104 (March 10, 1988), p. 91.

13. Ibid., p. 60.

14. Robinson et al., *Industrial Buying and Creative Marketing* (Boston: Allyn & Bacon, 1987), p. 49. Also see Corey, *Procurement Management*, pp. 120, 214. Use of this practice also came out of the interviews with computer managers at the firms I visited.

15. Dobler et al., *Purchasing and Materials Management*, p. 664.

16. Macauley, "Non-Contractual Relations," pp. 55–67. These figures appear on p. 60.

17. Bid protest decisions have consistently held that as long as the evaluation criterion is itself valid for selecting a contractor, the simple fact that the criterion favors an incumbent vendor does not make it illegally restrictive of competition.

18. The two books where Williamson presents these ideas are *Markets and Hierarchies* (New York: The Free Press, 1975), and especially, for concepts relevant to the argument here, *The Economic Institutions of Capitalism* (New York: The Free Press, 1985). Okun's ideas appear in *Prices and Quantities* (Washington, D.C.: Brookings Institution, 1981), particularly chap. 4. The

Jackson book is *Winning and Keeping Industrial Customers* (Lexington, Mass.: Lexington Books, 1985).

19. E. Raymond Corey, *Industrial Marketing,* 3rd ed. (Englewood-Cliffs, N.J.: Prentice-Hall, 1983), p. 60.

20. Rodgers, p. 135.

21. Corey, *Industrial Marketing,* p. 526.

22. This point is emphasized in Dowst, "Early Supplier Involvement," p. 77.

23. Williamson, *Economic Institutions,* p. 63.

24. The Internal Revenue Service computer support services contract in the case studies is an indefinite-quantity, task-order contract, albeit mostly for studies and not for software development.

25. $N = 148$ and 31, respectively.

26. As noted earlier, a higher proportion of the most recent major acquisitions in the Private-Sector Computer Managers Survey involved mainframes. I thought that statistics comparing vendor involvement might be distorted in that vendors were more likely to suggest replacing existing mainframes with new generations of equipment. An examination of the data showed, however, that in only 27 percent of the cases involving mainframe acquisitions did the private-sector managers rate the involvement of the vendor in the idea for the acquisition between 1 and 4 on the scale ($N = 77$), a figure actually slightly below the 30 percent figure for acquisitions other than mainframes.

27. For comparison, the mean for needs identification for nonincumbent vendors in the Government Computer Managers Survey was 6.45. The smaller gap between the needs identification means for incumbent and non-incumbent vendors in the public than the private sector is another indication that incumbent vendors exert no particular efforts to make conscious site-specific investments in developing capabilities for idea-generation.

28. On value engineering, see *Oversight of Value Engineering Programs in Federal Agencies,* Subcommittee on Oversight of Government Management, U.S. Senate, Committee on Government Affairs, 100th Congress, 1st session, April 29, 1987.

29. Although I am using the metaphor somewhat differently here, I adopt the phrases "creating value" and "claiming value" from David A. Lax and James K. Sebenius, *The Manager as Negotiator* (New York: The Free Press, 1986). The discussion in Charles J. Goetz and Robert E. Scott, "Principles of Relational Contracts," *Virginia Law Review,* 67 (September 1981), pp. 1089–1140, is also very helpful in illuminating some of these issues.

30. See Williamson, *Markets and Hierarchies,* particularly chap. 5.

31. Kirk Monteverde and David J. Teece, "Supplier Switching Costs and Vertical Integration in the Automobile Industry," *Bell Journal of Economics,* 13 (Spring 1982), pp. 206–13.

32. Robert G. Eccles, "The Quasifirm in the Construction Industry," *Journal of Economic Behavior and Organization,* 2 (1981), pp. 335–57.

33. Thomas M. Palay makes a similar point with regard to vendor behavior in rail freight contracting in "Comparative Institutional Economics: The Gov-

ernance of Rail Freight Contracting," *Journal of Legal Studies*, 13 (June 1984), p. 276.

34. For those not familiar with game theory, in the prisoner's dilemma game players who choose to cooperate do better than those who do not, but each player may be driven to noncooperation by a fear that cooperation will subject him to exploitation by the other player. Two confederates are kept in separate cells. If both refuse to confess (the cooperative behavior), the police will not have enough evidence to convict either and they will be tried only for some minor offense with a short prison term—a good outcome for both. If one confesses, however, and the other does not (exploitive behavior by one player), the police will let the one who confesses off lightly for turning state's evidence and throw the book at the one who does not. This is the best outcome for the one who confesses but the worst for the other. The possibility of getting the best outcome for oneself if one is the only one to confess, combined with fear of the worst outcome if one fails to confess and the other does, provides an incentive for each of the prisoners to confess. But if they both confess, they both get sent to jail for a long term.

35. Robert Axelrod, *The Evolution of Cooperation* (New York: Basic Books, 1984).

36. Site-specific investments occurred because, say, the physical shape of the product was such that railroad cars had to be specially configured to make the product's transportation possible or because the location of the factory was such that dedicated rail lines to the factory had to be built.

37. Palay, "Comparative Institutional Economics," p. 275.

38. *FAR*, 7.102.

39. This is analogous, I think, to the problem of lack of seriousness about relative valuation weights prior to actual evaluation of alternatives that I raised in the previous chapter in the context of making the best decisions about contract awards.

40. Corey, *Procurement Management*, p. 20.

41. Leenders et al., *Purchasing and Material Management*, 8th ed. (Homewood, Ill.: Richard D. Irwin, 1985), p. 209.

42. My attention was first called to this through a report on IBM issued by the investment firm Alex Brown & Sons (July 1987). An article in *Business Week* on Zenith Data Systems, which sells heavily to the government market, also noted the low margins in government business. "Zenith Is Doing Quite Well, Thank You—In Computers" (July 11, 1988), p. 80. A source at EDS confirmed for me that EDS margins on government business are half those on its commercial business.

Chapter 5: Conclusions and Recommendations

1. Good discussions of this general issue are Henry Mintzberg, "Crafting Strategy," *Harvard Business Review*, 65 (July 1987), pp. 66–77, and James Brian Quinn, *Strategies for Change: Logical Incrementalism* (Homewood, Ill.: Richard D. Irwin, 1980). Recently the General Services Administration has identified itself with skepticism regarding "grand design" projects. See General Services

Administration, Information Resources Management Service, "An Evaluation of the Grand Design Approach to Developing Computer Based Application Systems" (Washington, D.C.: September 1988).

2. These are indeed, two separate problems and not simply different ways of stating the same thing. If changes in the world made old rules inappropriate, the solution might simply be different rules. An example is a license fee rendered obsolete by inflation, or rules requiring payment by cash or check after credit cards became more common. Of course, one argument against rules is that they are difficult to change, even into other rules.

3. General Services Administration, Information Resources Management Service, "The Trail Boss Program: Getting Ready for the 1990's" (Washington, D.C.: July 1987). An unfortunate amount of "trail boss" training involves getting officials better equipped to deal with the procurement regulatory system itself, but to its credit the training also significantly deals with methods for better project management during the contract implementation phase.

4. The elimination of such rules would not, of course, prohibit officials from choosing to use traditional techniques such as sealed bids where appropriate—say, in buying pencils or toilet paper. But it would give people much greater discretion in deciding how to go about the acquisition process.

5. There are, of course, cases where the group's ideal may be laziness, as with the much-studied instances of restriction of output among blue-collar workers. Such group ideology, however, sees bosses as exploiters and establishes an ideal of restricted output to restore justice against slavedriving. Such ideals are unlikely in the setting discussed here, although they might, at least on occasion. The dominant effect of the pressures toward group ideals would, however, be in the other direction.

6. Steven Kelman, *Regulating America, Regulating Sweden: A Comparative Study of Occupational Safety and Health Policy* (Cambridge, Mass.: MIT Press, 1981), p. 13.

7. I am grateful to Mark Walker of the Environmental Protection Agency for calling my attention to this clause at his agency and to Frank McDonough of the General Services Administration for the information that use of such a clause is not common.

8. I am grateful to Howard Metzenbaum for this suggestion.

9. I am grateful to Jack Donahue for suggesting this point to me.

10. Herbert Kaufman, *Red Tape: Its Origins, Uses, and Abuses* (Washington, D.C.: Brookings Institution, 1977).

11. See, for example, M. R. Darby and E. Karni, "Free Competition and the Optimal Amount of Fraud," *Journal of Law and Economics*, 16 (April 1973), and George Stigler, "The Optimum Enforcement of Laws," *Journal of Political Economy*, 78 (May 1970).

12. Issue advocates frequently attempt, in a manner sometimes bordering on intellectual dishonesty, to wish away trade-offs in public policy by making light of the losses suffered by choosing the policy the advocate supports. Thus, environmentalists not only praise the health gains to be achieved by environmental regulation but also routinely come up with low estimates of

the cost of environmental cleanup, while business bemoans the cost of regulation but also belittles the health gains such regulation would achieve. Since I do believe this occurs, I was prepared to accept the existence of a genuine trade-off. What was important, I thought, was to make the case that a trade-off did indeed exist and that the avoidance of corruption and procurement effectiveness were not both served by the current system.

13. Arthur M. Okun, *Equality and Efficiency: The Big Tradeoff* (Washington, D.C.: Brookings Institution, 1975), p. 60.

14. Revealing this inside information may have caused vendors to improve their offers and get the government a better deal than it would otherwise. In 1988 an employee of the General Services Administration apparently revealed inside bid information without having been paid for it, in the hopes of getting a vendor to lower his bid. This was clearly a violation of the procurement regulations, but it is unclear (and I am not familiar enough with the literature on auctions to have an opinion on the question) whether this official was behaving inappropriately from the point of view of getting the government the best value.

15. Interview with William Block, U.S. Attorney's Office, District of Columbia.

16. See Stephen Engelberg, "Inquiry into Pentagon Bribery Began with a Telephone Call," *New York Times*, June 19, 1988, p. 1.

17. Interview with Block, who is also the source on the observation of the inspector general.

18. I am indebted for this point to Robert Reich.

19. On the research regarding certainty and severity, see Daniel Nagin, "General Deterrence: A Review of the Empirical Evidence," in A. Blumstein et al., eds., *Deterrence and Incapacitation: Effects of Criminal Sanctions on Crime Rates* (Washington, D.C.: National Academy of Sciences, 1978).

20. The response of a wary government official to an effort at political influence might look the same under the existing system as the one I am proposing. Under my proposal, government agencies would still need to issue a statement of reasons explaining the contract award choice made. The response, "I'd like to help, but I just wouldn't be able to justify selecting your guy over his competition," is still available.

21. Leonard D. White, *The Republican Era: A Study in Administrative History 1869–1901* (New York: Macmillan, 1958), pp. 221, 256.

22. See Robert K. Merton, "Bureaucratic Structure and Personality," in *Social Theory and Social Structure* (New York: The Free Press, enlarged edition, 1968), especially pp. 252–53.

23. In the vernacular, this is often referred to as "covering your tail." For more scholarly discussions of the phenomenon and its origins, see Donald P. Warwick, *A Theory of Public Bureaucracy* (Cambridge, Mass.: Harvard University Press, 1975). See also the discussion in Kelman, *Making Public Policy*, pp. 282–85.

24. I am indebted to Robert Reich for making this point to me.

25. See, for example, General Accounting Office, *Senior Executive Service: Executives Perspectives on Their Federal Service* (Washington, D.C.: General

Accounting Office, 1988), p. 12. Fifty-eight percent of senior executive service respondents were dissatisfied or very dissatisfied over "working within the government's administrative system (that is, paperwork, regulations)," while only 18 percent were satisfied or very satisfied. See also Timothy B. Clark and Marjorie Wachtel, "The Quiet Crisis Goes Public," *Government Executive*, 20 (June 1988), pp. 16–17.

26. Eliot Freidson, *Profession of Medicine* (New York: Dodd, Mead, 1973), p. 368.

27. See, for example, Alvin Gouldner, *Patterns of Industrial Bureaucracy* (New York: The Free Press, 1954).

28. See, for example, Hugh Heclo, *A Government of Strangers* (Washington, D.C.: Brookings Institution, 1977), and Joel D. Aberbach et al., *Bureaucrats and Politicians in Western Democracies* (Cambridge, Mass.: Harvard University Press, 1981).

29. Information in this section is based on interviews with John Weiss, Federal Deposit Insurance Corporation, and Bruce Beardsley, Federal Reserve System. I am grateful to John Weiss, whom I had originally planned to interview for my Government Computer Managers Survey, for enlightening me about the situation at these two agencies.

30. Information in this section is based on an interview with a source not for attribution in the General Services Administration, and on Robert V. Head, *Federal Information Systems Management: Issues and New Directions* (Washington, D.C.: Brookings Institution, 1982).

31. See *Federal Information Resources Management Regulation*, 201–30.012–1.

32. Robert V. Head, *Federal Information Systems*, p. 21.

33. For a discussion, see Acquisition Team Report, "Federal Data Processing Reorganization Study" (Washington, D.C.: President's Reorganization Project, stencil, June 1978), p. I1–13.

34. On the change in General Services Administration policy, see Joseph J. Petrillo, *Government Information Systems Procurement* (Washington, D.C.: Federal Publications, 1987), p. 126.

35. See General Services Administration, Information Resources Management Service, "Go for 12: Final Report" (Washington, D.C.: November 1988).

Appendix A

1. "Fixed-format" questions are those where responses are placed into prearranged categories, such as "yes" or "no," "often," "sometimes," "seldom," or "never," or on numerical scales where, say, the number one represents one extreme and the number ten the other. "Open-ended" questions are ones where the respondent formulates his own answers in his own words to queries such as, "What changes would you like to see in the way the procurement system is organized?" For the purposes of quantitative analysis of such open-ended questions, responses were later coded into categories.

2. Respondents were not asked to name the vendor or to give many specific details about the contract.

Case Study 1: U.S. Department of Agriculture
Local Office Computerization

1. For background about these organizations, see U.S. Department of Agriculture, no title, RFP–00–85–R–13 (November 17, 1984), pp. 7–17.

2. This and subsequent materials in this paragraph on SCS are based on an interview with John Okay, Soil Conservation Service.

3. USDA, RFP, p. 12.

4. Information on FmHA comes from an interview with Lynn Furman, Farmers Home Administration.

5. Material in this section is based on an interview with John Okay.

6. Information in this section is based on an interview with Lynn Furman.

7. Ibid.

8. Ibid.

9. "Integrated" software packages allow people to interrupt, say, a word-processing text they are working on in order to do a spreadsheet calculation, and also easily to incorporate results from one application to another.

10. The materials in this section are based on an interview not for attribution and on an interview with Erlend Warnick, FmHA. In a future downloaded environment, changes in files on a given day (such as receipt of loan payments) would then be sent in an overnight batch to the mainframe in Kansas City, which would continue to serve as the official repository for loan records.

11. In technical terms, FmHA wanted "record lockout" but not "file lockout."

12. Materials in this section are based on interviews with Daniel Stoltz and Elizabeth Prigg, SCS, and with John Okay.

13. Material in this section is based on interviews with Dan Stoltz, Elizabeth Prigg, John Okay, and an interview not for attribution.

14. USDA, RFP, pp. 399–400.

15. Ibid., pp. 385–87.

16. Interview with Clem Munno, USDA Contracts Division.

17. Ibid.

18. Ibid.

19. See, for example, USDA "Amendment of Solicitation No. 8" (RFP–00–85–R–13, July 12, 1985).

20. I asked Lynn Furman, John Okay, Dan Stoltz, and Clem Munno about this.

21. Interview with Lynn Furman.

22. Material in this section is based on an interview with Lynn Furman.

23. Ibid.

24. Material in this section is based on interviews with Erlend Warnick, Dan Stoltz, and an interview not for attribution.

25. Material in this section is based on interviews with Erlend Warnick and Dan Stoltz.

26. Interview with John Okay.

27. Interview with Erlend Warnick.

28. Interview with Dan Stoltz.
29. Interview with Warren Lee, USDA.
30. Ibid.
31. The material in this section is based on interviews with Erlend Warnick, Dan Stoltz, Elizabeth Prigg, Clem Munno, and an interview not for attribution.
32. Interview not for attribution.
33. RFP, p. 47.
34. Interview not for attribution.
35. Interview with Clem Munno.
36. Ibid.
37. Interview with Warren Lee.
38. Interview with Clem Munno.
39. Interview with Dan Stoltz.
40. Interview with Warren Lee.
41. Interviews with Erlend Warnick, Clem Munno, and sources not for attribution at USDA and EDS.
42. Material in this section is based on interviews with Dan Stoltz and Erlend Warnick.
43. Interview with Clem Munno.
44. Material in this section is based on interviews with Lynn Furman, Dan Stoltz, and Elizabeth Prigg.
45. Interview with Lynn Furman.
46. Ibid.
47. Ibid.
48. Interview with Mark Boster, FmHA.

Case Study 2: U.S. Customs Service
Local Office Computerization

1. This procurement, the contract for which was also let during FY85, will be discussed later.
2. Interviews with Ken Malley and Ray Arnold, Customs Service.
3. Interview with Ray Arnold. See also U.S. Customs Service, RFP-CS–85-2 (no title) (December 14, 1984), Section C.
4. See ibid., pp. C-4–C-16.
5. Interview with Jim Ryan, U.S. Customs Service.
6. U.S. Customs Service, RFP, p. C-109.
7. Interview with Barbara Lasky, Customs Service.
8. See U.S. Customs Service, RFP, p. M-1.
9. Ibid.
10. Interview with Ken Malley.
11. Interview with Barbara Lasky.
12. Ibid.
13. Interview with Ken Malley.
14. Ibid.
15. Ibid.
16. Interviews with Ken Malley and Barbara Lasky.

17. Interview with Jim Ryan.
18. Interviews with Ken Malley and Jim Ryan.
19. Material in this paragraph is based on interviews with Ken Malley and Ray Arnold.
20. Interview with Ken Malley.
21. Interview with Ray Arnold.
22. Ibid.
23. Ibid.
24. Interviews with Jim Ryan and Ray Arnold.
25. Interview with Stan Livingstone, Customs Service. Customs in fact had other alternatives as well, because they could have bought stand-alone personal computers off a Department of the Treasurywide indefinite quantity contract for stand-alones. In fact, Customs negotiated a lower price with EDS than what they had originally offered for the stand-alones in response to a threat by Customs to buy the stand-alones off the Treasurywide contract.
26. Interview with Ray Arnold.
27. Interview with Ken Malley.

Case Study 3: Immigration and Naturalization Service Hardware Computerization

1. Material on INS activities appearing in this paragraph is based on Immigration and Naturalization Service, *ADP and Office Automation Equipment, Facilities Operations Support, and Systems Engineering and Integration* (RFP CO–1–84, January 25, 1984), Attachment 7, and an interview with John Miller, INS.
2. Ibid., see the organization chart in INS, *ADP and Office Automation*, p. 7-4.
3. Information in this section is based on an interview with John Miller.
4. OMB Circular A–109 called for design competitions on major acquisitions with a significant developmental component. This approach was used in the acquisition of the Federal Aviation Administration's replacement host computer for the air traffic control system, to be discussed in another of the case studies.
5. Interview with John Murray, INS.
6. Ibid.
7. Interview with John Murray.
8. Interview with John Miller.
9. Ibid.
10. Interviews not for attribution.
11. Interview with John Miller.
12. Ibid.
13. For RFP evaluation criteria, see INS, *ADP and Office Automation*, Pt. V. I have calculated the corporate experience weight to make it comparable to the other procurements examined. Actually, the RFP counted "corporate experience" as part of two of the management-related factors, "systems engineering and integration experience and approach" and "facilities operations systems

experience and approach," each of which included information from bidder proposals about how they planned to organize these functions, as well as the experience they actually had doing so. The scoring of actual corporate experience within these factors was not listed in the RFP, and I have arbitrarily assumed that half the score was based on actual experience at other sites. In addition, it may be noted that the evaluation criteria also included one called "management capabilities and approach," but it was strictly based on the overall management plan in the proposal.

14. Interviews with John Miller and John Murray.

15. Interview with John Miller.

16. In response to a question, John Miller stated that he did not believe that the decentralized solution was economically more advantageous to IBM (in the sense, for example, that they would have been able to sell more hardware than with a centralized solution).

17. Interview with John Miller. In fact, INS did have a contract at the time with EDS to print green cards for aliens. Miller states he does not believe he knew about that contract at the time and adds that even if he had, he did not regard the kind of work EDS was doing on that contract as at all relevant to his project.

18. Ibid.

19. Interview not for attribution.

20. Interview with John Miller.

21. On the evaluation criterion, see INS, *ADP and Office Automation*, Pt. V.2.1.a.2. Miller provided information on how the criterion was used in the evaluation process.

22. Interview with John Miller.

23. This discussion is based on an interview with John Miller and also on Miller's "Statement" (n.d.) in response to the later EDS bid protest.

24. John Miller, "Statement." One interesting question is why IBM did not simply go ahead and bid the smaller number of terminals the way EDS did. Apparently, the reason was mostly a fear by IBM that the government might conceivably hold IBM responsible for delivering the larger number even though the company had bid only the smaller number, or at least that the government would not allow IBM to charge for the additional equipment it needed to support the larger number. In addition, IBM could offer a smaller per-unit price (because of quantity discounts) for the larger than the smaller number. (Interview with Sterling Phillips, IBM.)

25. Interview with John Murray.

26. See the account in Miller, "Statement."

27. This is quoted from Miller, ibid.

28. For the EDS arguments, see Electronic Data Systems Federal Corporation, "Further Memorandum of Plaintiff Electronic Data Systems Federal Corporation in Support of Its Motion for Preliminary Injunction" (Washington, D.C.: stencil, June 28, 1984).

29. Material in this section is based on interviews with John Murray, John Miller, and Terry Appenzeller, Department of Justice Office of Information Resources Management.

30. Material in this paragraph is based on interviews with John Miller and Alan Miller, EDS.

31. General Accounting Office, *ADP Acquisitions: Immigration and Naturalization Service Should Terminate Its Contract and Recompete* (Washington, D.C.: March 1986).

32. Ibid., pp. 13–14.

33. General Accounting Office, *ADP Study for INS Needs Validation* (Washington, D.C.: April 1988).

34. Interview with Terry Appenzeller.

CASE STUDY 4: CUSTOMS SERVICE CONSOLIDATED DATA NETWORK

1. Information in this paragraph is based on I. Richer et al., "Network Alternatives for the U.S. Customs Service" (Cambridge, Mass.: Bolt, Bernaek, and Newman, 1983), especially pp. 45–47, and on an interview with Roger Malatt, Customs Service.

2. Interview with Roger Malatt.

3. Ibid.

4. U.S. Customs Service, "Consolidated Data Network" (RFP CS–85–1, December 14, 1984), p. C-1-2.

5. Ibid., pp. C-13–14.

6. Ibid., p. M-5a.

7. Interview with Roger Malatt.

8. Interview with Roger Malatt and Customs Service, "Consolidated Data Network," p. M-1.

9. Ibid., p. M-3.

10. Ibid., p. M-1.

11. Information in this section is based on an interview with Roger Malatt.

12. Interview with Roger Malatt.

13. Customs Service, "Consolidated Data Network," p. C-34.

14. Interviews with Roger Malatt and Charles Dubay, Customs Service.

15. See, for example, Customs Service, "Consolidated Data Network," p. C-13, in terms of assumptions about traffic growth.

16. Interview with Roger Malatt.

17. Interview with Werner Schaer, Computer Sciences Corporation.

CASE STUDY 5: VETERANS ADMINISTRATION OFFICE AUTOMATION CONTRACT

1. Information in this paragraph is based on an interview with Buddy Edwards, Veterans Administration.

2. Material in this section is based on interviews with Buddy Edwards and Eliot Christian, Veterans Administration.

3. It would theoretically have been possible for different vendors to have had differing mandatory features, such that—in the worst-case scenario—no vendor would have met all the mandatory requirements. In practice, though,

the requirements were generally basic enough so that there was no trouble getting vendors who would meet all of them.

4. For these examples, see Veterans Administration RFP 101–22–84 (n.d.), pp. C-15, C-18, C-55–56.

5. Interview with Eliot Christian.

6. Interview with Buddy Edwards.

7. On the technical evaluation criteria, see VA, RFP 101-22-84, p. M-2.

8. Interview with Buddy Edwards.

9. VA, RFP 101-22-84, p. M-8–9

10. Information in this section is based on interviews with Buddy Edwards and an interview not for attribution.

11. Interview with Buddy Edwards.

12. Ibid.

13. Interview not for attribution.

14. Interview with Jeff Ryan, Veterans Administration.

15. Interview with Buddy Edwards.

16. Interview with Jack Sharkey, Veterans Administration.

17. Material in this paragraph is based on interviews with Jack Sharkey, Buddy Edwards, and Phil Edenfield, Veterans Administration, who is in charge of the VA's technical interface with Wang.

18. Interview with Buddy Edwards.

19. Interview with Jack Sharkey.

20. Interview with Buddy Edwards.

CASE STUDY 6: INTERNAL REVENUE SERVICE CENTER MAINFRAME REPLACEMENT SYSTEM

1. Material in this paragraph is based on an interview not for attribution.

2. Assembly language is programming language closer to direct instructions to the machine. Higher-level programming language, which is based on code that is closer to the machine, allows a programmer to write in more natural logical commands rather than requiring that he mimic the machine's operation. Higher-level languages allow the system to do more of the work, while lower-level languages such as assembly language require the programmer to do more of the work. An advantage of assembly language, however, is that it uses up less computer power for a given set of computations.

3. Interview with Roger Howard, IRS.

4. Interview with Doug Southerland, IRS.

5. Interview with Lou Kuttner, IRS.

6. Internal Revenue Service, *Service Center Replacement System* (RFP No. IRS–80–38, February 1980), pp. E-39–4.

7. Interview with Roger Howard.

8. IRS, *Service Center Replacement*, p. E-39.

9. See ibid., p. E-38.

10. Vion has exclusive marketing rights for Hitachi machines sold to the federal government. NAS (National Advanced Systems) markets the same Hitachi machines to the private sector.

11. Information in this section is based on interviews with Doug Southerland, Roger Howard, and an interview not for attribution.

12. Information in this section is based predominantly on interviews with Roger Howard and Doug Southerland, and with a source not for attribution of Unisys Corporation (of which the former Sperry is now a part).

13. Interview with Doug Southerland.

14. Interview with Roger Howard.

15. Interview not for attribution.

16. Interview with Lou Kuttner.

17. I raised this question in interviews with Roger Howard, Lou Kuttner, and Doug Southerland, and the material is based on their speculations.

18. Interview not for attribution, Unisys Corporation.

19. Material in this section is based on an interview with Doug Southerland and on General Accounting Office, *Tax Administration: Replacement of Service Center Computers Provides Lessons for the Future* (GGD–87–109, September 1987), esp. pp. 16–19.

20. Ibid., GAO, p. 18.

21. The information on which this section is based comes from the Statement of Johnny C. Finch, General Accounting Office, "IRS Service Center Operations," Subcommittee on Oversight, Committee on Ways and Means, U.S. House of Representatives, December 16, 1985, particularly pp. 1–7.

22. Information in this section is based on interviews with Doug Southerland, Roger Howard, and an interview not for attribution.

23. IRS officials reject, however, the suggestion in the above-cited General Accounting Office Report that new applications that IRS developed for the computers, despite the injunction that the replacement system not expand existing computer requirements, were a significant cause of the difficulties. IRS officials argue that these new applications used very little computing power.

24. Interview not for attribution.

25. Interview with Fred Martin, IRS Contracts.

26. Interview with Lou Kuttner.

Case Study 7: Federal Aviation Administration Host Computer Replacement

1. For a good background on the projects, see Subcommittee on Aviation, House Committee on Public Works and Transportation, "Review of National Airspace System Plan" (Washington, D.C.: stencil, March 1987).

2. The material in the remainder of this paragraph is based on interviews with Jim Cain, Mike Perie, and Art Simolunas, all of the FAA.

3. Interview with Mike Perie.

4. Interviews with Mike Perie and Jim Cain.

5. Interview with Mike Perie.

6. Interview with Mike Perie.

7. Interview with Arthur Simolunas.

8. Interview with Mike Perie.

9. Federal Aviation Administration, *Host Computer* (RFP A01–85–R–00200, December 13, 1984). It might be noted that FAA was engaged toward the end of this period in a dispute with the GAO on whether the testing required in the design competition phase was sufficient to proceed to the production award phase, with the General Accounting Office claiming that FAA should delay the procurement further to conduct more rigorous testing. See General Accounting Office, *Federal Aviation Administration's Host Computer: More Realistic Performance Tests Needed before Production Begins* (Washington, D.C.: GAO IMTEC–85–10, June 1985). The FAA believed that the design competition phase had reduced the risks of the procurement significantly and that the mission-oriented demands of the air traffic control system argued against further delay. (Interviews with Mike Perie, Jim Cain, and Dan Trainem, House Public Works and Transportation Committee.)

10. FAA, *Host Computer,* p. 138.

11. Interviews with Mike Perie, Jim Cain, and Arthur Simolunas.

12. Interview with Mike Perie.

13. Interview with Arthur Simolunas.

14. FAA, *Host Computer,* p. 138.

15. See ibid., pp. 138–41.

16. Interview with Mike Perie.

17. FAA, *Host Computer,* p. 141.

18. Interview with Mike Perie.

19. Interview with Mike Perie and interview not for attribution.

20. Interview not for attribution.

21. Interview with Mike Perie.

22. Material in these paragraphs is based on an interview with Mike Perie.

23. Interview with Mike Perie.

24. Ibid.

25. Interviews with Jim Cain, Mike Perie, and Arthur Simolunas.

26. Interview with Mike Perie.

27. Interviews with Jim Cain and Mike Perie.

28. Interviews with Arthur Li, General Accounting Office, and Dan Trainem.

29. Interview with Jim Cain.

CASE STUDY 8: ENVIRONMENTAL PROTECTION AGENCY COMPUTER OPERATIONS AND MAINTENANCE SERVICES

1. On the features of the contract, see the EPA RFP, *Systems Operation, Software Maintenance, and Document Processing Center Operations* (RFP WA84–199, September 1984), Attachment A. I have also relied on interviews with John Hart and Charles Tobin of the Environmental Protection Agency.

2. Material in this section is based on interviews with John Hart, Charles Tobin, and Art Payne, all of EPA. Individual comments will not be attributed to specific sources.

3. Interview with John Hart.

4. Ibid.

5. Ibid.

6. Interview with Mark Walker, EPA Contracts.
7. Ibid.
8. Interviews with Mark Walker and John Hart.
9. The impression that the evaluation criteria did not address areas of dissatisfaction with the contractor's past performance was confirmed by John Hart.
10. Interview with John Hart.
11. Ibid.
12. Interviews with John Hart and Mark Walker.
13. Interview with John Hart.
14. Interviews with John Hart and Mark Walker.
15. Interviews with John Hart, Mark Walker, and Adriana Fortune, EPA.
16. Interview with Mark Walker.
17. Interview with John Hart.
18. Interview with Mark Walker.
19. Interview with John Hart.
20. Interview with Ed Hanley, EPA.
21. Interview with John Hart.
22. Ibid.

CASE STUDY 9: INTERNAL REVENUE SERVICE COMPUTER SUPPORT SERVICES

1. See Internal Revenue Service, *ADP Support Services* (TIR 85–0289, July 5, 1985), p. 11.
2. See ibid., pp. 39–40.
3. An "8(a) firm" is a minority-owned firm that contracts with the government through Section 8(a) of the Small Business Act, which authorizes agencies to award sole-source contracts to such firms.
4. Interview with Emory Miller, IRS.
5. Ibid.
6. IRS, *ADP Support Services*, p. 93.
7. Ibid., p. 94.
8. Ibid.
9. Ibid., p. 95.
10. Internal Revenue Service, "Benchmark Materials for Solicitation No. IRS-84-0118" (n.d.).
11. Ibid., p. 1.
12. IRS, *ADP Support Services*, p. 93.
13. Ibid., p. 96.
14. Ibid.
15. Ibid.
16. Ibid., p. 99.
17. Ibid.
18. Interview with Emory Miller.
19. Interview with Fred Martin, IRS.
20. Interview with Sue Ensslen.

21. IRS, *ADP Support Services,* p. 93.

22. Interview with Emory Miller.

23. Interview with Fred Martin.

24. Interview with Emory Miller.

25. Ibid.

26. Interview with Emory Miller. The surprise was confirmed in an interview with Joseph Skovira, Vanguard Technologies.

27. Ibid.

28. Interview with Emory Miller.

29. Ibid.

30. Interviews with Sue Ensslen and Emory Miller.

31. Interview with Emory Miller.

32. The material in this section is based on interviews with Emory Miller and Betsy Beckman, IRS.

33. Interview with Betsy Beckman.

34. Interview with Emory Miller.

35. OAO Corporation (GSBCA 10186-P, September 1989).

36. Interview not for attribution.

Index

Source selection officer, 22
Southerland, Doug, 203, 204
Specifications
  changes in FmHA/SCS request for
    proposal (RFP), 116
  for Customs Service local office pro-
    curement plan, 124–25
  for Customs Service network linking
    procurement, 144
  effect of requirement for complete,
    89
  as limit to discretion, 19, 56
  for IRS computer mainframe pro-
    curement plan, 155
  in private-side purchasing, 65–66
  problems with, 32–33
  SCS personnel develop, 110
  vendor assistance with development
    of, 81–83
  vendors as source of information for,
    81
Spending, government
  on computer technology, 1–2
Sperry Corporation, 116, 117–18, 118–19,
  120, 153, 155–60, 161, 163–66
Stigler, George J., 195
Stoltz, Daniel, 118, 120, 198, 199
Surveys of computer managers, 3–4
System performance
  prediction of, 31–32

Technical assistance, 71, 72–73
Technology refreshment clauses, 30, 92–
  93
Teece, David J., 193
Tobin, Charles, 205, 206
Trainem, Dan, 205
Twain, Mark, 13
Tymnet, 134

Unisys, 8
UNIX, 112–13, 115, 117, 122, 126–28
USDA. See Department of Agriculture

VA. See Veterans Administration
Value engineering change order pro-
  posal, 76–77
Vanguard Technologies, 42–43, 65, 180–
  83
Vendor competition

  for FAA software design, 163–64,
    167
Vendor elimination process
  at FmHA/SCS, 120
Vendor knowledge, 69–71
Vendor performance, 29–38
  customer abuse and coddling in, 32–
    36, 53, 67–68
  incentives for, 63–68
  quality of, 53–55; surveys of, 6–8
  use of information about, 40–47, 51–
    52, 63–67
Vendor personnel, 53–54
Vendor protest, 170
  INS procurement plan, 134–36
  impact of, on INS procurement plan,
    140–41
Vendor-provided references, 48–50
Vendors, third-party, 76, 83
Verba, Sidney, 12, 186
Veterans Administration (VA)
  procurement goals, 148
  procurement problems, 5
Vion, 155–58
Viscusi, W. Kip, 189
Von Raab, William, 129

Wachtel, Marjorie, 196–97
Walker, Mark, 170, 172–73, 195, 206
Wang Laboratories, 148, 149–52
Warnick, Erlend, 118, 198, 199
Warwick, Donald P., 196
Weber, Max, 26–27, 188
Weighting. See Federal Acquisition Regula-
  tions (FAR)
Weighting methods
  of EPA recompetition plan, 170–71
  in evaluation criteria, 56, 68–69
  in FAA procurement plan, 164–65
Weiss, John, 197
White, Leonard D., 186, 196
Wicker, A. W., 191
Williamson, Oliver, 69, 71–72, 78, 192,
  193
Wilson, James Q., 28, 188
Wilson, Woodrow, 14
Wind, Yoram, 191–92
Witte, Eberhard, 57, 191
Wyse Technologies, 130

Zanna, Mark P., 59, 191

A Note on the Book

*This book was edited by
the publications staff of the American Enterprise Institute.
The index was prepared by Shirley Kessel.
The text was set in Palatino, a typeface designed by Hermann Zapf.
Coghill Book Typesetting Company, of Richmond, Virginia,
set the type, and Edwards Brothers Incorporated,
of Ann Arbor, Michigan, printed and bound the book,
using permanent, acid-free paper.*

The AEI Press is the publisher for the American Enterprise Institute for Public Policy Research, 1150 17th Street, N.W., Washington, D.C. 20036: *Christopher C. DeMuth*, publisher; *Edward Styles*, director; *Dana Lane*, editor; *Ann Petty*, editor; *Andrea Posner*, editor; *Teresa Fung*, editorial assistant (rights and permissions). Books published by the AEI Press are distributed by arrangement with the University Press of America, 4720 Boston Way, Lanham, Md. 20706.